FAITH
AND THE FAITH

Roy E. Cogdill

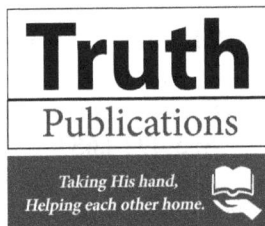
Truth
Publications

Taking His hand,
Helping each other home.
TM

ISBN 10: 1-58427-330-5

ISBN 13: 978-158427-330-1

Truth Publications, Inc.
CEI Bookstore
220 S. Marion St., Athens, AL 35611
855-492-6657
sales@truthpublications.com
www.truthbooks.com

Roy E. Cogdill
1907-1985

Dedication

To Nita, my faithful
wife, companion, and
co-laborer in the
gospel.

Table Of Contents

Introduction

Men are saved by the grace of God when, and only when, they exercise their faith in "the faith" or in the gospel of Christ. That is the theme of the Book of God and of this book of sermons on **Faith and The Faith.** Roy E. Cogdill conceived the idea for this series on "Faith" while driving alone toward California to preach the gospel of Christ in a protracted meeting many years ago. Thinking about Romans 10:17, "Faith cometh by hearing, and hearing by the Word of God," he compared other passages which refer to salvation by faith. The series which evolved has been preached from one side of the country to the other, blessing untold thousands of people through the years. Many more will be blessed by the book.

These sermons are preeminently scriptural. *"The Debt of Faith"* focuses on Romans 1:8-12, *"The Hearing of Faith"* on Galatians 3:1-4, *"The Spirit of Faith"* on 2 Corinthains 4:13-5:10, *"The Law of Faith"* on Romans 3:1-31, *"The Obedience of Faith"* on Romans 16:25-26, *"How Faith Purifies"* on Acts 15:7-9, *"Walking by Faith"* on 2 Corinthians 4:13-5:9, *"The Failure of Faith"* on Hebrews 3:12, and *"The Victory of Faith"* on 1 John 5:1-5. *"Measuring the Temple"* (Rev. 11:1) is a sermon brother Cogdill used on Sunday morning when he preached the *"Faith"* series week nights. The two sermons entitled *"Christianity Is Undenominational"* focus on 1 Corinthians 1:10-15 and on Acts 2:37-42, and were broadcast over the radio from the Church of Christ in Lufkin, Texas in 1949. Each lesson is practical and down-to-earth. Everyday applications are calculated to save the lost and to strengthen the saved.

Roy Cogdill and the Alamo City
The series as transcribed here was delivered in 1971 at the Highland Blvd. Church of Christ in San Antonio, Texas, a city where brother Cogdill had preached since 1924. Christians lived in the Alamo City as early as 1857 and a church meeting twenty-five miles south of

town on Lucas Creek reported progress in 1858, but no congregation met in town until 1883. The church's existence was tenuous because of Catholicism, liquor, and indifference. A building was erected the next year, but none of the 50-75 members met in it during the Spring of 1889 unless "some good brother preaches that happens to pass this way." Digressives gained control of it in 1893. A faithful group was growing again in 1897 with Johnson or "Joe" Harding's (b. 1832) help and moved away from the noisy railroad to Flores Street during 1908.[1]

Brother Cogdill never knew "Weeping Joe" Harding but heard of his emotional exhortations which earned him the nickname. One of the "preacher stories" Cogdill heard was about Joe's visit to hear John W. Denton (b. 1853) of Bonham, Texas in a gospel meeting. When no one answered the invitation, brother Harding asked to say a few words. Several people came forward to obey the Lord in response to his emotional appeal. Not wanting the harvest to be cut short, brother Denton urged, "Don't quit now, brother Harding, cry some more!"[2]

After the church on Flores Street, among the new works established was one in the Denver Heights area. A building went up at 401 Porter Street. While selling Bibles in the Fall of 1924 for the Southwestern Publishing Company of Nashville, Tennessee, a preacher only seventeen years old came to town and preached some at Flores Street, at Denver Heights, and at Floresville (about 25 miles southeast of San Antonio). Roy Cogdill had entered the picture. Arthur Slater (b. 1880) was the regular preacher at Denver Heights. Later while A. Hugh Clark (1895-1967) was the regular preacher, Denver Heights moved into its new building at 1226 Highland Blvd. and became the Highland Blvd. Church of Christ. Roy held the first gospel meeting in that new facility and continued to hold meetings there through the years.

The series on "Faith" was delivered during the week of 18-24 January 1971. At sixty-three, brother Cogdill was still in his prime as a preacher. Three evangelists — Stanley Lovett, W.L. Wharton, and John Witt — worked with Highland Blvd. at the time. Lovett, Wharton and Cogdill had been good friends for many years. Dr. George Bernard was an elder and Roy had known his father when George was in medical school. Roy stayed with Roy D. Spears, a close friend who had come there from Lufkin and was serving as an elder. W.A.L. Graves had his ninety-second birthday during the week and Roy quipped that he had known brother Graves "nearly all that almost 100 years." Many of Roy's friends from the West Ave. Church attended the meeting; he had preached for them during the period of October 1954-October 1956.

Roy Cogdill was intimately associated with the cause of Christ in San Antonio, especially with the brethren at Highland Blvd., through the years.[3] His contribution has been significant. Through the publication of these sermons, the good accomplished during that week of 1971 will be multiplied to many people in many places for years to come.

Accurate Reproduction

When brother Cogdill gave me the opportunity to edit these sermons, they were in typed manuscript form as taken from tapes practically verbatim (except for the radio addresses which were prepared in manuscript form originally). Every possible effort has been made to preserve the original style, content, and flavor of the sermons as delivered. The style of expression in speaking is more open and flowing than in writing. As much of brother Cogdill's speaking style has been preserved as is possible, the chief difference in the published speeches being that running sentences (100 or more words at times) have been broken down to make them more suitable for reading. Sometimes Bible passages were quoted verbatim and sometimes paraphrased, as we all do in preaching. Paraphrasing appears as originally given, to preserve the original style. The reader can easily turn to his Bible to distinguish verbatim and paraphrased quotations. Roy generally used the King James Version in the pulpit.

In editing these sermons, I worked very closely with brother Cogdill and followed his counsel. Had his health permitted, he could have edited them himself. We worked in a very warm relationship to insure the accurate reproduction of the sermons. He first considered publishing them under the title *Salvation By Faith* but finally decided that *Faith and The Faith* best expresses his theme.[4] Brethren far and wide testify to the power of this series on "Faith" as the lessons were orally proclaimed. Brother Cogdill often pointed out that the ultimate power of preaching is *in God* and *in the Word He revealed.* The same power of Divine truth is in these printed sermons that was in their oral presentation *because they are true to God's Word.*

The Importance of This Book

As Solomon noted, new books are always appearing. When we see a new one, we wonder about its value and whether it is worthy of our time for reading. Books like *Faith And The Faith* are a medium for preaching Christ, saving souls, and strengthening saints. There cannot be *too* many books for such work!

It is fitting that these sermons be printed because of their quality and because of the impact for good of Roy Cogdill's life upon so many people. Such lessons need not be slavishly memorized to be useful, but can provide models for young preachers and will stimulate Bible study for anyone.

To increase the usefulness of these Bible lessons both in personal and classroom studies, questions have been added by the editor at the end of each chapter. We hope this feature will adapt the material to an audience much wider than those who are accustomed to reading books of sermons. It would be hard to find Bible study literature which is more provocative and enriching than brother Cogdill's lessons on "Faith."

Faith and The Faith is a book to be prized. It is tragic that so few of Alexander Campbell's sermons, "which produced such profound and far-reaching results," were preserved in printed form.[5] The world and the church are richer because many other discourses by strong preachers did not suffer the same fate. Roy Cogdill's *Faith and The Faith* will join other significant sermon books in the literature pleading for a restoration of New Testament Christianity — books like Robert Milligan's *Scheme of Redemption* (1868), Benjamin Franklin's two volume *Gospel Preacher* (1869, 1877), T.W. Brent's *Gospel Plan of Salvation* (1874) and *Gospel Sermons* (1891), J.W. McGarvey's *Sermons* (1894), David Lipscomb's *Life and Sermons of Jesse L. Sewell* (1891), E.G. Sewell's *Gospel Lessons and Life History* (1908), N.B. Hardeman's five volumes of *Taberncale Sermons* (1922-42), Z.T. Sweeney's three-volume collection of restoration sermons by many preachers under the title *New Testament Christianity* (1923-30), and Foy E. Wallace, Jr.'s *Certified Gospel* (1937, rev. 1946), *God's Prophetic Word* (1946), and two-volume *Bulwarks of the Faith (1951).*

Faith and The Faith — and the volumes projected to follow — will join these and similar books in pleading for the gospel of Christ in its purity and simplicity. Never were such sermons more needed. Exhaustive studies show strong trends in American preaching toward pop psychology, salesmanship jargon, interpersonal relationships, and group dynamics — and away from strict teaching of the spiritual and eternal values based on Scripture.[6] Such trends are rampant among professed churches of Christ, especially among institutional churches, but even to a noticeable degree among some conservative brethren. Cogdill's sermons can help to turn back the tide of pop psychology in the pulpit and of pallid faith in the pew, *and to revive true Bible preaching.* As Benjamin Franklin aptly said (in the introduction to his first volume of sermons),

> The following discourses are aimed to be simply *Gospel discourses,* stating, unfolding, advocating, maintaining, and defending the *Gospel of Christ,* and opposing, exposing, and repudiating every thing in the way of it, or in opposition to it. This is done in kindness, but in plainness, and with earnestness and force.

Faith and The Faith is just such preaching. It needs no apology, but plenty of emulation!

Since this book will take its place with other important books of sermons and since other books by brother Cogdill are projected, a biographical sketch is included in this volume. A full-length biography by Steve Wolfgang, of Danville, Kentucky, will appear later. He offered helpful information in the preparation of this sketch, as did the Troy C. Irvins, of Birmingham, Alabama (longtime friends of Roy Cogdill), who provided access to a complete set of the *Gospel Guardian.* Fred A. Hutson of Alto, Texas, another longtime friend, also supplied information. Mrs. Terral Smith of Dayton, Ohio, worked long hours typing the sermons in their final form.

The Guardian of Truth Foundation has been intensely interested in seeing sermons and other valuable materials by brother Cogdill published as a blessing to present and future generations. The Foundation is happy to see the fruits of his rich studies preserved in published form and is honored to help him make them available.

Faith and The Faith will be a valuable aid to anyone who is determined to preach God's holy, pure, and powerful Word!

Ron Halbrook

West Columbia, Texas
June 1986

Notes

1. A.P.H. Jordan, "Texas," *Millennial Harbinger* 4th ser., VII, 5 (May 1857): 297; John Henshaw report, *Gospel Advocate* IV, 7 (July 1858): 221; Stephen Daniel Eckstein, *History of the Churches of Christ in Texas, 1824-1950* (Austin, TX: Firm Foundation Publ. House, 1963), pp. 147-50, 300; Colby D. Hall, *Texas Disciples* (Ft. Worth, TX: Texas Christian Univ. Press, 1953), pp. 380-82. See also reports in *G.A.* XXXI, 16 and 25 (17 April and 19 June 1889): 243 and 390.

2. Interview of Roy E. Cogdill by Ron Halbrook, 31 Dec. 1983. A sketch of Harding's life appears in *Gospel Preachers of Texas and Oklahoma* (Clifton, TX: Mrs. C.R. Nichol, 1911).

3. Basic outline of Cogdill's work in San Antonio taken from interviews of Cogdill by Halbrook, 10 Apr. 1982 and 31 Dec. 1983. The 1971 meeting date was confirmed by records at the Highland Blvd. Church of Christ, San Antonio, Texas, as per James R. Trigg letter to Halbrook, 9 Jan. 1984.

4. The final title was suggested by a book Roy Cogdill found in a used book store many years ago. The book by Thomas Treadwell Eaton (1845-1907) is *Faith and The Faith* (New York: Fleming H. Revell Co., 1906). Eaton was prominent and potent both as a preacher and as an educator among Baptists of the South. His 78-page book is a stirring call for the defense of biblical certainties in the face of modernists' doubts.

5. Archibald McLean, *Alexander Campbell as a Preacher: A Study* (Chicago: Fleming H. Revell Co., 1908), p. 9.

6. "A Pallid but Personable Faith," *Time Magazine,* 29 Sept. 1980, p. 85.

CHAPTER ONE

The Debt of Faith

I should like in the very beginning this morning to express my gratitude to brother Bernard for the very kind words of introduction and to the elders of this congregation for the honor that they have extended to me in inviting me to come for this meeting. I express to all of you the very genuine pleasure that I have in my heart for the privilege of being here and once again preaching the Gospel from this pulpit, and to this congregation. My association with this church has extended through a long period of years. I feel like I have among the members of this congregation some of the very best friends that I have anywhere on earth. It will be a genuine pleasure to me to be associated with all of you in these services and I trust that we will each one undertake individually to do our very best to make every service what the Lord would have it to be.

To fulfill the expectations of others is not our goal and our aim, and it ought not to be. But to please God is the thing that ought to challenge us in the things that we do and say. We want to make that our aim in every service that we participate in. I could not go anywhere and be associated with a congregation, or with the preachers of a congregation — and I put it in the plural here at Highland—with any more personal pleasure than it affords me to be here. I want you to know that I feel that way about it, and I will do my very best at every service to make the service worthwhile from the viewpoint of the truth that shall be preached, and pray that God will bless our efforts and attendance with His good providence, in making every service a blessing to you, and to the hearts and souls of us all.

The Text:
Romans 1:8-21

In the first chapter of Paul's letter to the church at Rome, I want to read a passage of Scripture as a basis to some of the things that we want to say, and I shall begin reading with verse 8:

> First, I thank my God through Jesus Christ for you all, that your
> faith is spoken of throughout the whole world. For God is my
> witness, whom I serve with my spirit in the gospel of his Son, that
> without ceasing I make mention of you always in my prayers; mak-
> ing request, if by any means now at length I might have a prosper-
> ous journey by the will of God to come unto you. For I long to
> see you, that I may impart unto you some spiritual gift, to the end
> ye may be established; that is, that I may be comforted together
> with you by the mutual faith both of you and me. Now I would
> not have you ignorant, brethren, that oftentimes I purposed to
> come unto you, (but was let hitherto), that I might have some fruit
> among you also, even as among other Gentiles. I am debtor both
> to the Greeks, and to the Barbarians; both to the wise, and to the
> unwise. So, as much as in me is, I am ready to preach the gospel
> to you that are at Rome also. For I am not ashamed of the gospel
> of Christ; for it is the power of God unto salvation to every one
> that believeth; to the Jew first, and also to the Greek. For therein
> is the righteousness of God revealed from faith to faith: as it is
> written, The just shall live by faith. For the wrath of God is revealed
> from heaven against all ungodliness and unrighteousness; because
> that which may be known of God is manifest in them; for God
> hath showed it unto them. For the invisible things of him from
> the creation of the world are clearly seen, being understood by the
> things that are made, even his eternal power and Godhead; so that
> they are without excuse: because that, when they knew God, they
> glorified him not as God, neither were thankful; but became vain
> in their imaginations, and their foolish heart was darkened.

Recognition of Personal Responsibility

In these verses we have Paul speaking of his own personal responsibility, the obligation that he felt in the work that he was undertaking to do, and the attitude that he had toward it. He had in mind
the consequences which would attend his work when done in harmony with the will of God, if the attitudes of saints at Rome were what
they ought to be toward God and toward the Word of God. It is
about this matter that I want to talk to you this morning, as we may
from these verses have impressed upon our hearts as deeply as possible *a recognition of personal responsibility in the service of God.*

Sometimes those of us who have already obeyed the Gospel and
become God's children take for granted that our part in the Kingdom

of God is a matter which only challenges and requires of us attendance at the services, participation in the worship of God regularly, and the use of at least a part of our money for the advancement of the purposes that the Church of our Lord has been charged with fulfilling upon this earth. When we are a part of the Church, the body of the saints, the body of the saved, and when we participate in the assemblies that the saints hold for the purpose of edification and for the purpose of honoring and worshipping and glorifying God, too many times we feel that this is the fulfillment or discharge of all the obligations that Christianity places upon us.

It is a sad thing that even about matters of this kind, too often we are negligent. People sometimes—because they have been baptized for the remission of their sins and because they count themselves to be Christians, because they have been added to the Church—feel they have a title, abstracted and guaranteed, to the mansion in the skies. Thinking that they are bound to go to Heaven eventually, they give no recognition, no time, and no consideration, to the responsibilities or obligations of assembling for worship. But there are too many of us who feel that we have fulfilled the law when we assemble for worship. Then we wonder why the Church does not grow as it ought to grow, why we do not become stronger in our faith as we ought to from day to day, and why more good is not accomplished and more souls are not saved.

Paul was an example of an individual who felt *a compulsion in his own conscience*—because of his gratitude toward God and because of his recognition of the duty which God had laid upon him—*that was so great that he turned away from any other consideration.* He left every personal matter completely apart, forgot it, crucified it, put it to death. He gave up the right of a home and a family and made a eunuch of himself, for all intents and purposes, for the sake of the Kingdom of God.

There would not have been any companionship on earth that would have been important enough to him to have stood between him and the service to which God had called and appointed him. There was not any obligation to any family, or to any neighbor or to any friend, or to any organization on earth, or to any kind or sort of association that he had formed with anybody, at any time, anywhere, that was important enough to interfere with that which

God wanted him to do. This was the paramount consideration.

I hear him expressing it in Galatians 2:20, telling us his fundamental attitude and what the essence of Christianity was to him, and what it ought to be to you and me, when he said that he died with Christ: "I have been crucified with Christ; and it is no longer I that live, but Christ liveth in me; and that life which I now live in the flesh I live in faith, the faith which is in the Son of God, who loved me, and gave himself up for me." I do not know of a verse in the New Testament that more clearly expresses the very essence, the meaning, and the heart of what it means to be a Christian than that very verse. It means to turn away from self, from selfish interests, selfish purposes, selfish desires, selfish ambitions, the fulfillment and gratification of selfish appetites, and to give ourselves without reservation to serving the will of the Lord in our lives. This is Christianity.

"That I Might Have Fruit Among You"

So, Paul said to the Romans, "I have often wanted to come unto you that I might have fruit among you." I have in mind that probably he meant the entire Roman nation. He had visited the other parts of the world and had preached the Gospel. I think that he did not limit the fruit that he intended to be borne by his efforts in Rome simply to the bestowal of spiritual gifts upon the Romans, though that may have been a part of it. But, his desire was that through the preaching of the Gospel in Rome he might both edify the saints of God and save those that were lost.

The New Testament record reveals to us the fact that his work did bear fruit. For years, in the city of Rome, even as a prisoner, he had some unusual opportunities. While he was in prison chained to a guard (or to a soldier of the guard) known as the Praetorian guard, he did not cease to teach and preach the Word of God. He announced upon one occasion that he had preached it to the whole Praetorian guard. For a while he was allowed to live in his own hired dwelling, and this was a place where people could come to him and hear him as he taught the Word of God. He gave his time to it in spite of the circumstances that would discourage, that would hinder, and that you and I would probably use as an excuse to give up the battle.

Were you to visit Paul's prison as traditionally identified (and I have an idea that if it was not the exact spot, it was at least one very much like the exact place where Paul was imprisoned in the Mamertine prison in the city of Rome), you would find a very small room with a door that shut out the light. A very small window, high in the wall, gave the only light that he had. But even then, he busied himself writing letters to brethren in whom he was interested and to churches which he had helped to plant and in which he had taught the Word of God.

This probably was during the time of his second imprisonment. The battle was not done; the fight had not been finished. His obligation had not been fulfilled until he was ready to lay his head on the chopping block and give his life for the sake of the faith. He had proclaimed it from the very time that Jesus had revealed himself to him on the road to Damascus and made it known that it was his will that Paul should carry the glorious light of the Gospel of Christ to the Gentile nations of the world. So, he was very faithful in executing this obligation and this responsibility.

Were you to turn to the last part of the eleventh chapter of the Second Corinthian Letter, and read the sufferings that Paul listed from his experiences as a preacher, as an evangelist, and as an Apostle of the Lord, you would be impressed with the tremendous sacrifice that Paul made—even from the viewpoint of personal suffering. Every indignity on earth, every physical punishment that could be brought upon him, every hardship you can possibly imagine, he endured. He did not ask for an easy road to travel.

He did not ask for favors or for special consideration. The only distress that I know anything about that ever did fill his heart so full that he besought the Lord to remove it was the "thorn in the flesh" (and what that was, we do not know), of which he writes, but even then it was not taken away and the Lord assured him, "My grace is sufficient for thee." And it was! It stood by him and strengthened him even until the end of his journey had been completed and his work was finished, and he could say, "The time has come for my departure."

Through all of that suffering, and in all of that devotion to the work to which he had given himself without reservation, and to which the Lord had called him, the attitude of his heart was always as it is expressed here: "I have longed to come unto you that I might bear fruit among you, even as among the other Gentiles." He said that he had been hindered in fulfilling that purpose. His plans were always made in harmony with the will of God.

False brethren had come to the Corinthians and had tried to undermine their confidence in and their respect for Paul. Paul's Second Corinthian Letter was given over very largely to a defense of himself. He was not interested just in defending himself for his own honor's sake or for the sake of his own good name, but he was interested in protecting his influence over the Corinthian church for truth and righteousness. These false brethren came along and said *many* things about him that were dishonorable and that would destroy confidence in him—none of which were true. Among their charges was this, "He promised to come. He told you he was coming and he has not come; therefore, he is fickle, he is changeable, he is not reliable."

Paul called to their attention that his plans were always made in harmony with and conditioned upon their being the will of God. That ought always in our lives to be understood. He had often purposed, but he had not been allowed. He had been hindered. There had been other work to do; there had been other things that God had in mind for him. Divine providence had overruled in his life and caused him to go to places that he would not have gone and to leave off that which perhaps he would have done, but he was always willing to do whatever was made known to him to be God's will, and he never questioned it.

"I Am Debtor"
This was his disposition. He said, "I am debtor both to the Greeks and to the Barbarians." They represented the two different poles, or the ends, the very ends, of human culture and society in Paul's day. They included, from that point of view, *everybody,* the whole human race from one pole to the other and all in between. "To the wise and to the unwise," and there was no one else. To all humanity, Paul said, *"I am debtor,"* or, *"I am in debt."*

Now, you know we like to think about not owing anybody anything. I struggled through the most of my life and I never have quite reached the point where I could say that I do not owe anybody anything. That would be a wonderful occasion, would it not? It would be a very fine and comfortable feeling from a financial point of view to have every debt paid and every obligation met. Paul did not have in mind the financial part of his life when he made this statement, but he had in mind the debt that no man can ever pay.

No matter how long you live, no matter how diligent you are in teaching others the truth, no matter how many sermons you might preach, or how much service you might render to the Lord or how faithful you might be in it, the time will never come while the strength is yet yours and while life still exists that you can say, "I do not have any obligation that has not been fulfilled entirely to the souls of all men or to the soul of any man; my debt is paid." It never will be!

Spiritually, your obligation to serve God and to work in the interest of the salvation of others will never be discharged until you lay your armor down—until your life is over and until you are ready for the reward that God has for those who thus serve. "I am debtor—I am debtor to all men." Well, Paul, why are you in debt? I think there are several basic considerations, and I suggest them to you for your study.

In Debt Because Saved By Grace
First, Paul felt that he was in debt to all men because God, through His grace and mercy, had saved him. God has saved me! Not because I deserve it. Not because my soul is any more valuable than anybody else's. But the grace of God has made it possible for me to be a Christian. This puts upon me an obligation—an obligation born of and based upon the gratitude that I ought to have in my heart to God Almighty to do His will, to please Him, to accomplish His purposes, to serve in my life the ends and the aims that God would have me to serve. This ought to take precedence over everything else.

What will result if I am as grateful to God as I ought to be for the forgiveness of my own sins, for my own salvation, for His goodness and for His mercy, for the illimitable long-suffering and mercy and grace that He has extended unto me? If I feel toward God the gratitude that I ought to feel for all of this and for the hope that I have in the world to come, then I will be obligated out of that gratitude, devotedly and faithfully to serve His purposes in my life as long as I live. Paul said, "I was the chief of sinners." Even though he was the chief of sinners, Paul said that the Lord appeared to him as one "born out of due season" and made him a minister and a witness of the glorious Gospel of Christ to the Gentiles.

Paul never forgot the mercy and the grace of God. He mentions it in almost every sentence. He argues it all the way through every Epistle. He talks about the grace of God and the peace of God constantly and continually in all of his writings. He was never unmindful of it, and he never forgot that it was by God's grace that he had been saved, and that by the grace of God he had the hope of eternal life.

You and I ought not to forget it. We cannot deserve what God has done for us. There is not any way to merit the blessings and the mercy and the goodness of Almighty God. What you have in the world and what God has granted you from day to day, both among the good things of physical life and among the perfect, spiritual provisions for the eternal salvation of your soul, are not of your own making. You have not earned them, and there is not any way that salvation can be earned. It is a matter of God's grace making it possible and our faith accepting it on the conditions that God has stipulated.

I need to know all the while that if ever I gain Heaven, it is going to take the grace and the mercy of the Almighty God to get me there. I am not going because of any personal excellence or worthiness. I am not going because of any distinctive service or sacrifice on my part. I am not going because it is possible for me to merit what God has offered. I am going by the grace and the mercy of God, and that is the reason I am a Christian.

Paul is especially mindful of that. God's grace had put him under a great debt. It has you and it has me. I cannot appreciate what salvation means or how gracious and merciful God has been in extending to me the privileges of being a Christian, of having my sins forgiven, and of entertaining in my heart the hope of Heaven after a while, I cannot appreciate that and be grateful for it without recognizing the obligations that arise out of it.

There is not any relationship in life that is worth having that does not involve obligations. God in His wisdom provided the marriage relationship for man's good. One of the greatest blessings that God has ever bestowed upon us is the privilege of a home and family, but it involves responsibility. There is not any way to enjoy its privileges without accepting and discharging its obligations. The same thing is true in the business world. When advancement comes, when

our salary is increased, and when we prosper, we face greater responsibilities and greater obligations. And this is true from a spiritual
point of view. The greatest obligation you have is the obligation to
be faithful in God's service, out of the gratitude of your heart for
God's grace which makes it possible for you to be saved.

In Debt Because All Men Are Lost

But there was another consideration. *Paul based his debt upon
the fact that all men are lost and need to be saved.* The need of others
was recognized. "All have sinned and fallen short of the glory of
God." There is not a solitary individual, within or without my acquaintance, but who needs to be saved exactly as I have been saved!
Whether it is a member of my own family, the neighbor next door,
the man down the street, the man with whom I am in business or
with whom I work, or a chance acquaintance on the street or on
some means of conveyance, I need to know that he has sinned. He
has fallen short of the glory of God and needs to be saved more than
he needs anything else on earth.

The greatest favor that I can do any individual is to teach him
the truth, giving him the opportunity to be saved! This is always
so. I do not mean that we need to make out of ourselves offenses
to others, that we need to be radical or fanatical, that we need to
try to force and push upon people the truth when they do not want
it and will not hear it. I simply mean that we ought not to allow
any situation ever to deter us from recognizing our duty to teach
the truth to anybody, anytime, anywhere, that we have the opportunity to do so. If we do not use it, God will hold us responsible.
All men need to be saved.

In Debt to Preach the Gospel of Christ

*The next principle upon which Paul placed his debt and his obliga-
tion is that the Gospel of Jesus Christ is the only power that can
save anyone.* There is not any way to save a man, except by teaching
him the truth. Jesus said, "Ye shall know the truth and the truth
shall make you free." You can pray for your loved ones, friends,
and neighbors the rest of your life. They can pray for salvation all
they want to, but without the knowledge of the truth, the Word of
God, it will never be a reality. Salvation does not come simply
through prayer. Salvation comes through the power of Divine truth
as it produces faith in our hearts and brings our lives into submis-

sion unto the will of God. That is the only way any man can be saved, and I need to recognize it. God proposes no other way!

You may use your good influence to teach the truth and make the truth more effective; it is your obligation to safeguard that good influence and through it to promote the gospel. Whether you have more or less ability than somebody else, to the extent of *your* ability, you are under obligation to teach the truth that is able to save to the man that needs to be saved by it. This is the only way that he can be saved.

Perhaps fathers and mothers in their homes need to recognize more than any of us do, that the only way children will grow up to be what they ought to be (they may not anyhow) is to teach them the Word of God as we have opportunity to do so while they are young and while we have influence over them. I need to recognize that if there is some person in my family who is not a Christian, until he learns the truth he cannot be saved. If he does not know the truth, then he cannot be a child of God. Without it, nobody can be!

God's way of making men righteous, or of bringing men to justification, is *the truth, the plan revealed in the Gospel.* That is what Paul says about it.

I hear Paul saying, "I am not ashamed of the gospel of Christ: for it is the power of God unto salvation to every man that believes." Only those who believe the truth can be saved by it. You will probably make an effort to teach it to a lot of people who will not have it, but their failure to obey is not your responsibility. You cannot believe, you cannot repent, and you cannot obey the Gospel *for others;* but, you can teach the truth to others, as they are willing to listen to you. And that is exactly what God has obligated everyone of us to do! We are to spread, to disseminate, to propagate, and to tell the story of God's plan for man's justification.

That story is in the Gospel. Paul said, "I am not ashamed of the gospel, for"—the reason he was not ashamed of it is that—"it is God's power to save men and women who believe it." And then he tells us why it is the "power of God to save." It is the power of God to save because "therein"—*in the gospel* — is made known God's way of making men just, holy, and righteous. God's plan for saving mankind is God's design for making men holy, just, and righteous as revealed in the Gospel.

It is revealed in the Gospel *in order that men might have faith in it.* The intent and purpose—the *very purpose* of it being revealed—is in order to produce faith in the heart of the individual! Only those in whose hearts the Gospel produces faith can be saved by it. It is the power of God to save only those who believe it! It will not save anybody who does not believe it! But it will save, it is able to bring men to justification, to righteousness, and to holiness in the sight of God, *if* they will believe it, *if* they will accept it. That faith is the kind of faith that works by love in doing whatever is required in the revelation of God's will to mankind!

You and I need to recognize, then, that it was *constantly impressed* upon the heart of Paul that *only the gospel* can save those who need to be saved! There is not any other way to do it. Teach them everything else you want to teach them, let them learn all the science and all the knowledge that man has accumulated, but salvation is only by *divine truth.* There is not any justification or righteousness that can be attained except through faith in Divine truth as God has revealed it in the Gospel. And so, the Gospel *is the only* power that can save anybody. That is the reason Paul proposes to pay his debt by preaching the Gospel.

"I am in debt." Well, Paul, to whom are you in debt? "To all men." Why? "Because *all* men need to be saved." How are you going to pay that debt? You cannot save them. "No, but I can save men that are willing to believe, by teaching them the Gospel, God's plan for salvation. That is the only way I can help to save anybody." It is the only way anybody can be saved, and so Paul said, "I am going to pay my debt by teaching men the truth."

Are You Personally Paying Your Debt?
Now, I want to say something to you this morning and I want to say it to *you personally.* I do not care what congregation you are a member of; I do not care how many preachers the Church supports; I do not care how much the Gospel might be preached by it publicly or what its program of work may be. *If you individually and personally are not doing what you can to teach people the truth and influence them to accept it, you are failing in your life as a Christian!* You will not go to heaven, if the Word of God is so and God's promises can be relied upon. It is as much an obligation of the Chris-

tian life to spread the Gospel as it is to break bread on the first day of the week. To teach people the truth and save others is as much an obligation of the Christian life as it is to live right and to leave off immorality, ungodliness, unrighteousness, and lasciviousness in your life.

What are you doing about it? Are *you* paying *your* debt to the souls who are lost that are about *you?* Are you even concerned? Are you even making an effort in that direction? The Church in the New Testament that exists, the attitude of mankind. We make a lot of excuses. It is because of the location in the community that we have and in which we are situated. We excuse ourselves all the time because the Church does not grow like it ought to grow.

I do not care in what place the lost live, do you know what happens anywhere when saved men and women institute the kind of a program that the New Testament Church in Jerusalem carried on? As men learn the truth, among them will be many who will accept it! Humanity is just about the same that it has always been. Human nature does not change. The Gospel of Christ is the same. And while I get discouraged many times, yet, among the people that I meet and I know, there are many who have good and honest hearts.

If I would only plant in that good and honest heart the seed of the Kingdom, I know what the result would be, and I ought not to question it. The good of preaching the Gospel ought never to be doubted! It will do what God knows it will do! And what God expects it to do! God knows what the results will be, and I can fulfill my duty by doing it. I can pay *my debt* by doing it!

Well, what is the measure of my responsibility? Responsibility is personal, but how can I measure my responsibility as an individual? I think Paul put his finger on the point when he said, "So as much as in me is, I am ready." Paul was ready. The Bible teaches that we ought to be ready, ready to every good work. Ready for *every* good work! Prepared for any opportunity to do good which God has appointed us to do! This ought to be the constant state and constant attitude of mind on the part of every child of God. I am ready! Are *you?*

Are you ready to do any good that comes along, ready to do any good that arises, or is there something else in the way? My mother used to have an expression that I have never forgotten. She talked about people who could not serve the Lord because they had "other fish to fry." And you know what that expression means? It is an old-timey one. They had something else that they gave precedence, that was more important to them. A lot of us cannot serve God because it is too important to us to have a good time, too important to us to make money, too important to us to fulfill our other ambitions and to gratify our other appetites. We just do not have time to serve God.

To the extent of my ability, "so as much as in me is," I must act in faith. It must be to the *full* extent of that which I have been granted by grace and the mercy of God. Concerning the privilege, the ability, and the opportunity of doing, Paul said, "I am ready." I am not going to let anything stand in the way. I want to say to you this morning that when you get that sort of a spirit into the hearts of those of us who make up the Church of God in any community—I do not care whether it is large or small—you will see things happen. You will *see* things happen! And the reason they do not happen when they do not, is not because of the fact that God has failed.

It is not that God's plan will not work, not the fact that there is not anybody yet on earth who will hear the truth, not the fact that we do not have opportunity, but the fact that *before* all of this, there are *other* considerations. I serve God with reservations, I serve God making certain exceptions in my life. I want to be a Christian, I want to do my duty, *if* it does not demand too much time of me, *if* it does not cost me too much money or require too great a sacrifice. If it does not involve too much persecution and too much suffering, I would like to go to Heaven. But, if it is going to cost me too much, I am not as interested in it as I was when I started.

What Is Your Attitude?

What is *your* attitude? If you will say to yourself and before the Lord this morning, that to the extent that I am able, I am ready, your hope of Heaven will be much stronger and much brighter as the days come and go. But you must not relinquish that purpose. It is more important than any obligation. It ought to transcend any earthly relationship. There is not any duty that you owe to anybody that is any greater, that ought to take precedence over your serving the Lord and doing His will. May God help us that such may be our attitude.

But sometimes, we need to do something else in order to serve the Lord. We cannot have any part or lot in the service of God until we are fit vessels, meet, and prepared for God's use. As long as there is sin in my life that I have not repented of—sin in my heart that I have not repented of—the things that are wrong that I have not crucified—wrongs that I have done and guilt attached to my soul that I have not received pardon for—I cannot serve God. Sin cannot come into God's presence. That is the reason the eyes of the Lord are over the righteous and their prayers are acceptable in His sight, but the prayer of the wicked man is an abomination in His sight. You cannot live in rebellion to God and expect God to accept your worship, your prayers, your sacrifice, anything you do. And if you converted a million people while you lived and did not do the will of God yourself, you would go to Hell just the same. Just the same!

So, if you have not given yourself with all of your heart believing and trusting in Him, in the provisions of His grace, and in the salvation that he has provided in the Gospel which was offered to you and to me; if you have not thus trusted in the Lord, if you have not repented of your sins, and if you have not confessed and acknowledged Jesus Christ as Lord before men; if you have not been buried with Him by baptism into His death—into *your* death to sin—and been raised up, justified, made holy, and righteous; *then you are still lost in your sins*. These are God's conditions. This is God's offer and you have to comply if you are to accept His terms. If this you have not done, you cannot serve God until you do it.

If once you began, but you have fallen by the wayside and you have become negligent, careless, unfaithful, and untrue to the Lord, then you have denied Him by not rendering the service you so faithfully ought to render. You need to come back and ask the mercy and the forgiveness of a kind, loving, prayer-hearing and prayer-answering Father. God is ready to forgive those whose hearts are perfect before Him, and whatever your failure may have been, if you repent of it and ask God's pardon and mercy, he will not withhold it. He promises so. We can even pray one for another, as we confess our faults one to another. God has made this possible. If it is this you need to do today, we invite you to come and do it.

If you want to be identified with this congregation, you want this to be your place of work and worship with the saints of the Lord, to be a part of this church, to accept your responsibility as such, to be under the eldership of this congregation, to work in harmony with its program insofar as it is in harmony with the will of the Lord, you ought to let that be known if you have not already done so.

If you are a subject to the invitation, we invite you to come while we stand and sing.

Further Study On Chapter One

1. Each class member should be ready to quote Rom. 1:14-15 from memory. Begin class with 1-2 minutes of silence to let everyone write down the passage. Each student may check his own work. Then, call on a few to quote aloud.

2. The student should outline chapter 1 at home by listing the headings, a point or two made under each heading, and the main passages used under each heading. Call on class members to briefly explain what each heading means (such as "That I Might Have Fruit Among You") and how some passage was used to support the heading.

3. Each student should write and bring to class a brief "commentary" on Rom. 1:14-17. Explain in your own words what each line or phrase in the passage means. Discuss any connection of thoughts between verses 14 and 15, then 15 and 16, then 16 and 17. The teacher can call upon various students to read all or part of what they have written.

4. What thoughts in Gal. 2:20 help us to recognize and accept our personal responsibilities as Christians? What are some of those responsibilities? If we accept one or two, may we reject or neglect others?

5. Discuss some things Paul suffered in order to bear fruit in gospel preaching. Which were hardest to endure? Which are we likely to face today? Which would be most likely to cause some of us to give up?

6. Each student should have prepared a list of questions and answers on chapter 1 (5 true-false; 3 brief answer; 2 asking "What passage

teaches us that. . .?''). The teacher should ask students to read some of their questions for the class to discuss.

7. Why was Paul and why are we in debt to God? Discuss some blessings in life which bring duties and responsibilities.

8. What is the only message or power that can save a sinner? Explain the difference between our being held accountable to teach the message, and being accountable for the reaction or decision of people whom we teach.

9. What are some things we can do to help people learn the truth today? How can we be more effective in reaching the lost? (If possible, the teacher may break the class into small groups of 3-5 for about 5-7 minutes of discussion; then let each group leader tell the whole class one or two important points developed by the group.)

10. The teacher should assign someone to prepare 3 review questions on chapter 1 to be read at the next class period.

CHAPTER TWO

The Hearing of Faith

I would like again this evening to express my genuine appreciation for your presence, for the interest that you manifest in this service by being here, and for the good providence of God that makes it possible for all of us to be assembled in His presence to study His Word and to worship Him. In these services throughout this week, both day and night, we have in mind but one thing, and that is to make every contribution that we can make to the salvation of every possible soul by plain preaching of the Word of God.

If you are a Christian, we want to help deepen your conviction, strengthen your faith, increase your zeal and your diligence and your courage, and to help you to be a better Christian than you have been. We believe that the only way to accomplish that is through the truth. If you are not a Christian, you need to be one more than you need everything else on earth. Our hope and prayer in every service of the meeting will be that we may be able to encourage you by helping you come to a better knowledge of the truth. Our aim is to persuade you to believe God's Word and to put all of your trust in the provisions of His grace extended through the promises of His Word. If you yield yourself by such a faith in obedience to His will, you may plant your feet upon His promises and have hope of eternal life in the world to come.

These are our hopes and our prayers. This is what we will be seeking, praying, and working to attain during this meeting. We believe that in such an effort, if we will give it our very best, God will certainly bless us.

The Text: Galatians 3:1-4
In the third chapter of Paul's letter to the churches of Galatia, I hear him saying in the first verse:

O foolish Galatians, who hath bewitched you, that ye should not

obey the truth, before whose eyes Jesus Christ hath been evidently set forth, crucified among you? This only would I learn of you,
Received ye the Spirit by the works of the Law, or by the hearing
of faith? Are ye so foolish? having begun in the Spirit, are ye now
made perfect by the flesh? Have ye suffered so many things in vain?
if it be yet in vain.

In this particular passage of Scripture, Paul suggests to us the theme
of our lesson tonight, and that is *the hearing of faith.* By a knowledge
of the truth and by faith in it, these people had turned away from
every other consideration. Some of these people turned from the
Jewish religion and some of them from the world of heathenism;
overcoming unbelief and even idolatry, they accepted the Lord and
rendered obedience to His will. Thus they became the children of
God.

To these same Galatians, in the third chapter of this letter, the
26th and 27th verses, Paul said, "We are all the children of God
by faith in Christ Jesus. For as many as have been baptized into
Christ, have put on Christ." This is the way they had become the
children of God: *through their faith in God's Word and by their
obedience to His will.* This is the way, of course, that God makes
it possible for all of us to be His children. It is the way to begin
the Christian life. It is only the beginning, but it is the only beginning there is. There is not any other way to start obeying God except
to put our trust in Him and to begin our obedience by compliance
with the primary requirements of the Gospel of Christ.

To these children of God had been bestowed spiritual gifts—
ordinary and extraordinary, endowments that were beyond their
ability to appreciate, that were beyond their comprehension as to
the blessing involved and the blessing conveyed by them, opportunities and privileges they enjoyed in Christ that they had never even
imagined to exist. Yet, having begun in the Spirit, the Galatians were
turning back to things of the flesh. Some of them turned to the old
system of carnal laws and outward ceremonies that constituted the
Jewish religion. Others of them returned to the works of the flesh
and the things of the world, which they had supposedly "died unto" when they became the children of God.

And so, Paul raises the question, "Having begun in the Spirit,
having become the children of God by hearing what the Spirit has

revealed, by believing it, and by obeying it, *do you now expect to attain perfection by turning away from things that are spiritual and eternal?* Having begun to walk as the Spirit directs, do you now foolishly expect to make progress by walking after the things of the flesh?'' The answer to that question, of course, is obvious.

Another question he raises, "How did you receive the Spirit? Did you receive the Spirit by doing the works of the law, those of you who would turn back to Judaism?'' Judaizing teachers had followed Paul everywhere he had gone. They had taught that Christianity was an adjunct to the Jewish religion; that the Gospel was simply a suffix to the law of Moses; that Judaism constituted the door of admission into the Church or into the Kingdom of God; that a man had to receive even Jewish circumcision, fleshly circumcision, in order to have the pardon of his soul from the guilt of sin and to become a child of God. Thus, they were seeking to undo, to sabotage, and to destroy the work that Paul had done and to lead astray those who had been converted by it.

Paul was dealing with this when he said, "While you were doing the works of the Law, keeping all of your ceremonies, and complying meticulously or sometimes Pharisaically with all of the outward demands and ceremonies of the Law, did you then *by that means* receive the endowment of the Spirit of God which was bestowed upon you later when you became God's children in Christ?'' The answer, of course, to that question is also obvious. It is a rhetorical question. They did not receive the Spirit by the works of the Law. They received the Spirit *by the hearing of the faith.*

There is not a more important subject than the subject of faith in the Word of God. Nothing more fundamental! God has summed up all that was done in the interest of our redemption in the one word, "grace." The Gospel sums up all that God requires or all that man can do in obedience to the will of God in the one word "faith." *Grace is God's part.* It means that God provides. *Faith is man's part.* It means that man puts his trust in the provisions that God has offered and that he accepts them. He complies with the terms upon which God's provisions have been offered, upon which the promises rest, in the full commitment of that faith that causes him to obey or yield himself to the will of God Almighty.

So, faith is the very heart and substance of the religion of Jesus

Christ, and I want to talk to you about it in all of the night services
of this meeting. We will study tonight what "The Hearing of Faith"
means. One night we want to study on the subject, "The Spirit Of
Faith." Another night we want to talk about "The Law Of Faith."
Another night we want to talk about "How Faith Purifies The
Heart." Another night we want to talk about "Walking By Faith."
And still another night, on the subject, "The Failure Of Faith." Still
another night, "The Victory Of Faith." Faith will be the theme and
the subject of lessons and study together in the evening services of
this meeting.

Faith Is Conviction

In the Word of God, there is a Divine definition that tells us what
"faith" is so that we cannot misunderstand it. Paul said in Hebrews
11:1 that "faith is conviction in unseen things, and confidence in
things hoped for." *Faith is conviction.* That is one element of faith,
but that is not all there is to it. To be convinced concerning the provisions of God's grace and the truth revealed in God's Word, to be
convinced concerning His existence and the revelation of His
nature—this, too, is a necessary element of the faith which comes
through His Divine Word. Conviction in that which God has revealed
in His Word, conviction in the truth that is taught in it, is an *essential* element of faith.

But conviction cannot exist without knowing the ground upon
which our conviction rests. It is utterly impossible for a man to have
faith without knowing *what* he believes! It is even impossible, as we
shall see in the second element of faith, for him to have faith without
knowing *why* he believes it. He must not only know what he believes,
he must know why he believes it!

Peter, in the third chapter of his First Epistle, says that we are
to consecrate in our hearts Jesus Christ as Lord, and that we ought
to be ready to give an answer to every man who asks us a *reason*
for the hope that is within us. So many times people come around
and say to me, "What do we believe about this or that or something
else?" Well, I do not know. I do not know "what *we* believe" about
anything. I must know what *I* believe. But just like I must know
what I believe, *you* must know what you believe; and you must not
only know what you believe, you must know *why you* believe it.

Faith is, not only to be convinced of the truth of that which God has revealed, but faith is to put your trust in the provisions that God has made known in that truth for your salvation. Paul said that "faith is conviction in unseen things," faith in things that God has revealed that man could not otherwise know.

Now, I hear people talk about the process of learning, and how we arrive at what we believe. Modernism, the new orthodoxy, a lot of the existentialism, and the other theories in religion that are modern in nature (and yet are ancient infidelity in principle), all of these will tell you that the way we arrive at what we believe is to assimilate all of the facts by our natural senses that it is possible for us to gain. When we have gathered the facts together, then we are to rationalize or reason upon them until we reach leaps of inference or are able to draw certain conclusions. This is the way they say we arrive at what we are to believe. Now, *that is exactly opposite* to what the Bible teaches, as we shall see in the course of our lesson.

The Bible does not teach that through the wisdom of man faith is made possible in any sense, in any of its elements, or through any of its particulars. The wisdom of man is not to be the basis. Faith moves, operates, and acts in the realm of things that are unseen— things that are purely, and simply, and only, matters of Divine revelation that God had made known—things that man could not know without the Word of God. This is faith in the sense in which the Bible uses it. "Conviction in things unseen." And if our faith rests upon any other basis, then it is not a saving and a justifying faith in the sight of God.

Faith Is Trust
But not only is it conviction. *Faith is also trust*. It is made up of a second element, and saving faith has to have both. I may know what the Bible teaches and be convinced that these things are true. Yet, I may not be willing to submit myself to the truth, for reasons that are purely selfish. My thoughts and desires would conflict with what God would have me to do. I do not wish to surrender, out of the selfishness and stubbornness of my heart. I may not be willing to surrender to that which God would have me to accept and to do, and to put my trust in the provisions of God's grace. If conviction is all there is to my faith—I am but convinced and do not have the trust that will lead me to step out upon the promises of God's Word—*then my faith will not justify me*. It will not save me!

When Paul said, "Being therefore justified by faith, we have peace with God through our Lord Jesus Christ" (Rom. 5:1), he was talking about a faith that was conviction *and* confidence, conviction *and* trust, conviction *and* surrender. Our trusting in God and the provisions of God's grace can bring about in our lives and in our hearts such surrender and such complete commitment. That is what faith is! These are the two elements that must compose it.

Now the Bible gives us some demonstrations of conviction alone. John 1:42 teaches that among the rulers of the Jews there were many that believed on Jesus. And, the expression is as strong an expression as you can find in the Bible from the viewpoint of faith as mere conviction. The preposition is the preposition *"eis"* and it literally means those who believed in Christ. They believed concerning the identity of the Lord.

Many of the rulers of the Jews were convinced concerning the identity of Jesus, but they loved the praise of men more than they did the glory of God. They did not allow their conviction to become trust. They refused to put their trust in the Lord and to walk in His way. They were convinced, but they did not place their trust in Him. They loved the praise of men more than they did the glory of God; hence, *they would not confess Him.* They were believers in the sense that they were convinced concerning His identity.

They gave *assent* or agreement to the person and identity of the Lord, but they did not *confess* Him. They would not. That suggests impenitence, doesn't it? That suggests a rebellion of heart, an impenitent heart! It not only suggests an impenitent heart, but it also suggests that they loved the praise of men more than they did the glory of God. Their affections were not surrendered to the Lord. They did not place their trust in Him; *they would not confess Him.*

For three reasons they were lost. Jesus said, "Unless ye repent, ye shall all likewise perish" (Lk. 13:3). They had not repented; therefore, they were perishing. Jesus said, in effect, "Unless ye confess me before men, I will not confess you before the Father" (see Matt. 12:32-33). They would *not confess Him;* therefore, the Lord will *not acknowledge them.* And the Bible teaches, "If a man love the world, the love of God is not in Him" (1 Jn. 2:15). John says so by inspiration of the Spirit of God. You cannot love the world and love God, and they loved the praises of men more than they did the glory of God.

So, because they had not repented and would not, because they did not and would not confess Christ, because they loved the world more than they loved the Lord, they were lost. *They were condemned men in spite of the fact that they were believers!* They were believers in the sense that they had conviction. The Bible sometimes uses faith, then, in the sense of mere conviction, but it uses faith in other senses also.

Faith Is Persuasion
The Bible uses faith in the sense of full persuasion. For example, in Romans 14 the Apostle Paul said, "Let each man be fully persuaded in his own heart." He was talking about matters of personal conviction, personal judgment, or personal opinion in that fourteenth chapter of Romans. One man thought it was all right to eat meat. Another thought that he ought to eat only herbs. One man thought that it was all right to observe a particular day that had some personal significance to him from the viewpoint of custom. Another man would condemn him for doing it. And in this realm in which God did not legislate a thing, where the word of God had not specified, where man had been given a choice, Paul said that men were to act in harmony with their own conviction or persuasion. They should not offend their conscience by doing the thing that they judged to be displeasing or wrong in the sight of God. So, the definition in Romans 14 is faith or full persuasion. But this is not all.

Saving faith is conviction plus trust. I find this definition of faith in Hebrews 11:6, "He that cometh to God must believe that he is, and that he is a rewarder of them that diligently seek him." God will do what He says He will do. He will keep His promises if you will do His will. You can trust God for the fulfillment of His promises. If you are to come to God, you must believe that He is, and that He will do what He has promised He will do! You can put your trust in Him that He will keep His word and will perform it. This is necessary in order to come to God!

We have seen that faith is defined as mere conviction, and saving faith as both conviction and trust. Also, in the instance of matters of human choice where we are to be guided by human judgment, faith may refer to a persuasion determined by our own consciences.

Faith Is Commitment

But more than that, faith, in the Bible is defined as full commitment—the complete resignation of a man's heart in all of its functions to the Lord and to the will of the Lord, full and unreserved commitment. This, I think, is what Peter implied or stated in the second chapter of the Acts of the Apostles in his sermon on the day of Pentecost, when he said to the Jews—commanded all Israelites in that audience—to believe beyond a doubt, "to know assuredly that Jesus is the Christ."

Not only does Acts 2 suggest the idea of faith being the full commitment and surrender of the heart, but also you will remember another such occasion in Acts 8. When the Ethiopian eunuch asked Philip, the inspired evangelist, "Why can't I be baptized?", Philip said, "If you believe with all of your heart, you may." If you believe "with *all* of your heart." Now, what does believing with all of the heart mean?

Well, it means first of all an understanding and a conviction as to the truth. It is the surrender of the intellect of man to the knowledge of the truth, to that which God has revealed. Man must be convinced concerning the truth which God has revealed. But it means more than that. It means the surrender of his intelligence to trust in the provisions that God has made and the promises that God has offered.

But it means even more than that. "Faith with all of the heart" means that faith is able to beget in our hearts the love that we ought to have for God and for things that are spiritual and eternal. One of the functions of the heart is the emotions, the ability to love or to hate, the ability to sorrow or to rejoice, the whole scope of the emotional nature of man. Faith not only conquers the *intellect*—to be convinced to bring it into agreement with the will of God and the Word of God, and to place the trust of the individual in God's Word and in God's wisdom, rather than in his own or in the wisdom of man—but it also means the surrender of the *affections* of the heart.

Paul, you remember, wrote to the Colossians, as he exhorted them to walk in Christ even as they had received Him, and he said, "Set your affections upon the things that are above where Christ is seated at the right hand of God'' (Col. 3:1-3). Let the affections of your heart be placed upon the things that are in harmony with God's will, not upon the things that are upon the earth. For if the world is a friend of yours, you are guilty of spiritual adultery and you are an enemy of God Almighty, James says. ''Friendship with the world is enmity with God'' (Jas. 4:4). So, we need to understand that faith with all of the heart means not only the surrender of all of the intellect, to be convinced and to trust in that which God has revealed and in God's provision for our salvation, but it means also the surrender of our affections to put God *first* in our hearts.

We are to love God with all of our hearts, souls, minds, and bodies, and to serve only Him. We must love Him as Jesus challenged Peter to love Him, when He said, ''Simon Peter, lovest thou me more than these?'' Jesus challenged Peter with a word in the New Testament which means ''a love that is supreme, to ardently adore.'' This is not just brotherly love, not just a feeling of affection, but the kind of love and the degree of love that will put the Lord first. This is what faith demands—the surrender of our affections!

But it demands more than that; it demands the surrender of the will. Faith must conquer the will and surrender the will of the individual in obedience to the will of God. Trust demands this. As long as I walk willfully in my own way, after the vanity of my own mind, in the deceit of my own ego or conceit; if I live to do what pleases me and what in my judgment I want to do rather than seeking to please God, then I have not been crucified with Christ. My will has not been surrendered. I am not able to say, ''Thy will be done on earth as it is in heaven,'' and be sincere about it. I am not willing to say what Jesus prayed in the Garden, ''Thy will be done.'' This is not the attitude of my heart. Until faith causes me to do the will of God in full surrender and commitment, and to take my stand upon the promises of His Word in trusting obedience, I do not have true faith.

Different Degrees of Faith

Then, I think we need to consider the fact in the lesson that *faith has different degrees*. In the New Testament this is noted. For example, on four occasions in the ministry of our Lord among men, I hear him rebuking his disciples for ''little faith.'' One time they tried to cast out a devil. They were unable to do it, not because they did not have the power, but because they did not have enough faith to exercise the power that the Lord had promised them. This was an evidence of "little faith," of weak faith, upon their part. Simon Peter stepped out of the boat upon the bidding of Jesus to walk to the Lord on the water; but when he saw the waves dashing about him, his faith was so weak that he began to sink. He did not have enough faith to carry out the commandment of the Lord when the Lord commanded him to come, and Jesus rebuked him for his "little faith."

Once when Jesus was weary with the trials and the toils and the travels of the day, he fell asleep upon a cushion on the deck of the little vessel in which he was sailing across Galilee with his disciples. A storm suddenly arose, which is not an unusual thing on Galilee, and the little boat seemed about to be swamped. His disciples became afraid. They awakened him and asked, "Carest thou not that we perish?" They seemed to know that he had the power to save them. Why they did not understand and accept with the same faith in the Lord whether he was asleep or not, that they would not be allowed to perish in the storm, I do not know. But they awakened Him in their fear, and Jesus rebuked them for their "little faith."

Upon another occasion the Lord, you remember, talked about the leaven of the Pharisees and the Sadducees. He was not talking about bread to eat. They thought he was. They lacked spiritual discernment. They had their mind upon earthly things rather than upon heavenly things. This is so often our difficulty. It makes it so much harder to teach people the truth. Like Peter, we mind the things of men rather than the things of God and we are unable spiritually to discern and to receive the things of God simply because we are carnally and worldly-minded. And God said that was the cause of it— "that the carnally minded man cannot receive the things of God." And that is true in all respects. A man cuts himself off from the ability to understand and to drink deeply from the fountain of truth and to eat of the "strong meat" of the Word of God because of the worldliness—the worldly considerations of carnality—that fills his mind. He is not spiritually minded.

And this was the trouble with the disciples. They thought the Lord was talking about the bread of the Pharisees and the Sadducees, and he rebuked them and explained that he was not talking about their bread but was talking about their false teaching. He rebuked the disciples for their inability to understand what he was talking about.

So, the Bible talks about weak faith. But the Bible not only talks about weak faith, the Bible talks about *great faith*. I remember in Matthew chapter eight and in Luke chapter seven that the Lord healed a centurion's servant. It is a very outstanding incident in the life of Christ. One of the captains of the Roman army, the army of occupation in the land of Palestine, had a servant that was very near death. He sent his Jewish neighbors to get Jesus. He had accommodated them by his generosity and favor and thus placed them under obligation. He had even built a synagogue for them. Though they despised him, they were under obligation to him, and he requested of them that they go to Jesus and request of Jesus that he heal his servant. You remember that they went and they said to the Lord, "He is worthy that thou shouldst do this for him."

Jesus started with them back to the man's house, and as he approached the house, the Gentile centurion or army captain sent his servant out with the word, "I do not consider myself worthy to come unto you." This is why he had sent the Jews. "Neither do I consider myself worthy that you should enter into my house. Only speak the word and it shall be done."

This soldier describes, in his message to Jesus, his concept of the Word of the Lord and its power and its authority. He said, "I am a man of authority, I have soldiers under my command, a hundred of them. I say to them to go, and they have to go, or they are guilty of insurrection, sedition, or rebellion, punishable by death. I command them to come and they have to come; they do not have any choice about it. They are subject to my command and responsible for doing what I tell them to do. They have no appeal from my authority."

Then he added further, "I have servants, slaves, chattels, property in the person of individuals who belong to me. I say to one servant, 'You do this.' He does not have any appeal from it; he belongs to me; he cannot deny, refuse, rebel, or appeal from my decision and from what I tell him to do. I say to another one, 'Do this,' and he does it. There is no appeal for my servants from the authority of my word. It has the power and that authority over those who are subject to it. So it is," he said to the Lord, "that if you say it shall be done, that is all that is necessary; it will be done."

Jesus turned to the Jews that were with him, and he said, "In all Israel"—among all of the Israelites that I have had contact with, among all the Jews that I have seen—"I have not seen or found demonstrated such great faith." Here was a man who knew what faith in the Lord and in the Word of the Lord meant.

The Source of Great Faith

But, I want to talk in the closing moments of our lesson, about this faith—this *great faith*. First of all, the source of faith needs to be kept in mind. Paul said, "Faith comes by hearing, and hearing by the Word of God" (Rom. 10:17). Peter said, "God made choice that the Gentiles by my mouth should hear the word of the Gospel and believe" (Acts 15:7). The foundation for all that it is possible for a man to believe, for all of the faith that you can exercise, is the Word of God. There is no other source and no other power that is able to plant faith in the heart of an individual! And I need to keep that in mind.

Sometimes we use the words "I believe" very carelessly. "I believe" thus and so, and God never said anything that remotely sounded like it. If you believe it on that basis, you believe it for some other reason than the fact that you have found it in the Word of God, and that *is not* faith in God.

So, faith that is acceptable to God, that is able to save, and that will justify our hearts before God and make us righteous in God's sight, is a faith that is based upon hearing the Word of God. This Word is the source of faith! This is the source of all spiritual blessings: *faith in that which God has said in the Word of God!* When you begin to look at that fact, it is significant that I need the proper attitude in order for the Word of God to produce faith in my heart.

Nothing makes it any clearer than the parable of the sower. In four different kinds of soil, the same seed was sown. Three of them produced no harvest at all. All of that seed was lost. Only one kind of soil was able to produce any seed or any fruit from the seed, and that was a good and honest heart.

Now, I have an idea that the Lord was talking about those who had heard and believed his Word, and probably not about unbelievers primarily in that parable. If so, the application (instead of being made to the fellow out here who never has become a Christian) needs to be made to those of us in the Church who have the seed or the Word of God planted in our hearts. At times those of us who in some measure have an opportunity through teaching to put our trust in God and to render obedience to His will, have the wrong attitude and hence do not profit by the Word of God as we ought.

But the principle would certainly apply to a man who, upon the mere hearing of the initial truths of the Gospel or the fundamental facts of it, rejects them. Certainly what he learns from the Word of God cannot produce any sort or kind of fruit unto God because of the wrong attitude of heart.

One of the most important things, then, that we could possibly talk about in connection with faith is *the importance of the right attitude of mind and heart.* Nothing is more important than for me to have in my heart toward God and toward the Word of God the right attitude! Now that eliminates a number of destructive considerations that could well be mentioned in connection with faith.

The Attitude of the Young Prophet

If you want an example of the wrong attitude, go back to the young prophet. There is in his story in 1 Kings chapter 13 a demonstration from the Old Testament of a wrong attitude. The young prophet went, when God told him to go up to Dan and Bethel and cry out against the altar, and he started out to obey God's instructions about his return. When the prophet's message had been delivered, the king commanded him to be seized. But as the king made the gesture his arm withered, and he could not draw it back again to his body. His arm was left useless and stiffened. He besought the young prophet to beseech God to heal and restore the arm to him. This was granted.

Then the king invited him to come into the palace to receive rest, refreshment for himself, and a reward, but the young man rejected this offer. There was just one reason why he rejected it: *God said for him not to remain at the palace after delivering the message but to return home immediately.*

That ought to be reason enough for anything. God said for me not to do it! And if God says for me not to do it, then faith in God, in the Word of God, demands of me that I do not do it!

So, the young prophet started home, by a different route, exactly as God had commanded him to do. But, you know, he was deceived. His faith in God was surrendered because he allowed himself to be deceived! As he journeyed on his way, with the intent and purpose of carrying out what God had told him to do, an old prophet who had been told by his sons what had happened set out in pursuit. When he caught the young prophet he invited him back. He wanted to talk with him. "I need to talk to you." He lived in this land. And the young prophet said, "I cannot go back." "Well, you need refreshment and you need rest," and he began to persuade him. But the young prophet steadfastly refused. Why? "Because *God said* for me *not* to do it!"

But the old prophet made up a pretty good lie in the time that he had, to deceive the younger man. He said, "I have received a later revelation. Since God told you that, He has spoken to me, and He told me something different. God told you this, but God has given me a later revelation." And the young man put his faith in the story and the claim of that old prophet. That meant that he surrendered his faith in God. When he put his faith in what the old prophet said, he surrendered faith in what God told him, didn't he? That is always the case! The basis of faith is not the wisdom of man, but the Word of God!

Paul said in First Corinthians 2 that he had preached "in weakness and in fear and in much trembling," and he explained, "I was determined when I came unto you to preach nothing but Jesus Christ and him crucified, that your faith might stand not in the wisdom of man, but in the power of God." That is the basis of our faith.

Later revelations are all fraud—I do not care whether it is Mormonism, or whether it is Christian Science, or whether it is Adventism, or whether it is some so-called "Holy Ghost filled" preacher who preaches something that the Bible does not say anything about. It does not matter whether it comes from Catholicism with its councils and hierarchy or where it may come from, if the Word of God does not teach it, you cannot afford to make it a part of your faith.

And so, we need to learn that the right attitude toward the Word of God is to stay with what God says and reject all claims that men may make to a later revelation or another revelation that says something that the Word of God does not say. My faith belongs in what God does say. That ought to be its limitations and its boundaries! What God says is the very foundation of faith!

The Attitude of Balaam

But I think of Balaam as another example of the wrong attitude. Balaam, you know, was invited by Balak to come up and curse the children of Israel who were encamped in the valley of Moab. He wanted them driven out of the land, and so he wanted the prophet to pronounce a curse upon them that he might get rid of them. You may remember that Balaam wanted to go and he asked God if he could go, but God said, "You cannot. They are my people." So Balaam came back and told the messenger of the king, "I cannot go."

But the king was not easy to refuse. He operated on the theory that every man has his price, so he raised the ante. He sent back the offer of a greater reward, and he sent more important messengers to make an impression upon Balaam. When they came and told Balaam what the king wanted, Balaam said he would go back and see what more the Lord had to say. Now, that just meant one thing: "I will see if God has not changed His mind."

And I have an idea that there are a lot of people in this world today who think they believe in God, but who in the recesses of their own mind have the idea that God somewhere and sometime between now and the Judgment will change His mind about some things. You take a man, for example, who is a Christian and who knows that the Bible teaches that adulterers, fornicators, liars, murderers, and drunkards *will not* enter through the Gate into the City. No liar will be in Heaven! That is what your Bible says about it.

Yet, we go right on lying. Why? Don't you believe in God? Oh yes, I believe in God. Well, don't you believe what God says about it? Yes, I believe what God says about it, but somehow or other I believe that God just will not enforce that. I do not believe that God will just carry that out to the letter. I believe that some way, somehow, because of something else as a consideration, that God will allow me to escape the penalty for lying.

Now, don't you sometimes feel that way, maybe subconsciously or unconsciously? Don't we think that way about things? I will just go on committing adultery or sinning in other ways—I will go on committing that thing that God commands me not to do, condemns me for doing, and tells me I cannot do and go to Heaven. Paul said those who practice such things "shall not inherit the kingdom of God" (1 Cor. 6:9-10).

But, sometimes we think, "I can do it, and maybe I will get by with it. After all, I am pretty liberal with my money," or, "I devote a lot of my time, I give a lot of my ability, and I surrender a lot of what I would like to do. God is not going to hold me strictly to this one little thing—this one little corner, this one little recess in my heart that I want for myself, that I want to be an exception. I expect that God sometime, somewhere will change His mind and will not just carry out His warnings to the letter of the law." Is that not the way we feel? I am afraid it is. You examine your own heart and see.

The Attitude of Israel
I remember another example of the wrong attitude, and that was the attitude of Israel. Israel rejected God as their king. They turned Him down. He had always come to their aid, met their needs, and delivered them out of the hands of their enemies. He had raised up one to lead them to victory every time that the enemy had assailed them, when they would do His will. There came a time when they wanted a king, to be like the nations around them. They cried out, "Give us a king!" God let them have their way, even as He will let you and me have our way if we do not let His will guide us.

You will recall that they built their hope, even concerning the promised Messiah, upon the basis of an earthly king. They expected the Messiah, when he came, to sit upon the literal throne of David. They thought that God would restore the old National Kingdom of Fleshly Israel, with all of the prosperity and the power and the glory that characterized it in the days of Saul and David and Solomon. This is what they thought.

When they studied the Old Testament prophets, every single passage of prophecy that they came to that said anything about a kingly and a glorious Messiah, they interpreted it to mean what they wanted it to mean: an earthly king and an earthly kingdom. They read that into it. When they read some passage from the prophets that described the coming Messiah as a man of sorrows and acquainted with grief, as one who would be smitten for our transgressions and bruised for our iniquity, who would give his soul up for a sacrifice for sin, who would pour out his soul unto death, they said, "Oh, I know that God said that, but that just cannot be the Messiah that God has promised, because He is going to be an earthly king."

They warped, twisted, wrested, and molded the Word of God to fit their idol, and so often we do the same thing. We go to the Bible to prove we are right about something instead of to prove *what* is right, to justify ourselves rather than to be justified in the sight of God. Instead of going to learn the truth, we go to prove our opinions. We study the Bible to justify our own ideas and read into it our own idols. God said in Ezekiel 14 that if my people come to me with idols in their hearts, I will reward them according to the multitude of their idols. Paul said, if we do not receive the love of the truth, we will be sent a working of error that "we might believe a lie and be damned because we believe not the truth" (see 2 Thess. 2:10-12).

What is necessary in order not to be deceived and led away from the truth? *A love of the truth!* "Buy the truth and sell it not!" That is the kind of faith we ought to have—I will take what God has said in His Word, plant my feet upon it, and not be moved away from it. I will not accept the word of the teaching of any man. I will not discount for one moment the fact that God means what He says and that His Word is steadfast. I will stand upon what God has said in language plain enough that I can understand it. I will build my hope upon God's promises! I will guide my life by that which I learn to be God's will, and not by my own desires! Because this is what faith demands! A full commitment!

That is *great* faith! The man who has faith that is able to save is the man who has faith that obeys. Faith works by love! And that does not mean just baptism. That means doing the will of God in your daily life as a Christian just as much as it applies to being baptized, or to anything else that God commands.

Do We Have Abraham's Faith?

Paul in Romans 4 describes the steps of Abraham's faith. There were at least two that I can see. One of them is that he believed what

God said in spite of the circumstances. God promised him a son by his wife, Sarah. He counted his own body as good as dead. Sarah had never conceived and borne any children, and now she was past the age to do so.

There was no reasonable ground upon which to accept God's promise. Human experience would not justify accepting it. Human wisdom would not justify accepting it. There were no facts to rationalize about, no inferences to draw that made faith in God's promise to Abraham reasonable. There was not any syllogism that he could fashion to prove it by. It could not be demonstrated.

Why did he believe it? There was just one reason. In spite of all the unreasonable circumstances that made it seem entirely unlikely and that made it look entirely unreasonable, Abraham believed it just because *God said it!* And that is the reason that we ought to believe all that we believe. *Just because God said it!!*

The second step of Abraham's faith is seen in that he not only believed what God said in spite of the circumstances, but he also did what God commanded him to do in spite of the cost. It did not make any difference how much it cost him. God said to Abraham later on, when that child had grown up into young manhood, "You take him yonder on the mountain and offer him as a sacrifice. Take his life, and burn his body on the altar."

Abraham could have objected, "He is the child of promise." "You do *what I say*," is what God would have replied to him. He could have said, "You told me that I would not only have a son from my wife Sarah, but that *through him* I would become the father of a great nation, and there would be a blessing extended to all the nations of the earth. If I kill him, you will not be able to fulfill your promise." He could have rationalized that way, but he did not.

It was the greatest sacrifice that he could have been called upon to make. God emphasized the enormity of it, saying, "Take Isaac, thy son"—and as if to emphasize to him what He was demanding, God said, "thine *only* son"—"and offer him as a sacrifice." Abraham did not falter; he did not hesitate. He did not even delay. He immediately gathered the company and the things that were essential and set out on the journey.

And, as if to test his faith once more, when he had left his servants at the foot of the mountain and started up the mountain to offer his son as God had instructed him to offer him, the boy said to him, "Father, we have everything but the sacrifice. What are we going to offer?" And Abraham, without faltering, said "Son, God will provide."

God will provide! God will take care of the situation. It is not our worry. Our responsibility is to do by faith what God says for us to do and let God take care of the contingencies and the results. Can you do it? *Can you do it?* Do you have that kind of faith—that I will do what God says for me to do, no matter what it costs, and I will not for one moment doubt the consequences?

How did Abraham do it? There is an explanation for it. The explanation is that he counted God able and faithful in the fulfillment of His promises to raise up Isaac from the dead, to bring him back to life and fulfill His promise anyhow (Heb. 11:19). He believed in God to the extent that he did not for a moment doubt the fact either that God *could* or that God *would* fulfill His promises. That is what faith is. That is the hearing that faith will accord what God says, and I ask you tonight, do you have it?

Have you in full surrendered yourself to the will of the Lord to do what God commands you to do?

Further Study On Chapter Two

1. A pre-assigned student should read 3 review questions on chapter 1, give the class a few minutes to write answers, then announce correct answers. Assign someone to prepare 3 review questions on chapter 2 for the next class.

2. Memorize Gal. 3:1-2 or some other passage in chapter 2 and be ready to quote it. (Give the class 1-2 minutes to write down their passage, then call on a few to recite.)

3. Outline chapter 2 at home (main points and Scriptures). The teacher will call on class members to explain what each heading means (such as, "Faith Is Conviction") and how some passage was used to support the heading.

4. Each student should write and bring to class a brief "commen-

tary" on every phrase in Gal. 3:1-4. Tell in your own words what each verse means. The teacher can call upon several students to read all or part of what they have written.

5. What facts, commands, and promises of the gospel are reflected in Gal. 3:1-4, 26-27?

6. Each student should have prepared a list of questions and answers on chapter 2 (5 true-false; 3 brief answer; 2 asking, "What passage teaches us that. . .?"). The teacher should ask students to read some of their questions for the class to discuss.

7. What three reasons did the author give for the believers in Jn. 12:42 being lost? Tell about similar cases of people who believe the truth but will not obey it today. Are the "reasons" they give for not obeying always the *true* reasons?

8. Explain what is meant by the author's warning against going to the Bible "to prove we are right about something instead of to prove *what* is right" (in section on "The Attitude of Israel").

9. What modern religious practices and denominations substitute the works of the Jewish law for the hearing of faith?

10. How does a person's attitude affect his hearing of God's word and his obedience to it? Compare audience attitude in Acts 2 and Acts 7. Will attitude *alone* save (consider Acts 10:1-2)? Explain how the attitude of hearers helps us understand "as many as were ordained to eternal life" and "I have much people in this city" (Acts 13:44-48; 18:9-11). (If possible, the teacher may break the class into smaller groups of 3-5 for about 5-7 minutes of discussion; then let each group leader tell the whole class one or two important points developed by the group.)

CHAPTER THREE

The Spirit of Faith

I am enjoying this meeting more than it is possible for me to express. I am enjoying a lot of things about it. One of them is the pleasant association that I am enjoying with friends of many, many years, and this is always, of course, pleasant to all of us. Then the interest that has been taken by so many of you in these meetings by your presence, your good attention, and your listening to the Word of God, as we undertake to preach it, is a source of encouragement, for which we are very grateful indeed. Tonight we are happy to have a number of visitors from various congregations, and we hope that you will come back to the services again and again.

Our interest in these services is by the plain preaching of the Word of God to make every contribution that we know how to make for the salvation of souls through the truth. If you are not a Christian, we are hoping that we may be able to help you to become one. *You need to be a Christian more than you need everything else on earth combined!* Until you become one, there is not a promise of God that you can claim, not a hope that you can have in your heart, based upon the Word and the promises of the Lord. And so we hope that you will not continue to rob yourself of the rich provisions of God's grace by rejecting His Word and refusing to do His will. If you are a child of God, our hope and prayer is that we may help you to be a better one.

The Text: 2 Corinthians 4:13-5:10

Tonight our text of scripture suggesting our subject of study is found in the fourth chapter of Paul's second letter to the church at Corinth. I want to read a few verses, beginning with verse 13:

> We have the same spirit of faith, according as it is written, I believe, and therefore have I spoken, we also believe, and therefore speak; knowing that he which raised up the Lord Jesus shall raise

up us also by Jesus, and shall present us with you. For all things are for your sakes, that the abundant grace might through the thanksgiving of many redound to the glory of God. For which cause we faint not; but though our outward man perish, yet the inward man is renewed day by day. For our light affliction, which is but for a moment, worketh for us a far more exceeding and eternal weight of glory; while we look not at the things which are seen, but at the things which are not seen: for the things which are seen are temporal; but the things which are not seen are eternal. For we know that, if our earthly house of this tabernacle were dissolved, we have a building of God, a house not made with hands, eternal in the heavens. For in this we groan, earnestly desiring to be clothed upon with our house which is from heaven: if so be that being clothed we shall not be found naked. For we that are in this tabernacle do groan, being burdened: not for that we would be unclothed, but clothed upon, that mortality might be swallowed up of life. Now he that hath wrought us for the selfsame thing is God, who also hath given unto us the earnest of the Spirit. Therefore, we are always confident, knowing that, whilst we are at home in the body, we are absent from the Lord; (for we walk by faith, not by sight:) we are confident, I say, and willing rather to be absent from the body, and to be present with the Lord. Wherefore we labor that, whether present or absent, we may be accepted of him. For we must all appear before the judgment seat of Christ; that every one may receive the things done in his body, according to that he hath done, whether it be good or bad.

I do not know of a passage of scripture in the entire Word of God that better expresses what a man's outlook or attitude toward life ought to be, than these verses that we have read. Surely Paul was moved, not only by the power of the Holy Spirit and by the will of God as he wrote them, but also by the faith of his own heart in God's will and in the provisions of God's grace.

Paul had exactly the right evaluation of the things of this life in mind. He was thinking about *the immortal nature,* the eternal nature of man's spirit, the spirit that dwells within us, the spirit which is to give God homage and of which God Himself is jealous. Man's spirit is a part of God's own breed in nature—made in the image of God — with which each one of us has been endowed. Only by proper appreciation for that eternal spirit can we recognize the need for its salvation through faith in God and in His Word, and enjoy the provisions He has made through His Word and offered in the interest of our salvation.

Paul said that we have received the "same spirit of faith," and it is the spirit of faith that brings about this whole discussion. Our spiritual concern should be awakened not only by the immortal or eternal nature of man's spirit, but also by the fact that man faces the eventuality of death and is unable either to long delay or ultimately avoid it; for, it is appointed unto men once to die and then the judgment. Paul calls that to our attention. In view of death's certainty, in view of the resurrection on the other side, and in view of the fact that we are accountable to God and shall stand in God's presence after a while to give an account of all that we have done in the body, whether it be good or bad, *in view of all these considerations,* Paul urges that we need to have in our hearts the same spirit of faith. And he tells us what it is.

"I Believed, And Therefore Have I Spoken."

Back in the Old Testament, as Paul quotes from it, it is written, "I believed, and therefore have I spoken." Paul said we also believe and therefore speak, as it is written—"according as it is written I believed, and therefore have I spoken." My faith can rest only upon the Word of God. This is the source of it. We gave emphasis to that in our study last night: "faith comes by hearing and hearing by the Word of God." This in itself impresses not only the importance of faith, because it means the right attitude toward God and toward the Word of God, but also it shows us the importance of it from the viewpoint of bringing us into *a proper relationship with God.* This is a relationship that is described as righteousness, as justification, as holiness, as being the children of God, as being redeemed or given pardon, and as those who belong unto God, having been purged from their sins by the blood of the Son of God.

But a great many people who readily agree that faith is essential and faith is important will deny the essentiality and importance of it by saying that it does not matter what a man believes, just so he is sincere. Their conception of the truth is that there is not any fixed, definite truth. It is all relative, and it does not matter what you believe about any given thing, if you are honest, earnest, and sincere.

This means, first of all, that truth cannot be determined, that it has not been revealed, and that there is no way to learn what the truth is. In such a view, it would be impossible for a man to exercise faith in truth—faith prescribed by it, faith founded upon it. If the truth is relative, there is not any fixed standard by which we are to learn what is right and what is wrong in the sight of God. If there is no medium by which truth can be ascertained, by which it can be tested and by which it can be tried, then certainly there is not any way that a man can determine what to believe. And if it is not important what we believe, then it is not important whether or not we do believe.

If believing one thing is just as good as believing something else, if it does not matter *today* what a man believes, it cannot and could not *ever* matter what a man believed. And it could not matter therefore, whether a man believed the Bible. Whatever the Bible said about anything would be of no importance, because it would not matter whether or not one believed. If one honestly disbelieved what the Bible teaches on any point, he would be just as well off as to honestly believe what the Bible teaches. Therefore what the Bible teaches would be of no importance.

Just so a man is honest and sincere, in this view it cannot matter what he believes—whether or not he believes this or that or anything. That is *equivalent to saying it does not matter whether or not he believes* what God says, and that is *equivalent to saying that it does not matter what God says!* So, you can throw your Bible on the junk pile and forget about it, go your way and do as you please, walk after the vanity of your own mind, and be just as well off as if you learned and believed everything the Bible records.

A man would be just as well off that did not believe that Jesus Christ is the Son of God, as he would be believing that Jesus is the Son of God, if it does not matter what a man believes. Yet, Jesus said, "Except ye believe that I am he, ye shall die in your sins" (Jn. 8:24). And He explained that if a person dies in his sins, "Whither I go, ye cannot come" (v. 21). It matters *what* a man believes about whether Jesus Christ is the Son of God or not!

Not only that, I remember that Paul said, "He that cometh to God must believe that he is, and that he is a rewarder of them that diligently seek him" (Heb. 11:6). I must believe in the God revealed in the Bible! I must believe in the provisions of His grace! I must put my confidence in the promises that His Word contains! I must believe that He is, that He will do what He said He will do, and that He will keep His promises!

There is plenty of ground upon which to believe and to trust the promises of God's Word. Solomon, you remember, said, as he called Israel together, "That of all the good things that Jehovah your God has promised, through Moses his servant, he has not failed to perform a single word" (1 Kgs. 9:56). Joshua bore testimony of the same thing, that God has kept every word of every promise that He ever made (Josh. 21:45; 23:14). Sarah received power to conceive seed after she was of age, for the reason that she believed that He was faithful who had promised. I need to put my faith in the Word of God and put my trust implicitly in it, and believe it *because I believe in the God who gave it.*

I remember that Jesus taught that if a man does not believe the Gospel, he will be damned, condemned, or lost eternally. He said to the Apostles, "Go into all the world, and preach the gospel to every creature. He that believeth and is baptized shall be saved; but he that believeth not shall be damned" (Mk. 16:15-16). Well, he that believeth not *what*? What disbelief is it that damns the soul of a man? He is lost if he does not believe what? It is not some opinion that some preacher may have. It is not some human creed that some man may have written. It is not some philosophy that some man may have invented. But it is the Gospel of the Son of God! "Go into all the world and preach the gospel to every creature. He that believeth"—the Gospel that you preach—"and is baptized shall be saved. He that believeth not"—the Gospel that you preach—"will be damned."

"The Love Of The Truth"
In the second letter to the Thessalonians, chapter two, Paul refers to "those who receive not the love of the truth"—those who do not put in their hearts the proper emphasis and value on the truth. They do not value it above everything, do not recognize that it is the pearl of great price. It is the treasure hidden in the field, which, when a man finds he ought to be willing to go and sell all that he has in order to possess it. Pay any price for it.

"Buy the truth and sell it not." When once you have learned the truth, refuse to part with it no matter what the reward may be that is offered. That is the value of the truth! Paul said that if we do

not so evaluate the truth that we will be sent a working of error that
"we might believe a lie and be damned because we believe not the
truth." A man must believe the truth in order to be saved. To believe
error condemns! To believe the truth saves!

There is just one standard by which that truth can be
determined—only one measurement that can be made of it. John
was given the measuring reed and the voice said, "Rise, and measure
the temple" (Rev. 11:1). And he did so, and measured also the altar
and them that worshipped therein. There is a measuring reed for
your faith and mine, and that measuring reed for Divine truth and
for our faith is the Word of God. Jesus said in John 17, "Sanctify
them through thy truth: thy word is truth."

You know, for everything there has to be a standard. We have
to have *standard time* or else we would not know what time of day
it is. We have to have *standard measurement* or we would not know
whether we got a gallon of gasoline when we paid for it, or a pound
of sugar when we paid for it. Standards of weight and measurement,
standards from every point of view, for all the affairs of life, are
essential and necessary. There would be utter confusion if it were
not for the fact that we have standards and these standards are fixed by law. When you cross over the line into another country, the
standard changes for the law is different. There is a different government, exercising a different authority, setting a different standard.

Drive across the line into Canada, and a Canadian quart is a fourth
larger than an American quart. Five American quarts are in a Canadian gallon. I thought they were robbing me the first time I bought
gasoline up there, until I found out that I was getting more for a
gallon than I do in this country. Somebody may say, "Well, do they
not know what a gallon is?" Yes. They have the right to determine
what a gallon is in their country. They have a government of their
own. That government has the authority to set the standard.

Even so, the sovereign of this universe! "And the earth is the
Lord's and the fullness thereof." God has the right to determine
the standard of truth, of your faith, of authority, of obedience, of
our service, and of our sacrifice. It is to be measured in every sense
and in every way and in every degree by the standard that God has
set: *the Word of God.*

I might ask tonight, "What time is it?" I look back at the clock on the wall and it says it is eight minutes after eight o'clock. You look at your watch and you way, "It is ten minutes after." I look at mine and I say, "It is five minutes after." Suppose we need to know *exactly* what time it is. How would we determine it? Perhaps there would be as many different times as there are timepieces in the audience. How would you know? Sometimes it is extremely important to know what the minute of the hour of the day is. How may we know? By what can we determine whether or not the time is right? You cannot go by every timepiece that you look at. Some of them are not accurate. But how can you determine if they are accurate or not?

Well, we go down the street and we find the clock on the wall at some public building or business house that has Naval Observatory time, such as Western Union. That means that it is kept correctly. Every few seconds, perhaps, or on the dot at stated intervals, it is corrected. If it gets off to the least degree, it is corrected, and put exactly on the second, the minute, and the hour. But what is the standard by which that standard is discerned? The Naval Observatory. How does the Naval Observatory do it? They have a chronometer that itself is regulated by the movements of God's universe, and that is the standard by which time is determined.

Now, you are not going to argue with that, are you? I do not care how much you paid for your watch, or how long you have had it, how reliable it has been, or anything else about it. You will pull the stem out of it, if you are very smart, and make it agree with that time, if you know that is what it is. If that is really Naval Observatory time, regulated by Western Union service, then you will do just what I will do. You will pull the stem out and make your watch agree with it. This ought to be our attitude in matters of faith. In matters of faith I am to be regulated by the standard that God Himself has given, and that standard has been so definitely determined in the Word of God that I can learn what the truth is.

Human Answers To The Question, "Who Is Jesus?"

Jesus helped us in one instance to determine it. In a very simple illustration we can get the idea before you. I remember that in Matthew, chapter sixteen, when He came into the parts of Caesarea Philippi, he asked His disciples saying, "Whom do men say that I

the Son of man am?'' And they answered, *"Men say"*—I want you
to notice—"Men say that you are John the Baptist." Others say,
"You are Jeremiah." Other men say that you are Elijah. Still others
say, "You are just one of the Old Testament prophets." This is what
men are saying.

They represent human doctrine. They represent human creeds.
They represent human standards, human ideas, human opinions,
human arrangements, and human institutions. This is what men are
saying. What one of them says is just as good as what another one
says. This is true of human creeds. One of them is just as reliable
as the other. None of them are reliable at all, for the reason that
they are written by man and the "way of man is not in himself."

Before noticing Peter's answer to the Lord's question in Matthew
16, let us stress that human creeds and human wisdom are the standards of faith in *the religions of men.* More than that, human creeds
are constantly being revised. They recognize their own insufficiency
and they are constantly changing. Sometimes human creeds teach
exactly the opposite to what that particular creed at one time taught.
I could produce a certain denominational discipline that in 1910 in
one of the Articles of Faith expressed by the official body of a certain organization of that denomination, was changed from saying
that a child was born in sin to the expression that children are born
in Christ. Now if it was right prior to 1910, it is wrong now. If it
is right now, it was wrong then. When you revise a matter of faith,
when you change a doctrine, *it cannot be right both times.*

So, human creeds are constantly being revised. I have in my library
a book that gives the confessions of faith of a certain denomination
all down from the very days of its beginning, from the day that it
started in England. It will not matter which one it is. It is true of
them all. Modifications have been made in the doctrines of that particular denomination, in the way those doctrines are expressed, in
the way they have been watered down, so to speak, and made a little more palatable. They teach the same principle and yet in many
respects have modified, changed, and revised the principle to suit
the times.

This is a rather remarkable thing to think about and to study upon.
It is true of all human creeds. They make provisions for amendment
and for revision. Those who wrote them, the bodies that authorized

them to begin with, have the right to revise them. Put your faith in one today, and it may teach exactly the opposite tomorrow. This is exactly what has happened over, and over, and over again.

But the Word of God is not subject to revisions. "The flower of the grass fadeth and withereth away, but the Word of the Lord endures forever" (1 Pet. 1:24). This is the way the Word of God talks about truth. Jesus said, "The word I spake unto you shall judge you in the last day" (Jn. 12:48). To the Apostles He said, "Whatsoever you bind upon earth will be bound in heaven, and whatsoever you loose upon earth will be loosed in heaven" (Matt. 16:19). He gave them the authority, as His ambassadors, to make known His Divine decrees to all the nations of the earth—decrees that will be binding upon all men of all nations in the judgment. Paul said that God will judge all men "according to my gospel," the Gospel of Christ, which Paul faithfully preached (Rom. 2:16). This is the standard of judgment.

Human creeds then are unreliable. They are insufficient because they are constantly amended; they are not worthy of our confidence because they are constantly changing; they are not authoritative. They are unenforceable. Suppose that a human creed tells you that it is all right to do a certain thing in worship to God. Just imagine any human practice. It is right; do it and you will please God—when you follow that creed. Then in the Judgment, God rejects it because it is not in His Word. What can you do about it?

Let us be definite in our illustration. Suppose some preacher tells you that it is just as good to be sprinkled with water as it is to be immersed when you are baptized. Now, no historian questions the fact that immersion was the unvaried practice in the New Testament Church. No authority says that the word "baptize" means to sprinkle. Regarding the original Greek word that Jesus used when he commanded it, no accepted authority says that sprinkling is included in its meaning. Certainly the Bible nowhere records an instance of sprinkling.

People were baptized in the New Testament day when they were in the water. Not out of it, but *in the water*. And after being baptized, as in the case of Jesus and the eunuch, both instances, they came up *out of the water*. The circumstantial evidence, the meaning of the word, the description of the action as a burial and a resurrection, as a planting and a coming forth, as the washing of the body in pure water, all of this confirms that baptism is immersion. It is plainly and definitely taught in the Word of God.

But suppose some preacher tells you, some creed teaches you, and you accept sprinkling instead of what the Bible teaches on the subject. You rely upon it. But when you get to the Judgment after a while, the Lord rejects it, and calls your attention to the fact that sprinkling is not taught in His Word, that it is not what He commanded you to do. What are you going to do about it? Can you call on the preacher that told you it was all right to come to your rescue? What could he do about it? Can you call upon the church that had that creed written, taught that doctrine, and persuaded you to accept it, to come to your rescue? What could they do about it?

What is going to determine in the Judgment the salvation of your soul? What does it stand upon: *the doctrine of men or the Word of God?* Human creeds and human doctrines are not authoritative. They are not enforceable. So, they altogether are lacking. One of them is just as good as another, but none of them are any good at all. Human doctrines in the realm of things spiritual and eternal are always wrong.

The Divine Answer: Jesus Is The Christ, The Son Of God

Now, turning back to the question of the identity of Jesus in Matthew 16, let us see that Jesus calls attention to the truth in contrast to human opinions. Jesus asked the apostles, "Whom do you say that I am?" And Peter answered, "Thou art the Christ, the Son of the living God."

Thou art the Christ, the Son of the living God! Jesus said, "Blessed are thou Simon Barjona, for flesh and blood did not reveal this unto thee." You did not learn this from men. It did not come from man, but from "my Father which is in Heaven." This is what His Word teaches, and that is the truth, because it is the Word of God. Now, there is the dividing line between truth and error! That is the dividing line always between matters Divinely authorized, that which God commands, and what men teach. The same line of division is drawn today.

In Matthew, chapter fifteen, you remember that Jesus was talking about the traditions of the elders and the commandments of the law of God. The Jews did not know the difference. They had covered up the law of God and its commandments and its ordinances with human traditions, just like we have covered up the truth today in the religious world with human creeds, human doctrines, and humanly authorized practices. Jesus spent much of his time drawing the line between human creeds, on the one hand, and on the other hand, Divinely ordained truths revealed in the Word of God and God's will represented in His commandments as He has ordained His will to be executed. In Matthew fifteen you have a fine example. The scribes and Pharisees came to Jesus and asked, "Why do you not teach your disciples to wash their hands before they eat?"

Jesus did not keep human traditions and he did not teach his disciples to observe them. He rejected them, and he did not bind them upon his disciples! They were human. They had no authority behind them. And so, the religious leaders raised the question: "Why do you not teach your disciples to wash their hands before they eat?"

Jesus explained to them, "Your traditions make void the Word of God. God said to honor your father and mother. But you say that if a man takes what he must provide his father and mother with, substance that he might give unto them to sustain them, and give it to another good cause, that he can claim freedom from that obligation, he can be excused. You excuse him from the thing that God commanded. You loose where God has bound and you bind where God has loosed." Now they loosed over here, when God bound "honor thy father and thy mother." They bound over here, where God had not bound. One of these actions of the religious leaders is as great a sin against God as the other. *Both* of them disrespect God's will. *Both* of them reject the Word of God.

Well, where is the line to be drawn? The line is to be drawn between that which God authorizes, which the Word of God teaches, and that which man has invented and of which man is the author. You must remember that Jesus said that "every plant that my Heavenly Father has not planted shall be rooted up" (Matt. 15:13). It does not matter who invented it. It does not matter who is pleased with it or how much good you think it does. Unless God planted it, unless it is taught, unless it is authorized, unless it can be found in the Word of God, then it will be rooted up and be rejected in the last great day!

This is the lesson that we need to learn: *to honor God's Word and to know what the spirit of faith is.* It is not enough just to say, "Oh, I believe the Bible to be the Word of God." Are you willing to honor it as such? Are you willing to let it settle every issue? Are you willing to let the Word of God resolve every question? Are you willing to let it find the solution to every problem? Are you willing to limit and prescribe your faith by what the Word of God says? This is what Paul was talking about when he used the expression "the spirit of faith."

You know it is one thing to talk about faith and another to exercise it. It is one thing to profess and to talk about believing, and another thing actually to believe and to honor the Word of God, to reverence it because of the faith that you have in it. You look at what he said. Let me just draw an illustration of it. Paul said, "According to that which is written, I have believed, and therefore do I speak." What are the limitations? "According to that which is written." This is the word of God. "According to that which is written, I have believed." The center and the circumference of my faith is what God has said. It should be. *It should be!*

"The Spirit Of Faith:" Speak What Is Written

But not only do *I believe* according to what is written, I also *speak* according to what is written. This, Paul says, is *the spirit of faith!* And unless I have this attitude toward the Word of God, I do not need to profess faith, because I do not have it. My faith is not sufficient. My faith is sufficient only when I let the Word of God become the center and circumference of all that I believe and do in the name of the Lord. And I do not have the right to sign the name of the Lord to anything, whether it is a matter of practice, of doctrine, or of organization, unless the Word of the Lord teaches it. I am committing spiritual forgery when I do. I am showing my disrespect for the will of the Lord and the Word of the Lord when I become guilty of going beyond it, for this is what God has prohibited.

Paul said in First Corinthians four that he had transferred "these things to myself and Apollos for your sakes," that in us you may not go beyond the things that are written. I hear Paul saying again in Galatians one, "If any man preach any other gospel than that which I have preached unto you, let him be anathema." If even "an angel from heaven, should preach to you any other Gospel than I

have preached and which you have received, let him be anathema.''
I do not care who the preacher is, how many degrees he has after
his name, or what his qualifications may be otherwise. There is not
any man who has the right nor who can escape being condemned
before God, if he preaches any other Gospel than that which he can
read in the Word of God in language plain enough to be understood.

Does the Word of God say it? Can you put your finger on the
passage that teaches it? Can you read it in the Bible in language plain
enough that you can understand it, and that all men can understand
it? If the Word of God does not teach a certain thing, then you stand
condemned if you do teach it. If you believe it, or you teach it, or
you practice it, without it being within that which is written, then
you show disrespect for the sovereignty of God Almighty and for
His Word. What does it mean to believe? It means to be satisfied
with the Word of God. It means to believe that His Word is inerrant, that there are no errors in it.

Have you ever stopped to think about what a tragedy it would
be if a man had to admit that there was, or that there might be, just
one error in the Word of God? Suppose you admitted in your own
mind that the Bible might be wrong about something. *How would
you find out what was wrong about it?* Now, just how would you?
Who is it that is wise enough to sit in judgment on the Word of God
and tell us when it is wrong and when it is right? There would not
be a possible way on earth. No man is wise enough to tell us what
God's Word is wrong about, what we ought to believe, and what
we ought not to believe.

And yet, men go through the Bible and pick out various things
and tell us that we are not to believe them or to take them at face
value: things such as Jonah and the big fish, Noah and the flood,
the miracles of Jesus, or the resurrection of Jesus Christ, or the virgin
birth of our Lord. We are not to take these seriously. We are not
to actually put our faith and our confidence in them. How did they
find out?

And if the Bible is wrong about the virgin birth of Christ, or the
resurrection of the Son of God, or if it is wrong about the authority
that he exercises at God's right hand, or if it is wrong about there
being a God, or about man's having a soul, or about sin's being
a reality, or about the guilt of sin and its ability to condemn us and

separate and alienate us from God—*if the Bible can be wrong about any of these things, then it can be wrong about all of them.* It will not be reliable about any of them.

How are you going to find out what the Word of God is wrong about, if there is a single mistake in it? I must either accept *all* of it or none of it. More than that, I must believe—if I have the spirit of faith in my heart—I must believe in the sufficiency of Divine revelation. God's Word is *all* I need. *All I need!* I must be entirely satisfied with it!

God's Word: All-Sufficient, Authoritative, And Final

Paul said, "Every scripture is inspired of God and is profitable for doctrine, for reproof, for correction, for instruction in righteousness, that the man of God might be perfect, throughly"— thoroughly, perfectly, completely—"furnished unto every good work" (2 Tim. 3:16-17). Where can I learn what good works are in the sight of God? Well, not in my own judgment. Not by the wisdom of man. Not by the doctrines of men or the creeds of men. *I learn only by that which God has breathed, by the breathing of God's own words!* What God has spoken! That is what it means!

So, I must rely upon the sufficiency of the Scriptures. And when you talk about their being sufficient for doctrine, for reproof, for correction, and for instruction in righteousness, that means that they are *all-sufficient*. That is the entire category! That is the whole catalog! And nothing beyond it is needed. The fact of the matter is this: *all the faith that I can have in the righteousness of God has to be grounded and rooted in the Gospel, in what the Bible teaches.*

Paul said, "I am not ashamed of the gospel of Christ, for it is the power of God unto salvation to everyone that believeth, to the Jew first and also to the Greek, for therein"—in the Gospel of Christ—"is revealed the righteousness of God from faith unto faith" (Rom. 1:16-17). God's righteousness has been revealed in the Gospel, and it has been revealed in *the faith* of the Gospel, in order that I might have faith in it. My faith in the righteousness of God has to be grounded upon and rooted in the Gospel. If I do not believe what is in the Gospel, and *that only,* I cannot believe only in God's righteousness. If I believe in anything that is not in the Gospel, then I put my faith in the righteousness of man and not in the righteousness of God. That is the test!

The only faith that I can exercise in the righteousness of God is the faith that I have in God's Word. That is where God's righteousness is revealed. And if a doctrine or practice is not in the Word of God, it is the righteousness of man and not the righteousness of God. When you put your faith in that unrevealed thing, whatever it is, your faith is in *man's* righteousness and not in God's righteousness, and that means you are not headed in the direction of Heaven. That is just the plain truth about the matter.

What must I believe if I have real, genuine faith in my heart? If the spirit of faith has actually taken hold upon my heart, and is rooted in my heart? What must I believe? I must believe in *the sufficiency of the Gospel!*

Not only that, I must believe in *its authority*. I must believe that it is without error. I must believe that it is sufficient, that I need nothing else besides it. I must believe that it is authoritative because it is the Word of God. Jesus said, "All authority is mine, both in heaven and on earth" (Matt. 28:18). There is not any authority in religion except the authority of Christ. Nobody has any but the Lord! He is the "head over all things to the church, which is His body" (Eph. 1:22-23). There is not any authority in the Church or in Divine affairs, except the authority of Christ! And if Christ has not authorized a thing, it does not belong in the Gospel, it does not belong in the Church, and you cannot practice it by faith! Not to save your life! It cannot be done!

So I need to recognize that I can respect Divine authority only to the extent that my faith is satisfied with the Word of God. Now you can call that legalism, if you want to. Paul calls it the spirit of faith! That is exactly what the Bible says it is! It is the real attitude of mind and heart, the real reverence in your mind and heart for the Word of God, that faith in God and in His Word will produce.

Not only that, I must believe in God's Word as *His final Word*. He is not going to give an additional revelation. The Bible affirms the finality of the Gospel just like it affirms the finality of the sacrifice of the Son of God. No wonder Paul said, "If any man preach any other gospel than that which I have preached, let him be accursed" (Gal. 1:8-9). No wonder John said, "He that goeth onward and abideth not in the doctrine of Christ, hath not God" (2 Jn. 9). Why? Because the revelation of the Gospel by the authority of Jesus Christ is God's final Word.

There was a time when God spoke to the fathers through the prophets, but He has spoken to us through His Son. That message, "through His Son," has been "once"—*one time, for all time to come* — "delivered unto the saints" (Jude 3). There will never be another truth revealed! There has not been another truth revealed since the Sacred Canon was closed, since John wrote "finis" across the face of the Book of Revelation, and the Word of God and Divine revelation was completed as a reality! There has *not* been *one* truth revealed since that time! There will not be until eternity dawns if this world stands for a hundred million years yet! *Truth is the Word of God!* John said, "If any man goes beyond the doctrine of Christ, he has not God." You cannot have faith in God's righteousness, you cannot have God; you cannot have Jesus Christ, the Son of God, unless you *are willing to abide in the doctrine of Christ.*

Do You Have The Spirit Of Faith?

Where is your faith? What do you believe? Why do you believe it? What is the spirit of faith? It is to *believe* and to *speak* according to *that which is written!* If your faith has embraced anything other than that, if it has been founded upon, or if it includes anything other than that which God in His Word has spoken, our prayer tonight is that you will turn away from it. No matter where you got it, no matter who taught it, no matter how strongly you have believed it, if God did not say it and the Word of God does not teach it, God's Word is right and you are wrong when you differ from it. That is the simple truth and the final message of God's Word tonight.

When a man differs from what the Bible teaches, that man is wrong and the Bible is right. Paul put it like that in the Roman letter, when he said in effect, "Believe the gospel or not, it still stands as the truth" (Rom. 1:16-17; 3:3-4). Does your unbelief make the Word of God of no effect? Can I invalidate what God says by refusing to believe it? His answer to that was, "No." And he affirmed it in language so clear and strong and plain that we need to have it reverberating in our minds and resounding in our hearts always. He said, "Let God be found true and every man a liar." When you are not willing to stand upon the Word of God, it is you that is wrong and it is not God's Book.

The Word of God is right. Our plea tonight is that you put your

faith in it, that you be willing to let every question be answered by
it and every issue be settled according to it. Every problem in life
can be solved by its prescription and by the Divine will revealed in
it. Take it, live by it, and treasure it in your heart. Pray that your
faith in God's Word may grow and that it may be increased, even
until it leads you finally into Eternal Day in the presence of God.
Only in this way will you enjoy that final salvation—as God alone
is able to grant and offer and promise it unto the souls of men—the
Eternal salvation of your soul.

The result of faith and the end of faith is the salvation of the soul.
But that faith has to be expressed in obedience. The faith that will
not obey cannot save. The faith that does obey is the faith that works
by love. Jesus said that "except ye believe that I am he" you will
die in your sins (Jn. 8:24). He said, "Except ye repent, ye shall all
likewise perish" (Lk. 13:3). He said, "Unless you confess me before
men, I will not confess you before the Father" (Matt. 10:32-33). And
He said again, "Except you be born again . . . . born of the water
and the Spirit, you cannot enter the Kingdom of God" (Jn. 3:3-5).

These are ultimatums. And when the Lord says "You cannot,"
you cannot! There is not any other way to do it! If you have not
met these Divine ultimatums, then you have not been born again,
you are not a citizen in the Kingdom of God, a child of God; and
your soul has not been saved. He summed it up in language so plain
and clear that we cannot misunderstand, when He said, "Go, preach
the gospel to every creature. He that believeth and is baptized shall
be saved."

This is the way the Lord said it. This is His promise. It can be
yours, if you have faith enough to do what the Lord requires you
to do in order that His promise may be yours. We pray that you
have obeyed Him, or that you will come tonight and do it while we
stand and sing a song.

Further Study On Chapter Three

1. A pre-assigned student should read 3 review questions on chapter
2, give the class a few moments to write answers, then announce
correct answers. Assign someone to prepare 3 questions on chapter
3 for the next class.

2. Memorize 2 Cor. 4:13, 2 Tim. 3:16-17, or Jude 3 and be ready to quote it. (Give the class 1-2 minutes to write down their passage, then call on a few to recite.)

3. Outline chapter 3 at home (main points and scriptures). The teacher will call on class members to briefly explain what each heading means (such as, "The Love of the Truth") and how some passage was used to support the heading.

4. Write and bring to class a brief commentary on each phrase in 2 Cor. 4:13, 2 Tim. 3:16-17, or Jude 3. Tell in your own words what each verse means. The teacher may call upon several students to read all or part of what they have written.

5. "It does not matter what a man believes, just so he is sincere" (see heading "I Believed, Therefore Have I Spoken"). List some errors and dangers of such an idea, and be ready to discuss them in class.

6. Each student should have prepared a list of questions and answers on chapter 3 (5 true-false; 3 brief answer; 2 asking, "What passage teaches us that. . .?"). The teacher should ask students to read some of their questions for the class to discuss.

7. What are some activities and areas of life which require the use of standards? Why is a standard needed in religion?

8. What are some weaknesses and dangers of human creeds?

9. Use a dictionary to define "inerrant," "authority," "sufficient," and "final." How does each term relate to the gospel or word of the Lord? List some passages which teach these ideas.

10. What was Jesus' attitude toward human traditions? What are some traditions which set aside the Word of God today? (If possible, the teacher may break the class into small groups of 3-5 for about 5-7 minutes of discussion; then let each group leader tell the whole class one or two important points developed by the group.)

CHAPTER FOUR

The Law Of Faith

This is another good audience tonight. We are grateful for your presence and for your continued interest. If I am able to judge correctly, the audiences have increased both in the morning and the night services, from the very beginning of the meeting, discounting the fact, of course, that our Sunday audience was a Sunday morning audience. We had a good crowd in the ten o'clock service this morning and we hope you can be with us tomorrow. We believe that these day services can be helpful to us and we will appreciate your coming and taking part in them with us.

I concur very heartily in the expression of gratitude that Brother Wharton made concerning the presence of so many visitors and I reciprocate fully the expressions of confidence and of regard that he made concerning me. Our relationship has been a very close personal one and one that has been of benefit to me and a great deal of encouragement to me through a long period of years, as has my relationship with a number of preachers in this audience tonight. Bob and Nola Craig are among my closest and very best friends and associates from the years past, and it is good to have them in the audience tonight. A number from the West Avenue congregation here in San Antonio are present, which is an encouragement to me. It is a congregation with which I lived and worked for a period of time [October of 1954—October of 1956], for which I have held a number of gospel meetings, and for which I hold a very high regard. From among them, I count a number of very close personal friends.

So, we are grateful for your presence, for the good providence of God that makes it possible to assemble in His presence to study His Word, and to worship as He has directed us in that Word. Brother Witt is doing a fine job of leading the singing and you have entered heartily into it, and I hope that you may enter just as heartily into this part of the service, as we study the Word of God together.

The Text: Romans 3:1-31

I want to read tonight from the third chapter of Paul's letter to the Roman saints, and we will read the entire chapter, beginning with verse one:

> What advantage then hath the Jew? or what profit is there of circumcision? Much every way: chiefly, because that unto them were committed the oracles of God. For what if some did not believe? shall their unbelief make the faith of God without effect? God forbid: yea, let God be true, but every man a liar; as it is written, That thou mightest be justified in thy sayings, and mightest overcome when thou art judged. But if our unrighteousness commend the righteousness of God, what shall we say? Is God unrighteous who taketh vengeance? (I speak as a man) God forbid: for then how shall God judge the world? For if the truth of God hath more abounded through my lie unto his glory; why yet am I also judged as a sinner? and not rather, (as we be slanderously reported, and as some affirm that we say,) Let us do evil, that good may come? whose damnation is just. What then? are we better than they? No, in no wise: for we have before proved both Jews and Gentiles, that they are all under sin; as it is written, There is none righteous, no, not one; there is none that understandeth, there is none that seeketh after God. They are all gone out of the way, they are together become unprofitable; there is none that doeth good, no, not one. Their throat is an open sepulchre; with their tongues they have used deceit; the poison of asps is under their lips: whose mouth is full of cursing and bitterness: their feet are swift to shed blood: destruction and misery are in their ways: and the way of peace have they not known: there is no fear of God before their eyes. Now we know that what things soever the law saith, it saith to them who are under the law: that every mouth may be stopped, and all the world may become guilty before God. Therefore by the deeds of the law there shall no flesh be justified in his sight: for by the law is the knowledge of sin. But now the righteousness of God without the law is manifested, being witnessed by the law ar d the prophets; even the righteousness of God which is by faith of Jesus Christ unto all and upon all them that believe; for there is no difference: for all have sinned, and come short of the glory of God; being justified freely by his grace through the redemption that is in Christ Jesus: whom God hath set forth to be a propitiation through faith in his blood, to declare his righteousness for the remission of sins that are past, through the forbearance of God; to declare, I say,

at this time his righteousness: that he might be just, and justifier of him which believeth in Jesus. Where is boasting then? It is excluded. By what law? Of works? Nay; but by the law of faith. Therefore we conclude that a man is justified by faith without the deeds of the law. Is he the God of the Jews only? is he not also of the Gentiles? Yes, of the Gentiles also: seeing it is one God, which shall justify the circumsion of faith, and uncircumcision through faith. Do we then make void the law through faith? God forbid: yea, we establish the law.

Basic Theme: "God Is No Respecter of Persons"

The book of Romans has as its primary theme, in my approach to it and in my study of it, the principle found in chapter two and verse eleven: "God is no respecter of persons." This argument or this promise is based upon three major considerations that Paul argues in the letter in the first eleven chapters. In chapters one through the twenty-third verse of chapter three, he argues that *God regards sin upon the part of all men alike.* Sin is no more sinful for a Gentile than it is for a Jew; and whether it is a Jew that sins or a Gentile that sins, God condemns alike and is the Judge of all them that are guilty of sin. They stand alienated from Him and condemned by Him, whether they are Gentile or Jew.

Then he argues, beginning with verse 23 of chapter three and running through chapter five, that *God has provided the same salvation, the same means of justification for all men alike, without any respect for any man's person.* He does not have one way of saving the Jew and another for the Gentile, one way for this man and another way for another individual. God has made the same provisions, through His Divine grace for the salvation of all men universally; the same offer of mercy and pardon has been extended to all men without any respect of persons.

The third argument, beginning in the last part of the fifth chapter through even the eleventh chapter, is the argument that *God requires the same thing of all men alike:* the same faith and the same obedience of faith, the same faithfulness, whether upon the part of the Jew or the Gentile. God has provided justification through Christ. By the blood of Christ the grace of God is offered to us for the remission of our sins. That offer has been made in the Gospel, which reveals God's way of making men righteous, including the stipulations and the conditions upon which God's offer of justification can be appropriated, through faith upon your part and upon mine.

But God requires the same thing of all men, in order that they may enjoy these provisions. He does not demand one way of you and another way of me, one kind of an act of obedience upon your part, and another upon mine; but we are all saved by the same revelation of God's will through the Gospel, the faith of God, the faith of Christ, as Paul refers to it. And he was not talking about what God believes, or about what Christ believes. He was talking about "the faith" which originated in the mind of God and which was delivered by the revelation and through the authority of Christ, which is the Gospel.

"The faith" and "the Gospel" are frequently used synonymously in the New Testament. Frequently "the faith" refers simply to *the system of faith of which Christ is the author*—to those Divine truths that reveal, make known, and offer unto men by the revelation of the Holy Spirit God's plan for human redemption. *The faith*—the system of faith—is revealed in the *Gospel of Christ*. It is the Divine arrangement, this way of God by which men are to be justified, this way by which God offers to recognize men as both righteous and holy, that Paul refers to as "the law of faith."

Grace, Faith, and Obedience

One of the frequent demonstrations, to me, upon the part of a great many people, that they do not study the Word of God with much profit is that they want to exalt *one* Bible doctrine to the discredit of—and to the setting aside of proper consideration of—*another* Bible doctrine. Consider the relationship between grace, faith, and obedience. I hear people sometimes talking about "faith" as being opposed to "works," even the "works of obedience." This is a false concept of what faith is, as we shall see in the course of our study. Faith is a motive. Faith must motivate the works of obedience to the will of God, or it is a dead faith and of no profit or benefit. When it does cause us to act, moving us like motivating power as God intends, there is always obedience to the will of the Lord upon your part and mine.

There is no such thing as saving faith, or justifying faith, without that *faith's moving a man to do what the Lord would have that man to do*, that which he learns to be God's will. Faith must motivate man to obey God's commandments. And so, one of the characteristics of faith is its motivating power. It is not opposed to the works of obedience. When you take the doctrine that is in the Bible that faith is essential to salvation and try to make it conflict with the necessary obedience which that faith must render to the will of God in order that man might be saved, you simply have not understood what faith is nor the effect that God intends for faith to produce.

Likewise, men sometimes treat the necessary obedience of faith as arrayed against the doctrine of Divine grace. The obedience of faith, conditions upon which grace is received, in no way mitigates against grace. God in His mercy and love toward men has provided salvation without any obligation upon His part to do so, without any indebtedness toward man. Freely and in an unmerited manner, God has provided for our redemption through His grace and by His mercy. He has made possible what we could not. He has offered what we could not find or what we could not provide. He has granted what man could not have been responsible for, and that is the redemption of man's soul.

This, in every sense, in all senses, is completely unmerited upon the part of mankind. Man did not merit the love of God. He was not worthy of it. He had been disobedient and rebellious and sinful, both Jew and Gentile. All had sinned and fallen short of the glory of God. Paul calls to our attention in Romans one the fact that the Gentiles sunk into the very depths of moral depravity. They were morally and spiritually bankrupt because they had turned away from God to walk in the vanity of their own mind and in their own way. And man cannot, walking in his own way, ever advance or make any sort or kind of upward progress at all.

Man's way always leads down. It is always degrading spiritually, always leading to moral and spiritual destitution. Men are not born into the world depraved. But men can practice sin, disregard the will of God, and *become* depraved — even until they become so hardened in heart and soul that it is impossible for them to have any appreciation for their own welfare or for the will of God or for any desire of salvation, until they are reprobate unto every good work. Men can become depraved as the result of the practice of sin.

So, on one hand, the Bible teaches certainly that God's grace is unmerited, the provisions of that grace could not possibly be deserved, and man could not be responsible for them or worthy of them—for that is what grace means—yet, on the other hand, certainly there is no conflict between the idea that God saves us by His grace and the necessity for the obedience of faith.

"The Law of Faith"

While redemption is indisputably by grace, at the same time the offer of God's grace and mercy has been made upon certain stipulations and upon certain conditions. God Himself has every right to name these stipulations and with these conditions man must comply by faith. He obeys out of the faith in God that he has in his heart and by faith in the Word of God, in order that he might find access into the provisions that God has made for his salvation. Paul says that by faith we have access "into this grace wherein we stand."

I can enjoy the provisions of God's grace through the exercise of proper faith in my heart, and without that faith all that God has done goes for nought. The *law of faith* is the exercise of faith that takes advantage of God's grace, accepts the provisions that grace has made in the faith that obeys, and works by love in obedience to the will of God. You can just lay it down here in Paul's discussion.

Grace and faith do not do away with the idea of conditional salvation. Grace does not do away with the necessity of a law to guide us in our obedience to the will of God, and in the service and the sacrifice that we render unto God, that we might honor and glorify Him. Law is essential and necessary. We pointed that out in the lesson last night.

Authority—the authority that has the right to make laws and to demand and to require obedience to them—*is necessary to guide men*, to give men a standard for their conduct, in order that they might do that which is their duty to do. The way of man is not in himself. God had revealed the way of man's justification and of man's righteousness. Man was not responsible for it. It did not originate with man. Man could not have provided it. It is God's arrangement, God's rule, God's way, God's scheme, God's plan for making men righteous. This Paul refers to as the *law of faith*.

In the first place, Paul emphasized the fact that in connection with faith there is a law. Law does not rule out faith. Neither does law rule out grace. The Bible refers to the Gospel, to the will of God, in many different passages. Sometimes men try to leave the impression, and even are under the impression, that there is no such thing as law today—that we are under grace means that there is not any law.

Well, where there is no law there can be no standard; where there is no law there can be no authority; where there is no law there is nothing to guide; where there is no law there cannot be any obedience or compliance to law. Faith itself would be powerless to render obedience to the will of God, had not the Word of God laid down those conditions that our faith must meet in order to enjoy the grace of God and its provisions. This is what Paul meant when he said, "By faith then we have access into this grace." The only access you can have into the provisions of God's grace for your soul's redemption is through faith in the will, the law, the revelation, the plan, the scheme that God has laid down for your redemption.

I remember that Paul refers to the "law of the Spirit of life in Christ Jesus"—*"the law of the Spirit in Christ Jesus!"* That is simply a reference to the same thing as the *"law of faith."* I remember that James refers to the "law of liberty" and the law that makes liberty in Christ possible for men. This liberty is freedom from the rudiments of the world and the traditions of men, freedom from human standards, and freedom from the love of sin—from its dominion in their lives and from its guilt upon their hearts. All the liberty that a man has in Christ, freedom from condemnation and the hope of life in the world to come, is based upon and made possible by the *"law of liberty."*

Not only this, I find it referred to in various other passages and in various other ways, that we have today a law and that it is a law to guide and govern human conduct in obedience and in harmony to the will of God. That we might enjoy a proper relationship with God is the whole point of the matter. Our *faith in God and in God's provision* must move us to accept that law as the standard of our conduct. Faith moves in obedience to the will of God and in harmony with it.

First Principle: Every Man Is A Sinner
But let us look at the principles that are laid down very plainly in the third chapter of Romans. **First of all,** *God's law is that every man is a sinner.* Not that he was born guilty of sin, but every man is a sinner because "all have sinned." *All* men have sinned. I do

not care how good you are. It does not matter how high a degree of moral perfection you have reached in your own life, or how much good you may have done, in the sight of God you are a sinner.

The very first thing that every individual must recognize in order to be saved is that he is guilty of sin. Until you can convince a man that he is guilty of sin, you cannot convert him. There is not any salvation for him. He will not move a single, solitary step in the direction of redemption until he realizes, believes, and accepts the fact that he is a sinner. So the basic fundamental principle of the whole scheme of redemption, and the very reason that God has provided it, is the fact that *all* have sinned! *All men are guilty of sin!*

Somebody said, "Well what about a baby or a child? Doesn't a child do things that are wrong?" Certainly so. But until the child reaches the age of ability to distinguish between what is right and wrong, there can be no accountability. A person who is not accountable cannot violate the law, cannot justly and righteously be held guilty under the law, and cannot be punished by the penalty of the law.

God can judge men and condemn men when they have sinned because they are in violation of His will, but *God does not hold* a person who is not accountable—who has no ability, no capability, and therefore no responsibility—*accountable for wrong*. The man is accountable who has the ability to learn, to distinguish, to understand in his heart. He is the only person who is a sinner before God, accountable for his wrong, and guilty. And only by his own guilt is he separated and alienated from God. He is the individual that God condemns, because of the fact that he has sinned. We need to recognize that our accountability before God is based upon our ability.

The mentally irresponsible individual is not accountable for his wrongs. The law would not hold him so. If he committed the most heinous crime, he would not be punished as other men are. He might be restricted in the liberty that he enjoys so that he could not do further harm; but certainly, he would not suffer the penalty of the law, and could not do so justly. Why?

Well, the test is, does he have the mental capacity to understand and know the difference between right and wrong. If he does have the capacity, the mental ability, the capability of knowing the difference between right and wrong action, then he becomes responsible under the law. Even so it is with God. Children are not held accountable for their wrongs, for the reason that they do not have the capacity (or at least *until* they have the capacity, at whatever age they may (reach it) of knowing and understanding the difference between right and wrong.

The possibility of sinning is based upon the ability to discern between good and evil, truth and error, right and wrong, and no man stands guilty before God who does not have the ability to discern. But when a man reaches the ability and the age where his capacity is sufficient for him to know what the will of the Lord is, for him to understand what is right and what is wrong, what is truth and what is error, he becomes responsible before God. When he does not do the will of God, he is a sinner in God's sight, and by that sin men are separated from and alienated from God.

Second Principle: Sin Separates From God
This is the second principle that Paul lays down: *the guilt of sin upon the part of an accountable person separates him from God Almighty!* You cannot be guilty of sin, and at the same time enjoy fellowship or companionship or acceptability in the sight of God. God is *perfectly holy*, altogether righteous. Sinfulness cannot appear in God's presence or come before God. That which is defiled, which is unclean, which is impure, which is unholy, is altogether rejected by the God of Heaven.

Just as long as we have sins in our heart as responsible individuals, sins that we have not repented of, just as long as we have upon our souls the guilt of sins that have not been forgiven, we cannot offer acceptable sacrifices unto God. We cannot render any kind of obedience to the will of God, and we cannot enjoy any saved relationship with God. We cannot be reconciled unto Him. Being just in God's sight, holy before the Lord, righteous in the sight of the Lord, depends upon our sins being forgiven. All have sinned and have come short of the glory of God because of the guilt of sin.

You know, in Romans 5:12, Paul said, "Death has passed unto all men." Here is the reason why spiritual death rests upon the soul of any man by the judgment of the God of Heaven: "for that all have sinned." Now this passage is very evidently talking about spiritual death. Men die physically whether they sin or not. Children, innocent babies, die. Death is no respecter of persons. But Paul is saying that the sentence of spiritual death, alienation from God, rests upon all men who have sinned, who are responsible before the Lord. And, of course, sin is not accounted unless they are responsible, so that *spiritual death* is for the sinner.

Well, what does that death mean? It means *separation from God.* When the Bible talks about a man's being dead in trespasses or sin, the Bible means that by sin, because of sin, a man is separated from God.

Sin separates men from God Almighty! And *death* is the *separation.* Physically, it is the separation of the inner from the outer man, the spirit from the body. That is physical death. Spiritual death is the separation of the soul of man from the God of Heaven. The Bible not only talks about man's being dead in trespasses and sin, but the Bible talks about man's being made alive unto God. Paul said in Romans six to count yourselves though once dead in sin, to have been made alive unto God—no longer separated from Him.

And then the Bible talks about man's dying or "being dead *unto sin.*" That simply means separated from sin, or that sin has been pardoned. Our sins have been forgiven, the debt of sin has been paid, peace has been made with God; we have been reunited with Him, reconciled to Him, and redeemed by Him. We stand justified as though we had not done any wrong at all. Not because we have been guiltless, but because through the mercy and by the provisions that God has made, forgiveness for our guilt has been provided.

We can escape the sentence of spiritual death though we are on death row as sinners, alienated from God, and subject to the sentence of spiritual death for all eternity when we are guilty of sin. This is what Paul said, that "the wages of sin is death," but that the free "gift of God is eternal life, through Jesus Christ our Lord." Paul said in 2 Thessalonians 1 that it is "God's pleasure to recompense them that afflict you with affliction, but you that are afflicted rest with us, when the Lord Jesus shall be revealed from heaven with his mighty angels...taking vengeance on them that know not God, and obey not the gospel of our Lord Jesus Christ: who shall be punished with everlasting destruction." Here is spiritual death: *eternal separation* from the God of Heaven. That is the sentence that every man faces as the result of the guilt of sin!

But, how do we escape it? Through the works of our own righteousness? Nay, the law of faith provides otherwise and requires otherwise. You cannot do anything that will win for you or merit for you the forgiveness of a single wrong. There is not any act of righteousness that you can perform upon your own part. There is no scheme that you could devise. There is *no way* that *you* could think it out and provide it. Man's wisdom is utterly incapable of making any provision for justification and righteousness before God. That is utterly impossible!

I care not how much good you might do, how much humanitarian mercy you might extend and how much benefit men might receive from your acts of beneficence and benevolence in the world, *you could not win one single, solitary moment of pardon from the God of Heaven by your goodness.* The goodness of man, the righteousness of man is as filthy rags before the Lord. God will not accept as the means of pardon the works of our own righteousness.

The Third Principle:
Men Are Justified By God's Grace In Christ,

This is why Paul in Titus 3:5 said that it is "not by the works of righteousness which we have done" that we have been saved, but in "mercy he saved us, by the washing of regeneration, and renewing of the Holy Spirit." God's mercy is our only hope of salvation. But how has the mercy of God been extended? **That brings us to the third principle: justification or redemption in Christ by the free grace of God!** All men have sinned and all men are under the sentence of spiritual death. This is the condition of mankind. Paul said both Jew and Gentile are under the sentence of spiritual death as the result of the guilt of sin, but God has provided for our salvation, justification freely "by his grace" (Rom. 3:24). He has provided the redemption that is in Christ Jesus.

Now the word *"redeem"* means simply to buy back. Man is sold unto sin, enslaved by sin, lost in sin, separated from God through sin and because of sin, and under the sentence of spiritual death. But God has provided pardon. Through His grace He provides for us pardon and redemption to buy us back from the clutches of Satan, to redeem us from the lost condition that is characteristic of us spiritually. How has He provided this?

Well, look at Romans 3:24-25. "Being justified freely by his grace through the redemption that is in Christ Jesus: whom God hath set forth...." God has set forth Jesus to be what? "To be a propitiation." Well, what does that word mean? To be a propitiation means to be *a complete satisfaction*. God set forth Jesus to be a complete satisfaction for the debt of sin, to pay completely the debt, to make possible our forgiveness and our pardon from all the guilt that sin has placed upon us.

Read it further: "whom God hath set forth to be a propitiation through faith in his blood...." How is it that Christ has provided for our redemption? "Through faith in his blood." He came into the world to die that He might deliver men who were in bondage.

Hebrews 2:14 says so: "Forasmuch then as the children are partakers of flesh and blood, he also himself likewise took part of the same; that through death he might destroy him that had the power of death, that is, the devil; and deliver (or release, loose) them who through fear of death were all their lifetime subject to bondage." Men were under the sentence of spiritual death as the result of the guilt of sin until the blood of the Son of God made it possible for them to escape it—until the blood of the Son of God paid the price of pardon and redemption for us.

It is through our faith in the blood of Christ that we have the hope of redemption, and in no other way does God purpose to provide it for us. I hear him saying, "once for all"—one time for all time to come, He has offered Himself as a sacrifice for sin (Heb. 10:10-12). He has been manifested. He has appeared *once*, to offer a sacrifice for our sins. He will not do so again!

There will be no other provisions! Paul said, "There remaineth no more sacrifice for sin" (Heb. 10:26). The *only one* that Heaven ever intends to make has been made in the coming of the Son of God into this world to live in human flesh. Jesus Christ came *not only* to set for us a perfect example and to demonstrate perfectly for us Deity, to show in his life the power and mercy and grace of Divinity, *but also* at the same time to die upon the cross that our sins by His blood might be atoned for, and that we might be allowed to go free as a result of that sacrifice. Justified in the sight of God! Made righteous before God through the blood of Christ!

Fourth Principle: "The Righteousness of God" Is Revealed
But now, I want you to notice that Paul said that the "righteousness of God" has been manifested without the Law (v. 2). Now the trouble with the Jew was that he thought that he could attain it by keeping the works of the Law. That is the reason he was so meticulous. In all of the ceremonies and in all of the rituals—not only those things the Law required, but in all that they had invented by their human traditions—they, especially the Pharisaic group, were very meticulous to comply carefully with every formality they could compile.

The spirit of obedience and the spirit of faith did not move them. They thought that they could *earn* consideration from God, and that they would *deserve* and *merit* consideration before God, as the result of their outward formality in complying with the traditions that had been invented and the requirements of the Law in a ceremonial or outward fashion. This was Pharisaic righteousness. They *said*, but they *did not*! They taught others, but they did not learn themselves what the will of God was.

They sought righteousness, but they did not seek it after due order, that is, by faith. They were very pious in tithing mint, anise, and cummin, but they did not observe and did not have any regard for the fundamental principles of righteousness that had been revealed in the will of God, such as justice and truth and mercy. So, the Jew thought that through keeping of the Law of Moses and by his practice of Judaistic traditions, he would attain unto righteousness.

Paul said in the tenth chapter of the Roman letter, when he discussed this Jewish attitude, that they set aside the righteousness of God and went about establishing their *own* righteousness. They turned away from the provisions that God had made, in their unbelief rejected what God wanted and what God offered for them as a means of pardon, and sought to attain it through their obedience outwardly to the Law of Moses and to their own tradition of the elders. But, they *were* and we *are* unable to attain it that way.

There are a lot of people in the world today who think that obedience to the Old Testament, at least a part of it, is essential to righteousness before God. Paul said the righteousness of God has been revealed apart from, *without* the Law, not in the Law or through the Law, but *without the Law!* The plan of God for making men righteous is not found in the Old Testament. Oh, it is there in promise, it is there in prophecy, it is there in type and in shadow. But the scheme that God offers, the plan for making man righteous that God evolved in His mind before the world was a reality and its foundations were laid, was *not fulfilled* in the Law of Moses.

The Law of Moses had two purposes, according to the passage, and they are generally taught in the Word of God. One of them was to reveal sin. Paul tells us that "through the law is the knowledge of sin." When the Law came, Paul said, I was made to know sin and became conscious of the fact that I had sinned. I was a sinner. God intended that the Jew, by the Law, should be convicted of sin. That is why He gave the Law — to bring them to the recognition of the fact that they had not attained righteousness, that they were lost, that they needed a Savior, and that their salvation would be provided in and through the promised Messiah. This is what he means in Romans ten, when he says that "Christ is the end of the law"— the purpose and the aim of it—"unto all them that believe."

And so, the Law was a schoolmaster to bring them unto Christ, but the Jew did not allow it to serve that purpose. He thought he would find righteousness in it, in the Law itself, in Judaism itself. He sought to find righteousness, and he was unable to find it. Some men today, our Adventist friends and a great many others, think that Christianity is a conglomeration of the Old and New Testaments. They believe and practice Christianity from the Old Testament as well as the New, according to *their* concept. They think that Christianity is an amalgamation of the two—some things taught in the Old and some things taught in the New—and that this is the religion of Christ.

So, God's righteousness has been manifested *apart* from the Law, and Paul calls to our attention the fact that even the Law and the prophets themselves "witnessed" this (Rom. 3:21). The "righteousness of God" without the Law is manifested, "being witnessed." This is what even the law and the prophets themselves taught.

Both Moses and the prophets *taught* that righteousness would be *only* through the coming of the Redeemer, the Seed of Abraham, that God had promised would be a blessing to all the nations of the world. They did not offer righteousness under the Law of Moses.

If they had, it would have been righteousness only for the Jew, and if it had been righteousness only for the Jew and not for the Gentile, then God would have been a respecter of persons. That is the reason Paul said that "apart from us" God did not make them righteous. God did not offer justification unto the Jew and leave the Gentile out. He would have been a respecter of persons, and the whole theme of the Roman letter would become false.

So, there was no righteousness to be attained under the Law. The righteousness is revealed in the Gospel. The righteousness is through Jesus Christ. By His blood we are made righteous. Justified through our faith in His blood, we claim the pardon that God has provided for us. And the righteousness of God—God's way of making men righteous—was not revealed in the Law, but it has been manifested in the faith of Christ.

Now, I want you to notice this expression: "The righteousness of God without the law is manifested, being witnessed by the law and the prophets; even the righteousness of God which is by faith of Jesus Christ...." Now, I submit that that passage is not talking about your faith in your own mind and heart. This is not subjective faith in the sense that it is the believing that we do, but the faith of Jesus Christ—like the expression "faith of God" in another passage earlier in this chapter.

The "faith of God" simply means the system of faith, the Gospel of the Son of God. *The faith!* Paul preached "the faith," of which he once made havoc (Acts 8:3; Gal. 1:23). The priests, a great number of them, became obedient to "the faith." "The faith" has been once delivered unto the saints. One time for all time to come! It is through *the faith* that *the Gospel* reveals, manifests, and offers to men the righteousness of God. *In the Gospel!* If you want to know how God makes men righteous, the only place you can find it is in the New Testament, in the Gospel of the Son of God! Through faith of Jesus Christ!

Fifth Principle: Grace Must Be Appropriated

Now, notice in the same connection and in the same context, Paul said, "by faith of Jesus Christ." That is the way God has manifested it and offered it unto men, and how did I appropriate it? **Here is the next principle: grace must be appropriated by the sinner.** All men have sinned. All men who have sinned are under the penalty of spiritual death, and therefore need to be saved. They need to be made alive unto God. They need to die unto sin and to be made alive unto God! That pardon which makes this possible—reconciliation, justification, righteousness in the sight of God—has been provided by the sacrifice of the Son of God that Heaven has made in Jesus Christ and by the shedding of His blood. And it has been revealed in *the faith, the Gospel* of the Son of God.

Now, how can I appropriate it? Through *my* faith in *the faith!* By believing what God has said! By accepting God's provisions and God's Word! And by putting my convictions to rest upon it, to be founded upon it, and my trust to abide in it! This is the way that I can appropriate it.

Paul said God's righteousness "hath been revealed," it has been "manifested apart from the law," without the law. "Witnessed by the law and the prophets," the righteousness of God is manifested by "the faith of Jesus Christ" *unto all* them "that believe." Now, the man who does not believe will never be made righteous. God's righteousness does not avail, it cannot be attained except through faith.

In Romans, chapter nine, the Apostle Paul reminded the Jews that they had not sought God's righteousness after due order. *They,* having had the law, and the goodness of God having been extended to them, and seeking the righteousness of God in the wrong way and in the wrong place, *had failed to attain unto it.* But *the Gentiles, multitudes of them, had attained unto it.* How? Because they sought it by faith. Faith in their hearts had been planted by the Word of God, and *the faith* of *the Gospel* cannot make a man righteous until he believes it with all of his heart. That is the reason Paul said it is by faith—our faith in *the faith*—that we have access into God's grace!

God's grace has provided the way to make us righteous in *the faith* of *the Gospel.* I have to put *my* faith in it. Now, I do not care what else you believe, it cannot make you righteous. You may believe all of the moral precepts that human philosophy can set forth. You may believe in all of the works humans can devise and that human intelligence can plan. You may believe in every system of religion for which man could possibly be responsible. You may have faith in anything and everything except the Word of God and still be in sin.

Lost! God's righteousness does not avail and the provisions of God's grace cannot be claimed until you believe with all of your heart.

But what kind of faith is it? Somebody said, "Does *faith alone* save us?" The answer is, *"No!"* Oh, I know men teach it, creeds teach it, denominationalism emphasizes it and certainly puts a *great deal* of emphasis on it. Their idea is that we are justified by faith only and that it is a most wholesome doctrine.

One time in your Bible God mentions the doctrine of justification by faith only. You can get your concordance and see. Just one time. That one time is in James 2:24, and in that passage God says it is not so. "You see then how that by works a man is justified, and not by faith only." That is, faith *without* the works of obedience. That is what James was talking about. He said that faith that does not work "is dead." Faith that does not work is barren; it is unfruitful; it is vain. Well, how can faith work and what work must faith do? It must work the works of faith, the work of God. Faith must motivate a man to obey the will of God!

Paul said in the first chapter of Romans, and in the latter part of Romans sixteen, that the Gospel was to be preached unto all men "unto obedience of faith" (1:5; 16:26). The margin says, "unto obedience to the faith." One of them means that I am motivated by faith. The other means that in the Gospel is the will of God that must be obeyed. It is *my* faith that moves me to do that which *the faith* teaches to do.

The faith of the Gospel embodies God's requirements, in order that I might claim His grace in the blood of Christ for the pardon of my soul. In passages plain and simple, that is made perfectly clear. I hear, for example, the Apostle Paul saying that "we are justified by faith and have peace therefore through our Lord Jesus Christ" (Rom. 5:1). And then he said, "For in Jesus Christ neither circumcision availeth anything, nor uncircumcision; but faith which worketh by love" (Gal. 5:6).

What is the faith that justifies? Well, it is the faith that works. The faith that works what? The will of God! The works of God! You know, the Bible mentions the works of man's righteousness and the works of God's righteousness. The Bible mentions, on one hand, the works that men devise, that men are responsible for, by which a man can walk in his own way; and, on the other hand, the works that God has provided, by which a man can walk in God's way.

The works of man cannot save but the works of God can save. Let me read a plain passage on that: Acts ten. Peter said that in every nation "he that feareth God"—he that respects or reverences the will of God, he that believeth—"and worketh righteousness is accepted of God." What is it? A man must have reverence for God and God's will. Reverence that is born of faith! Reverence that is willing to submit! Respect that will require us to yield ourselves to whatever it requires of us! That is the reverence that faith plants in a man's heart; and when a man has that kind of faith, and that faith moves him to do the righteousness of God, *acceptability before God is the result.*

Paul put it still plainer than that, when he said, "We are all the children of God *by faith* in Christ Jesus, for as many as have been baptized into Christ have *put on* Christ" (Gal. 3:26-27). As many as have been baptized into Christ have put on Christ! He said that those who walk in the steps of the faith of Abraham, our father— the father of all the faithful—are the children of Abraham. And he said, "If any man is in Christ he is a new creature," and more than that, "He is Abraham's seed, and an heir according to the promise."

Those who are spiritual Israelites, who are God's children today, spiritual Israel, are the ones who *by faith* have been baptized into Christ and have become the children of God. That is what it takes to be justified. When a man *in faith* yields himself at the feet of Jesus Christ, prostrates himself in full and unreserved submission, makes Christ the King of his heart and the Lord of his life, and does *the will of Christ,* and continues to do it, *that man is just!* He is righteous before God!

This is the reason that God laid down the rule: "the just" shall live or shall walk "by faith." And if a man does not walk and live and serve, and love and sacrifice and worship, by his *faith* in *the faith* of the Gospel, he cannot be just before God. I ask you tonight, have you been justified? Or, are you under the sentence of spiritual death? Have you been redeemed by the blood of Christ? Has He pardoned your soul from the guilt of sin? Are you tonight spiritually on death row, awaiting final judgment that will send you into an eternal Hell that God has prepared for the Devil and his angels—

and to which all men will be assigned who do not obey the will of our Lord Jesus Christ? We beg of you to give consideration to your own soul for the sake of the Lord that died to receive it, and that *by faith* in your heart you will come tonight to do His will and be saved by it.

Further Study On Chapter Four

1. A pre-assigned student should read 3 review questions on chapter 3, give the class a few moments to write answers, then announce correct answers. Assign someone to prepare 3 review questions on chapter 4 for the next class.

2. Memorize Rom. 3:27-28 and be ready to quote it. (Give the class 1-2 minutes to write it down, then call on a few to recite.)

3. Outline chapter 4 at home (main points and scriptures). The teacher will call on class members to briefly explain what each heading means (such as, "God is No Respecter of Persons") and how some passage was used to support the heading.

4. Write a brief commentary on or explanation of Rom. 3:27; 8:2; Gal. 6:2; and Jas. 2:25. Tell in your own words what each verse means. The teacher may call upon several students to read all or part of what they have written.

5. What three major considerations does Paul offer to prove that God is no respecter of persons?

6. Each student should have prepared a list of questions and answers on chapter 4 (5 true-false; 3 brief answer; 2 asking, "What passage teaches us that...?"). The teacher should ask students to read some of their questions for the class to discuss.

7. Define or explain the expression "the faith." List some passages where it is used (check a concordance for help).

8. Briefly state the role of each of the following in our salvation: grace, faith, and obedience.

9. Explain why we cannot be saved without God's grace. Explain why we cannot be saved without the "law of faith."

10. What did the Pharisee believe that kept them lost? How do the
following terms help you to understand why the Pharisees could not
be saved by their own righteousness: "propitiation" (Rom. 3:25),
"once for all" (Heb. 10:10-12,26; cf. Jude 3), and "the obedience
of faith" (Rom. 1:5; 16:26)?

CHAPTER FIVE

The Obedience Of Faith

For the good blessings of this day and for the privileges that are ours in this hour, as we assemble in the presence of God and to worship Him, I trust that everyone of us has come with gratitude in our hearts. I think sometimes we pass by in our consideration and take for granted some of the wonderful privileges we as the children of God enjoy that we ought to be mindful of and to be very grateful for indeed. One of them is the privilege of worship like we are engaging in, in this gospel meeting, in these services. I know of nothing that Christians ought to appreciate any more than the opportunity of gathering together to worship God and to sing God's praises in His service and in His honor, and to His glory. Surely from such a service there is always a blessing for our souls, if we come prepared in mind and heart to receive it.

Humility of heart and soul, along with our recognition of the truth and of our need for it, is the only means by which our salvation is made possible. We should have reverence for God as the One whose will is sovereign in this universe, as the One who has the right to rule in our lives and in our hearts, and as the One who ought to have His will and His way with us in all matters. In these dispositions, in such attitudes of mind and heart, as we gather together in God's presence to enjoy the privileges that His provisions have made possible by His grace, surely there ought to be a real and genuine blessing for every one of us. In it we ought to find a lot of joy and a great deal of satisfaction. It ought not to be a matter of necessity, or a matter simply of something that is required, as we strive to do what is demanded of us, but something in which we find real joy for the blessing and the good that we can get out of it.

Last night we talked to you about the law of faith and laid down some principles of the law of justification by faith that God's scheme of redemption included. It is based upon the fact that all men have sinned. Because all have sinned, all are under the sentence of spiritual death. God by His grace has offered but one means of pardon, one avenue and one power by which we can be redeemed from our sins, and that means is the blood of Christ. This offer of redemption and the provision of God's grace by which we might be redeemed has been made in the faith of the Gospel, the faith of Jesus Christ, our Lord—this is why it is God's power unto salvation to all that believe it! It can be appropriated upon the part of men who stand in need of it, only by faith. And, the faith that is able to appropriate it, and to find access into the provisions of God's grace, is the faith that obeys God's will.

Focusing On the Obedience of Faith (Rom. 1:5; 16:26)

Tonight we want to talk about *the obedience that such a faith must render, the principles that are involved in it, and the considerations that ought to move us to it by faith in God.* In the third chapter of the Roman letter, Paul tells us in verses 21 through 23, that the righteousness of God is manifested through the faith of Christ apart from the Law, witnessed by the Law and the Prophets, unto all them that believe. And so, God's righteousness is made possible through the exercise of faith in our hearts, when we are exercised by our faith to do the will of the Lord, as we shall point out and emphasize in this lesson. We suggested to you also that God's righteousness cannot be obtained by deeds of man. It was not attained by the Jew for the reason that he sought it not after due order. He sought it through the works of his own accomplishment, his own planning, his own will, his own traditions, and through simple outward conformity rather than being motivated by the faith in his own heart to do that which the Lord had provided for him to do.

The Gentiles who believed attained unto righteousness and became righteous in the sight of God because they sought the righteousness of God by faith. That is, they found it in the faith of the Gospel that was revealed and they appropriated it by faith in their own hearts.

We need to recognize that faith does not lead us to seek after and accomplish a righteousness of our own. Paul said that he prayed that he might attain the righteousness of God which is through faith in Jesus Christ, not having, he said, "a righteousness of mine own" (Phil. 3:9). Self-righteousness is of no benefit. So we need to understand that it is only the righteousness of God and that it is only by faith which works by love to do God's will—to obey God's commandments and to respect that which God has required of us—that can lead us to be righteous and holy and just in the sight of God. This is what the Bible means when it talks about being justified by faith. That justification—this relation with God of purity, holiness, reconciliation, and redemption—*is necessarily dependent upon the obedience which our faith is willing to render to the will of God.* Peter, you remember, said, "Seeing you have purified your souls through your obedience to the truth, love one another from a pure heart fervently" (1 Pet. 1:22). So, we are purified, made holy, clean, pure, righteous, and just before God, when faith obeys.

There is not any doctrine in the Bible, including the doctrine of justification by faith, that has been given any more emphasis than the necessity of obedience, the obedience of faith. I remember in the first paragraph of the Roman letter, that we find Paul talking about that in this manner: "Concerning His Son, Jesus Christ, our Lord, which was made of the seed of David according to the flesh, declared to be the Son of God with power, according to the spirit of holiness, by the resurrection from the dead, by whom we have received grace and apostleship for *obedience to the faith* among all nations for his name" (1:3-5).

And then over in the last paragraph of the sixteenth chapter, he states the same principle in a little bit different way, when he says: "Now to him that is of power to stablish you according to my gospel, and the preaching of Jesus Christ, according to the revelation of the mystery, which was kept secret since the world began, but now is made manifest, and by the Scriptures of the prophets according to the commandment of the everlasting God, made known to all nations for the *obedience of faith*" (16:25-26). God's plan is that men shall be made righteous through the faith of Jesus Christ, by their faith in the faith of Jesus Christ. But *our* faith in *the* faith must produce obedience to the gospel.

The man who is not willing by faith to obey simply cannot be righteous in the sight of God. Many passages emphasize this. In 1 John 3:7, John said, "Let no man deceive you: he that doeth righteousness is righteous." Peter preached at the house of Cornelius, "Of a truth I perceive that God is no respecter of persons, but in every nation, he that feareth God and worketh righteousness is accepted of him" (Acts 10:34-35). The righteousness of God, of course, is what the passage is talking about and not the righteousness of man, because man's righteousness cannot redeem, it cannot save. God does not save us by our own works of righteousness, but through faith working out in our lives the righteousness or the will of God as it has been revealed in the Gospel.

The Bible teaches also, and we emphasized in the lesson last night, that *faith alone*, simply to believe in God and to believe what God says without allowing that faith to motivate us or to allow us to do that which God wills for us, *cannot save anybody*. James, in chapter two, raises the question, can that faith save you? And the faith that he was talking about was the faith that does not work, the faith that does not perform, that does not motivate, that does not move a man to do the will of the Lord—*faith without works*. He was not talking about faith without the works of the Law. This was not his consideration. He was not talking about faith without the works of man's righteousness. The Bible teaches that neither the works of man's righteousness nor the works of the Law of Moses can possibly accomplish for any individual justification before the Lord. The Word of God says, "By the works of the law shall no flesh be justified" (Rom. 3:20). There was a reason for that. God did not intend that men should be justified by the works of the Law of Moses, even though they faithfully performed it.

The Gospel System: Grace, Mercy, and Pardon
The Law of Moses required perfect obedience in all things. It provided condemnation for every man who did not keep its every requirement. It extended no mercy. It was not a system of mercy and grace. It was the ministration of death and condemnation, and it said, "Cursed is everyone that doeth not all of the things which are written in the law" (Gal. 3:10). No man ever perfectly kept the Law of Moses and all of its requirements, save Jesus Christ while he was in the flesh. He kept the Law. He broke not a single, solitary point of it. His attitude was, "The commandments must not be broken" (Matt. 5:19; Jn. 10:35). He had that kind of reverence for the will of the Father, and submitted himself unto God. He said, "I do only those things which are pleasing in the sight of my Father" (Jn. 8:29). And so, he submitted himself and obeyed, and through his obedience, through his suffering, learned obedience or submission to the will

of Almighty God in order that human redemption might be provided.

You and I need to recognize that *our* faith must move us likewise to submit ourselves unto God, if justification is ever to be our lot. If justification is ever to become a reality in our lives, we cannot obtain it through the works of perfect obedience to the will of God. We can never merit it. We will never be righteous enough because of what we have done or what we are within ourselves. *But our only hope of salvation,* in view of our sinfulness, rebellion, and iniquity, and because of the imperfection of our obedience—our failure to meet the standard of righteousness that God has required of us in the Bible—*is the mercy and grace of Almighty God.* There is not any hope of salvation upon the part of any man who depends upon perfect compliance or perfect obedience to all the will of God.

The fact is, perfect obedience to God's standard of perfection in all things is no more possible today than it was under the Law of Moses. The reason is that we all sin and we all are incapable of working our way and earning our way back into a state of innocence or acceptability with God. But the Bible teaches that by the works of the Law "shall no man be justified." The works of the Law of Moses will not justify you. Neither will the works of man's righteousness. God cannot and does not offer righteousness upon the basis of our being perfect in our lives. The offer of heaven by means of perfection could leave the sinner only in despair! Of course, if we did live perfect lives, God would be in debt to us and under obligation to accept us as righteous. *If a man lived without ever sinning, without ever doing anything contrary to the will of God, without ever making a single, solitary mistake, he would have no guilt to be saved from. God in justice would be under obligation to accept him.*

But since we are not creatures of that sort and none of us can attain perfection—none will be as good as we may be or do all of the good that we may do—we still sin. We are guilty of sin and we need to be saved. The key to this whole discussion is the provision of perfect pardon—not available under any system except the Gospel system! God offers that salvation only when our faith submits us and yields us in obedience to the will of the Lord to walk by faith in *the* faith that reveals righteousness. The faith is the will of Almighty God or the plan of God for making men just and holy. This is the only way that it can be done. In the emphasis that the

Bible places upon obedience, we call your attention to a number of considerations, shown first of all in the consequences of obedience itself.

The Consequences of Obedience

As we begin to look at what obedience will do for us, Paul teaches in Romans 6:17-18 that "by obedience a man is made free from sin." Obedience makes men free from sin! And, it makes out of us the servants of righteousness. I recall that the Apostle, in that passage, very graphically pictured the condition of these people. He said that we give thanks to God that "whereas ye were the servants of sin...." That is what they were in their first condition. Bondservants of Satan in sin!

"Whereas, ye were the servants of sin, ye became obedient from the heart to that form of doctrine....and being made free from sin, ye became the servants of righteousness." Their status changed; their condition changed; their relationship changed. What brought it about? Well, they were made free from sin and became the servants of righteousness by obeying. "Ye became obedient...."

Obedient, he said, "from the heart." That carries a great deal of significance, as we shall see. From the heart, ye became obedient to the form or pattern or mold of doctrine "delivered unto you." Now, that doctrine was delivered in "the faith." When they had faith enough in it (and that is what "from the heart" signifies), when they were grounded in that form of doctrine "delivered unto them," and they "became obedient" to that which the form required of them, the result was that they "were made free from sin and became the servants of righteousness." Until a man obeys by faith the form of doctrine delivered in the Gospel of the Son of God, he is not freed from sin, he is not pardoned, he is not justified, he has not been forgiven, he has not been redeemed, he is unsaved and lost. He is in sin and under the sentence of spiritual death without obedience from the heart to the form of doctrine delivered in the Gospel of Christ!

But look at another passage. I remember that Jesus said, "If ye keep my commandments, then are ye my friends" (Jn. 14:15; 15:14). He is my friend that "doeth my commandments," says Jesus. *Friendship with God and friendship with Christ depend upon our doing the will of Christ.* The man who is in the world of sin is an enemy of Christ, an enemy of God. Friendship with the world is enmity with God! While a man lives in sin, he is in rebellion to God, walking contrary to God's will, disobedient before Him, rejecting and refusing the offer of redemption that God has made in His Word. As a result, that individual stands condemned and lost and is an enemy of God. I can be a friend of Christ, I can have friendship and reconciliation with God only upon the basis of obedience to God's will.

But not only is it true that obedience makes a man free from sin and reconciles him unto God and makes him a friend of God, but in addition to that, *obedience by faith gives a man access into the blood of the Lord Jesus Christ.* Romans 6:3-4 reads: "Know ye not that as many of you as were baptized *into* Jesus Christ were baptized *into* his death?" The Bible teaches baptism is *into* something. It is in order to initiate or inaugurate a man into a condition or state different to that in which he was. It is an act of obedience and also an act of transition. Obedience that moves a man from one state to another!

That is the design of baptism. It reaches the death of Christ. The death of Jesus Christ is reached by baptism! Paul says that we are "baptized into Christ" and that those who have been baptized "into Christ" have been baptized "into his death." Well, that is where His blood is. That is where redemption is. That is where there is pardon and forgiveness. That is where atonement was made. That is where justification or righteousness was made possible by the blood of Jesus Christ, which he shed by his death upon the cross!

This redemption is by the sacrifice that Jesus made of his own soul, which became a sacrifice for sin. When he poured out his soul unto death, dying as a sinner, separated from God, for your sins and mine which he bore in his body on the tree, he cried out, "My God, my God, why hast thou forsaken me?" Jesus was paying the penalty of your transgression and mine. The sun refused to shine upon the scene. God turned away His face and withdrew His presence. The Son of God was left alone upon the cross to die as a sinner would die, separated from God—not because of his sin, for he had committed no sin, but for your sins and mine, which he had taken upon himself. Though he had not sinned, he was made to be sin in our behalf! And so, he paid the penalty of our transgression.

82 *Faith and The Faith*

The Meaning of Baptism

But how do I reach the benefit of that death? *When I am baptized "into Christ."* I am not only baptized "into Christ"—and that is an act of faith—I am baptized into the death of Christ, Paul said. And, not only am I baptized "into the death of Christ," I am baptized "into death to sin." We talked last night about a man's being dead in sin and then being made alive. Paul said, "We were buried with him therefore, by baptism, into death." This time he is talking about our dying, not Christ's dying. I "die unto sin" in the act of baptism for the reason that I am separated from sin, made free from sin, when my faith thus renders obedience to God. That is the whole point! I am made free from sin, I "die unto sin," the guilt of sin is taken away.

If you want to know what death to sin is, look at Romans 6:4-7: "We are buried with him by baptism into death: that like as Christ was raised up from the dead by the glory of the Father, even so we also should walk in newness of life." We are raised up from death to walk in freedom from sin, "newness of life"—no longer condemned—to be the servants of righteousness. This burial and resurrection is the action of baptism. But the purpose of it is to reach the blood of Christ and to die unto sin; *and Paul said that when a man dies unto sin, he is "justified from sin."*

Justification, or holiness, or righteousness, then, becomes a reality when a man dies unto sin, and he dies unto sin when he reaches the death of Jesus Christ when he is baptized into that death. Baptized *into* Christ, *into* His death, *into* death to sin, *into* justification from sin! That is when a man becomes righteous! He becomes the "servant of righteousness," but it takes obedience from the heart in order to achieve it. Not just faith alone, but faith in our hearts prompting obedience to the will of Almighty God.

Not only is baptism in its action a resurrection, but it is a burial. Sprinkling will not meet the demand. Sprinkling is not obedience from the heart. If a man is sprinkled, it is not because of his faith in what God says, because God says nothing about a man's being sprinkled. There is not a passage in the Bible, Old or New Testament, in which God ever commanded clean, pure, unmixed water to be sprinkled on anybody for any purpose.

Now back in the Old Testament, in passages like Ezekiel 36 and

Isaiah 52, you can read about the sprinkling and the cleansing as the result of the sprinkling of the water of cleansing. But the water of cleansing was not plain, unmixed water. In the Old Testament, according to Numbers 19, it is water with the ashes of a red heifer. A red heifer was slain and all of her was burned, and the ashes were gathered up. Those ashes were mixed by the Law of God with water and scarlet wool and, by means of hyssop, sprinkled upon that which was defiled. And as it was sprinkled, that water of cleansing ceremonially or outwardly cleansed and purified and made a thing holy and sanctified unto God.

Now, that water of cleansing that you read about back in the Old Testament is not the water of baptism. The water of baptism is plain, clean, unmixed water. In Hebrews 10:22 Paul calls it "pure water." By "pure" water, he means just water, unmixed with anything else. He did not mean that it had been filtered to the point of purity, or that it had been purified by some particular process and that there were no germs in it. But in contrast to the water of cleansing in the Old Covenant or the Old Law, pure water in the New Covenant and in the law of Christ is simply water unmixed with any other element. Plain, unmixed water!

When a man washes his body in plain, unmixed water in the act of baptism, by faith, he is washed in that act of baptism by being buried in the element of water. And out of that grace into which he has been buried, he has been raised up, not only physically, but *spiritually*, for he was condemned and he has been baptized *into* death to sin, in order to *die to sin*. Oh, now, it is true that a man first dies to the *love* of sin through faith, and to the *practice* of it by repentance. That would certainly be true, but that is not what Paul has in mind, however, in this passage. He has in mind in this passage the design of baptism. It is to reach the blood of Christ! It is to die unto sin, to be justified from sin!

A man is buried by baptism *into* death or in order to die to sin, in order to be justified from sin. That is the purpose of being baptized. *When*, with that purpose in his heart and trusting to God's promises to that effect, *a man submits himself to that commandment*—intelligently, believingly, confidently, doing what God says for him to do that God might fulfill His promises to him—*then that man is cleansed and purified*. He becomes then free from sin by the blood of Christ and becomes righteous in God's sight. As a consequence, he is able to serve God in all righteousness. And as he continues to do so, the blood of Christ will keep him free from the guilt of sin. His past sins can never be called up again and he may apply to the blood for pardon and cleansing when he stumbles. So the consequence of obedience is to have access to the blood of Jesus Christ!

Continued Fellowship With God
Conditioned Upon the Obedience of Faith

Now, obedience is a necessary condition not only for the individual who has never been saved, but is a necessary condition in order that we also who have been saved might have access to the blood of Christ. That we might continue to enjoy its cleansing power, we are going to have to continue to obey the will of God. *Obedience is a life of submission that never ends as long as life lasts!* It is begun when obedience from the heart is rendered to that form of doctrine, when a man by faith is baptized into Christ. But the same spirit of obedience, the obedience of faith, must continue to characterize every child of God who desires to continue in contact, within reach, and within access to the cleansing power of the blood of Christ.

John teaches that, doesn't he? In 1 John 1 he said, "If we say that we have fellowship with him and walk in the darkness, we lie, and do not the truth: but if we walk in the light, as he is in the light, we have fellowship one with another." God then recognizes me as His own. I am a fellow laborer with the Lord and I can have fellowship with God. Friendship is the relationship! Reconciliation is enjoyed! That simply means to "make friends again." A man can enjoy friendship with God *only as long as his life continues to be submitted through faith to whatever God requires of him.* When the time comes that as a child of God you cease to walk or live by faith, by your faith in *the* faith, then you are separated by your sin from the blood of Christ and once again you stand alienated from God. You are guilty of sin until you submit to God in repentance. So we must walk in the light.

Now you look at the consequences of obedience in Hebrews 5:8-9, on that particular point. Paul said, "Though he was a Son, yet learned he obedience by the things which he suffered: and being made perfect"—that is, being perfected as a Savior, through his obedience and by his suffering—"he became the author of eternal salvation unto all them that obey him." We talk about obedience to the Gospel as if it were a thing that we do one time and get all over with, and it is all finished and done. That is not so. It has just begun. When a man obeys the gospel, he has just begun a life of obedience to the Lord. If he wants to go to Heaven, he is under just as much obligation to continue that obedience to whatever it is that God wills for him to do and to be, as he was to start it in order that he might become righteous in the sight of God to begin with.

And so, you and I need to recognize that it is only as we live by faith and walk by faith that we can maintain justification and continue to be just and righteous before God. And that is exactly what God teaches about it. But look at the consequences of failing to obey the will of the Lord—we ought to weigh them rather carefully.

The Opposite Consequences of Obedience and Disobedience

Paul, in Romans 2, points out a contrast to us. The fact of the matter is, it is an antithetical statement. You have some extremes. He says that through the hardness of your heart, in spite of the love of God, you have rejected God's will, and you are walking in disobedience and rebellion, despising the goodness of God. Then Paul asks,

> Despisest thou the riches of his goodness and forbearance and long-suffering; not knowing that the goodness of God leadeth thee to repentance? but, after thy hardness and impenitent heart, treasurest up unto thyself wrath against the day of wrath and revelation of the righteous judgment of God; who will render to every man according to his deeds.

I am writing my own destiny by whether I am doing the will of God. I cannot save myself by the works that I might plan, but I am determining whether or not I shall be saved, by whether or not I yield myself to God's plan for my salvation. God will "render unto every man according to his deeds." If you have been told that your works have nothing to do with your salvation, that what you do is not essential to being saved, you have been mistaught in that particular.

The Bible teaches that your destiny in the judgment will be determined according to what you have done. And there are many passages that teach that, but let us read on: "Who will render to every man according to his deeds: to them"—notice the contrast now—"who by patient continuance in well doing"—this is the way it is done, patient continuance in well doing; to those who thus patiently continue in well doing and—"seek for glory and honor and immortality, eternal life." Eternal life is the object of the verb "will render" in this sentence. God will render eternal life.

To whom will God render eternal life? He will render eternal life to those who patiently continue in well doing and who seek for glory and honor and immortality. To them, God will render eternal life. When will He render it? In the "day of wrath and revelation of the righteous judgment of God." That is when it will be rendered.

Now, look at the other side of the antithesis which Paul has set forth: "But unto them that are contentious"—rebellious, disobedient in attitude and mind— "and do not obey the truth, but obey unrighteousness"—unto them—"indignation and wrath." Here are some other objects of the verb "will render." God will render eternal life to them that patiently continue in well doing, but He will render wrath and indignation, tribulation and anguish, to them who do not obey the truth, but who obey unrighteousness. They do not obey the righteousness of God, the plan and the will of God by faith, but they obey unrighteousness; they are rebellious against God.

They refuse and reject God's will and do not conform to it. What will be rendered unto them? "Indignation and wrath, tribulation and anguish, upon every soul of man that doeth evil; of the Jew first, and also of the Gentile; but glory, honor, and peace, to every man that worketh good; to the Jew first, and also to the Gentile: for there is no respect of persons with God." He requires the same obedience of all men.

So the result of obedience is eternal life in the world to come. *If* I continue patiently, *if* I persevere patiently in my obedience to the will of God, *if* as a just and a righteous man before the Lord I continue to walk by faith, *eternal life* will be the reward by God's grace. But the result of not continuing in well doing, the result of failure to patiently seek for glory and honor and incorruption, the result of not faithfully walking in obedience to the will of God, of refusing to walk by faith all the days of my life, will be God's repaying me with *wrath and indignation, tribulation and anguish.* So, you see that we determine our own destiny by our attitude toward God and His Word. The deciding factor is whether or not we allow our faith—the faith in our hearts and our love for the Lord by which that faith works out its obedience to God's will—to lead us to do what God teaches us to do.

Look at another passage, a parallel passage both in thought and nearly in word: Second Thessalonians chapter one. Paul said that it is God's pleasure "to recompense them that afflict you with affliction; to you that are afflicted, rest." The object to the verb "recompense" or repay is affliction—those who *afflict* you will be repaid with *affliction*. They will be tormented as the result of the persecution that they brought upon you. But to those who faithfully endure the persecution which they are called upon to suffer, God will recompense *rest*. This rest is the object of the verb "recompense." It is God's pleasure to recompense rest. But read on.

I hear him saying not only that God will recompense you with rest, but also he adds, "....with us, when the Lord Jesus shall be revealed from heaven with his mighty angels, in flaming fire taking vengeance on them that know not God, and that obey not the gospel of our Lord Jesus Christ: Who shall be punished." What will happen to those, now, who will not obey the gospel, who will not by faith render obedience from the heart to the form of doctrine delivered in the gospel? As to those who do not live by faith, who do not patiently continue to do the will of God, Paul said they will suffer eternal destruction, death spiritually, separation from the face of God and the glory of His power. If you want to live with God in eternity, you had better do God's will, and you had better do it not simply to please somebody else, but out of the faith that you have in your heart and out of the love that moves that faith to obey the will of God. And so, we understand that the consequence of obedience is justification, righteousness before God, freedom from sin. And the consequence of disobedience is to be ungodly and unrighteous, and to be lost and condemned and under the sentence of spiritual death!

Obey From The Heart By Faith

But before our lesson tonight comes to a conclusion, in just a few moments I want to sum up for you as briefly as I can, what it means to obey from the heart by faith. First of all I would suggest (and we will discuss it in more detail in the lesson tomorrow night) that faith *purifies* the heart. The Bible teaches that it does. But how does faith purify the heart? Well, first of all, a man cannot do anything from the heart that he does not do intelligently. One of the functions of the heart is to understand. So, a man must do it *intelligently*. Another function of the heart is to believe. We believe with all of our hearts, and so, we must do it *believingly, confidently;* that is, with conviction, with assent, with agreement to God's plan and God's will and to God's Word; and not only with assent and agreement, but with complete trust. This is what it means to obey from the heart. It means to obey intelligently. It means to obey believingly, confidently, trustingly. It means to obey lovingly, for *faith works by love.* And it means to obey reverently, that is, to do it because it is God's will.

You know, the Bible uses the expression "faith" and uses that expression a good deal. In Hebrews 11, the Apostle talks about "by faith." "By faith," Abel offered; "by faith," Noah built; "by faith," Abraham obeyed; "by faith," Israel marched. The expression "by faith" needs to be considered a little more carefully, I think, than we usually do. It implies much more than is apparent to us at first consideration.

"By faith" is an incomplete sentence; it is an incomplete sentence, for in order to have a complete sentence, you have to have complete sense. And so, this sentence is incomplete; a prepositional phrase does not constitute a sentence, and it constitutes incomplete sense. You might say, "to town," but that would not tell anything. But if you say, "I went to town," then the sense becomes clear, and the sentence is complete. "By faith" has to be indicative of a number of things. There are a number of things implied by the expression, and I would like for you to see just what it does imply.

First of all, justification by faith means that it is "by faith" because God said it. *God said whatever I believe and whatever I do!* "Faith comes by hearing, and hearing by the Word of God"(Rom. 10:17). I cannot believe a thing that God has not said, and I cannot do a thing "by faith" that God has not commanded or authorized! To do a thing by faith means that God said it, that I believe it because God said it, and that I do it because I believe in the God who told me to do it. That is the idea!

And so, if God said nothing about it, then it cannot be by faith! You could not count beads "by faith" when you pray. You cannot burn incense "by faith." You cannot sprinkle for baptism "by faith." You cannot use mechanical instruments of music in worshiping God "by faith." You cannot build human organizations to do the work of the Church "by faith." There is not any way to do "by faith" anything that God says nothing about. And that is a principle that the world needs today as badly as it needs any other.

But not only did God say it, *the thing done must be what God said*. I might do something else, I might offer a substitute, but unless the thing I do is the thing that God Himself said for me to do, it is not "by faith." It is not simply something done with an attitude that I call "faith"; but when I do a thing "by faith," God said it and I do the thing that God said for me to do. Now, Abel's sacrifice was offered "by faith," because it was the kind of sacrifice that God said for him to offer. Cain's sacrifice was not "by faith," because it was a substitute for what God said. When men do not do *what* God says, they are not motivated "by faith." Faith moves a man to do *only what God says*! So I need to be careful that the obedience of my faith is the thing that God authorizes and that His Word teaches.

The next point that I want to emphasize is that "by faith" signifies not only that God *said* it and that it is *what* God said, but *it is done like God said do it* — in the manner in which *God said* for it to be done! I cannot even substitute another method. A man says, "I have been baptized." What did you do? "I had water sprinkled upon me." Not so—that is not Bible baptism! God said that baptism is a washing of the body in pure water. A man says, "I have offered acceptable praise unto God." How did you do it? "Upon a mechanical instrument of music." Not so! There is not any authority in the Word of God for it. When you praise God, you are going to have to praise God *like God says,* in the manner in which God says for you to do it. The sacrifice offered unto God must be not only the sacrifice that God has ordained, but it must be offered *like God says!*

Now, you could emphasize that in a number of Bible illustrations, but we will not take the time, because we will deal with them in another lesson, and that will be about Friday night when we talk on the subject, "Walking By Faith." But when Noah built the ark, he had to build it like God said. The thing would not have floated if he had not, and he would not have been saved by water in the ark. When Moses built the tabernacle in the mountain, God gave him the pattern of it and said, "See that you build it according to the pattern." If he had deviated from it, God would not have dwelt in it; but when he built it according to the pattern, God filled it with His spirit and accepted it as His tabernacle, as His dwelling place among His people. You could multiply demonstrations of the fact in Bible history that God has always demanded that men do *what He says, like He said* do it. And you cannot do it "by faith" and do it any other way.

But I suggest to you that "by faith" means even something else. "By faith" means not only that I do *what* God said and I do it *like* God said do it, but it means that *I do it for the purpose, or with the end in view, that God designates. I must do it with the end in view* that God assigns.

Now, the Lord's Supper has an end in view, a design. There is a purpose in it. We do not do it simply as a ritual or as a ceremony that within itself has any righteousness connected with it. Paul said that when you observe the Lord's Supper, unless you discern in the institution and in the elements that constitute it—the unleavened bread and the fruit of the vine—unless you discern in it the body and the blood of the Lord, and do it in memory of the death of the Son of God, you cannot do it without eating and drinking condemnation unto your soul. Now I cannot partake of the Lord's Supper simply because I am in the habit of doing it and please God. It is an appointment that the Lord has made that must be done "by faith." That means it must serve God's purpose. It must be a memorial service to the body and the blood of Jesus that was offered in His death for my sin. That is the meaning of it. That is the purpose assigned.

Baptism is another illustration. A man cannot be baptized to please his wife. He cannot be baptized to please a friend. He cannot be baptized acceptably in the sight of God for any other reason except *for, unto, in order to* the remission of sin. That is the design, the purpose, the end in view that God has assigned. That is the end that you must have in view and in which your trust must be placed, for that is *what* God said baptism is for, and that is *why* God told me to do it. Unless you do it for the purpose that God assigns, you are not doing it "by faith." But when a man renders the obedience of faith, it is *to* what God said, it is the *thing* that God said for him to do, it is done *like* God said for him to do it, it is done with the *purpose in view* that God assigned, and it is done—and I would emphasize this point—*only, only because God said* for him to do it! *Only because God said it!*

"By Faith" Exalts God, Not Human Reason

Faith does not operate in the realm of human reason. I think sometimes that we have glorified and deified education, human learning, human attainment, human wisdom, and human reason to the point that we want to test even the Word of God by it. We are not willing to take what the Bible plainly and very definitely says at face value and believe it, just because *God said* it. But you cannot obey God "by faith" without that sort of an attitude. Why should we do or not do a certain thing? Human reason answers, "Well, I can prove to you this and that about it. I will fix me some syllogisms, and I will logically reason it out." I am not decrying reason or logic *except when used as the source of religious authority,* and I have already indicated that we must obey God intelligently and understandingly from the heart. Christianity is a reasonable religion, but it is not a religion of reason! Somebody has said that it is not "unreasonable," but neither is it a "reasoning" religion.

Suppose a man did only what he could see and only when he understood the reason *why* God said for him to do it? You could not understand to save your life why God commanded men to be baptized rather than something else. You know *why* it is from the viewpoint of the end or the purpose that God assigns for it to serve (what God intends shall be accomplished by it), but why did God select baptism? Somebody says, "Well, I do not see how being baptized in water has anything to do with the salvation of the soul." Well, of course, *you* do not. Of course, *you do not!* And you do not see why breaking bread on the first day of the week in honor of the Lord's death has any spiritual value or benefit in it either. You could not reason that out.

There is not anything connected with the religion of Jesus Christ that rests upon human reason! Now, that does not mean that you do not have to do some thinking and studying in order to know what the will of the Lord is. Do not misunderstand me. But it means that nothing connected with the will of God or in the scheme of redemp-

tion depends upon human reasoning. "God chose the foolish things
of the world to confound and bring to naught them that are wise"
(1 Cor. 1:27).

You know, I read one time (I think it is Tennyson who wrote)
"The Charge of the Light Brigade." And there was an expression
in that that impressed me. As he told the story in poetry of that company of men who made the charge when the bugle was blown, in
the face of certain and imminent death, he said, "Their's not to
reason why, their's but to do or die." That is what faith is. *That
is what faith is!* When I learn a thing to be the will of God, when
I come to an understanding of what God teaches me to do, what
He says for me to do, and what His will is for me, *then, "by faith"
I ought to do it.* It does not make any difference what the consequences are.

Somebody asked an old black preacher down South one time who
was preaching right along that line: "You talk about faith always
obeying the will of God. What if God told you to jump through
that brick wall? What would you do about it?" And the old black
preacher said, "It would be my business to do the jumping and God's
business to make the hole." And that is just the point! That is *just*
the point! When I have enough faith to take God at His Word and
do what He says, whether I can see why God selected that or not,
whether there is any human reason that makes it all plausible or that
gives it any significance and meaning to me, *if God said it,* that is
enough for the man of faith.

I ask you tonight if you have that kind of faith? That is what we
have been talking about all week, and it is the only kind of faith
that can save a single, solitary one of us. Until you exercise that sort
of faith and yield yourself to do what God commands you to do,
you are in your sins. And if you die that way, Jesus said, "Where
I am, there you cannot come." And friend, when the Lord said you
cannot die in your sins and expect to go to Heaven, He means *just
exactly that!* No more and no less! You cannot be saved in the guilt
of sin or with the guilt of sin upon you.

If tonight you are not a Christian, if your faith has not led you
to be baptized into Christ, baptized into His death, baptized into
your death to sin that you might be raised up to walk in newness
of life, if your faith has not thus submitted to the will of God and

motivated you to do it, *our plea and prayer is that you come at this very moment,* the only time that God gives you. You have no promise of any other hope and your soul ought to be valuable enough that you would not reject this one. May God help you to accept it, while we stand and sing a song.

Further Study On Chapter Five

1. A pre-assigned student should read 3 review questions on chapter 4, give the class a few moments to write answers, then announce correct answers. Assign someone to prepare 3 review questions on chapter 5 for the next class.

2. Memorize Romans 1:15 or 16:26 and be ready to quote it. (Give the class 1-2 minutes to write down their passage, then call on a few to recite.)

3. Outline chapter 5 at home (main points and scriptures). The teacher will call on class members to briefly explain what each means (such as "Focusing on the Obedience of Faith") and how some passage was used to support the heading.

4. Write a brief commentary on or explanation of Romans 1:3-5 and 16:25-26. Tell in your own words what each verse means. The teacher may call upon several students to read all or part of what they have written.

5. Is the gospel a system of religion for perfect people, people who have never made and never will make a single mistake? *Why* or *why not* is the gospel such a system?

6. Each student should have prepared a list of questions and answers on chapter 5 (5 true-false; 3 brief answer; 2 asking, "What passage teaches us that...?"). The teacher should ask students to read some of their questions for the class to discuss.

7. Use Romans 6:1-4 to discuss what happened to Christ and what happens to the sinner seeking salvation.

8. Consider obedience "from the heart" (Rom. 6:17-18). Tell why sprinkling does or does not qualify as gospel obedience from the

heart. What about a person who claims he has been saved by his faith before baptism and then is immersed because it is a command of God?

9. What are some things which determine our eternal destiny and how is that destiny described? See Romans 2:1-11 and 2 Thessalonians 1:6-10.

10. What are some things God commanded or taught that men would have rejected down through history if they had followed a religion of human reason? Consider men in the Old and New Testaments, and men today. (If possible, the teacher may break the class into smaller groups of 3-5 for about 5-7 minutes of discussion; then let each group leader tell the whole class one or two important points developed by the group.)

CHAPTER SIX

How Faith Purifies The Heart

I want to again extend a very hearty welcome to you in this service tonight, and to express to you our genuine gratitude for your presence here. I trust we are as grateful as is possible for the good providence of God allowing us to assemble in His presence and to enjoy the rich provisions that His grace has made for us in a service of this sort—in the worship that He has taught us to render in spirit and in truth, by study of His Word.

We would like to remind you that if you are not a Christian, we are hoping to help you to be one. This is our aim and our prayer and why we are studying with you from the Word of God. Only by the power of the Gospel can a man be brought to believe in the Word of Christ and to be saved upon the terms of God's grace and mercy. So our aim is to help you to come to an understanding, if you do not understand it, and to persuade you to accept it by faith and to render obedience to its demands, if you have not done so. A man robs himself of the greatest blessings in life and of the only hope that the promises of God offer for eternity, when he fails to obey the Gospel in becoming a Christian, and when he fails to serve God in harmony with His will. And so we trust that, when we begin to sing the song that has been announced, you will have been able to make up your mind and to reach the decision that you are ready to do whatever God requires, that you may stand upon His promises and rejoice in the hope that they are able to sustain in your heart.

Faith In The Faith Purifies

I want tonight to talk to you about how faith purifies the heart. That it does, there can be no question or doubt. The *importance of faith* to any man who knows what the Bible teaches, and believes what the Bible says, cannot be doubted or for one moment questioned. It is essential to the salvation of every human soul; Jesus said, "Except ye believe that I am he, ye shall die in your sins"

(Jn. 8:24). Faith in the Christ as the Son of God is therefore necessary for the salvation of our souls from the guilt of sin.

The Bible teaches that the Gospel has been revealed in order that men might believe in the plan of God for making men righteous, holy, or just before Him. The Bible teaches that without faith it is impossible to please God, so certainly faith is the great essential. It embraces all that God requires of us, in fact. That is not to say that the Bible teaches man that faith is all that is necessary for the salvation of his soul. But faith from the Bible point of view, as it expresses man's hope for salvation and His means of justification, embraces all that God has planned and required that man must do in order that salvation might become a reality in his heart and life.

Jew and Gentile Purified Through Faith in the Gospel
(Acts 15:7-9)

The Gospel, of course, began to be preached on the day of Pentecost, in the city of Jerusalem, and you will find the record of it in Acts chapter two. Then, you will remember in the tenth chapter of the book of Acts that it was preached to the Gentiles for the first time. First, *to the Jews* on Pentecost in Jerusalem, and then *to the Gentiles* at the house of Cornelius by the Apostle Peter.

It was not long until, in spite of the growth of the Church, error had crept into it, and certain Judaizing teachers were going around teaching that men had to be circumcised and to accept Jewish circumcision in order to become children of God. They wanted to hold on-to their Judaism. They were trying to make the Jewish religion sort of an entrance-way into the Kingdom of God. They were preaching that Jewish circumcision was essential to the salvation of the soul—that a man first had to become circumcised and then by faith he could obey the Gospel, become a member of the Church of the Lord, and be saved by the blood of Christ. Of course, they had no Divine authority to sanction that.

Because of this Judaistic movement, there came together at Jerusalem a number of brethren. Paul was sent by the brethren and God revealed to him that He wanted him to go. Paul took with him others when he went to Jerusalem, and together with others thus assembled—first having met with the Apostles and the Elders, then the whole church was called together—this matter was laid before them, and God's law concerning it was made known. The decision

was rendered by the will of God in Heaven. The Holy Spirit revealed it, and the Apostles proclaimed it or made it known under the
guiding power of the Holy Spirit of God. This is recorded in the
fifteenth chapter of the Acts of the Apostles, and frequently is referred to as the "Jerusalem Conference," the Conference at Jerusalem
with the Apostles of our Lord.

I like to think of it as a case that was brought for a decision in
the Supreme Court of the Church of God. That is what the Apostles
constituted. Jesus said, "When the Son of man shall sit upon the
throne of his glory, ye shall sit upon twelve thrones, judging the
twelve tribes of Israel" (Matt. 19:28). The twelve tribes of Israel constituted the whole of fleshly Israel. To be a Jew today is not to be
one outwardly, but it is an inward or spiritual relationship.

Circumcision is not "of the flesh," Paul tells us in Romans 2,
but it is "of the heart." It is the cutting away of the guilt of sin
from the heart and in Colossians 2 he describes how it is done: Christ
circumcises our hearts when He cuts away the body of sin, the guilt
of sin. And, he tells us when this occurs: when we are buried with
him by baptism into death, wherein also we are raised up through
faith in the operation of God who hath raised him from the dead.
And you can read about that in Colossians 2:11-12. So spiritual circumcision is certainly essential. It means the cutting off of the guilt
of sin, the purifying and the cleansing of the heart.

Peter made a speech about purifying the heart by faith at this
"Jerusalem Conference." When certain things had been said and
done, Peter arose and rehearsed unto them certain things to which
he had been a party. The record said,

> Peter rose up, and said unto them, Men and brethren, ye know
> how that a good while ago God made choice among us, that the
> Gentiles by my mouth should hear the Word of the gospel, and
> believe. And God, which knoweth the hearts, bare them witness,
> giving them the Holy Ghost, even as he did unto us; and put no
> difference between us and them, purifying their hearts by faith.

Peter was simply saying that God's plan of salvation is exactly the
same for the Gentile as it is for the Jew.

The blood of Christ has been shed for all men alike. All men need
to be saved because "all have sinned" and "all have come short of

the glory of God" (Rom. 3:23). All are under the sentence of spiritual
death. All are in need of redemption. Only the blood of Christ can
take away our sins and can purge our hearts from the guilt of sin.
But Peter says that God's plan for men to be purged and cleansed
and purified by the blood of Christ is *through faith in the Gospel.*
So, he said that God put *no difference between the Gentile and the
Jew*, purifying the heart of the Gentile by faith, even as he had
purified the heart of the Jew by faith.

Now, we suggest to you first of all that *faith*, in both instances,
had come by hearing the Word of God (Rom. 10:17). As we have
repeatedly emphasized in this series of services in which we have
studied faith every night, there is not any other source from which
faith can come. Faith in God and in the righteousness of God must
be faith in "the faith" prescribed by the Gospel of the Son of God.
Only as I believe in "the faith"—and my faith rests upon the Gospel,
which has as its foundation the Word of the Lord and has been
planted in my heart by the Word of the Lord—can my faith be in
God's way of making men righteous.

Now, a lot of people believe that God will purify and cleanse and
make men holy and righteous in some other way, a way which they
cannot read about in the Word of God. This would be some way
that God does not teach and that God has not set forth, that some
man in his own mind's imagination has created and has planted in
the minds and hearts of others. It would be some human method
or human system by which they think salvation and righteousness
before God can be achieved. But there is not any!

Peter said God has just *one* plan! That plan, as we have already
learned, is by the blood of Christ. But that plan is set forth in the
Gospel of the Son of God, and I can appropriate that plan only by
my faith in the Gospel of the Son of God that makes the plan known.
Hence, the heart of a man is purified by faith.

What Is the Heart?
How is that accomplished? In the first place, I think it is essential
and necessary that we understand what the heart is in order that we
may be able to see what the Bible means by "the heart of man" and
not have the wrong impression, as a great many people do. We need
to look at a number of passages of Scripture.

I would suggest to you first of all that *the "heart of man" is his* intelligence. The heart is not the physical blood pump in your left breast. It is not a physical organ of your physical body. There is just as much religion and as much need for purification in one part of your physical anatomy as there is in another. When the Bible talks about purifying the heart by faith, it is not talking about this physical heart.

So many people think that this is the seat of religion, and I have seen people pat themselves where they thought would be at least in the vicinity of their hearts, and tell me how they felt, and tell me that they knew they had been saved because of some experience they had and because of *"the feeling" that they had in their heart.* But this is no evidence of salvation any more than any other physical feeling that you might have. A physical feeling is not evidence that a man's heart has been purified "by faith." There might be some reaction by this heart upon some good news that one learns, or upon some bad report that he hears. It might, perhaps, increase its beat. It might be affected to some degree by some shock or something sorrowful or a great catastrophe, but this is not the seat of religion. The heart, the Bible heart, the spiritual heart that needs to be puri-fied, is first of all the "intellect" of man. And we learn that from a number of passages.

In Matthew 9:4, Jesus said to the people whom He was address-ing, "Why think ye evil in your hearts?" So, I learn that the function of the heart is to think. That is a function of intelligence, intellect.

On another occasion, in Mark 2:8, Jesus perceived "that they reasoned within themselves." And another translation says "within their hearts." They *reasoned* in their hearts, a function of man's heart. That, too, is a function of man's intelligence. We reason by intelligence; we think by our intellect. Our intellectual ability, therefore, is our heart. At least, intelligence is a part of the heart, and to think and reason with our intellect is a function of the heart.

But still another passage. In Matthew 13:15, Jesus says that it is necessary for men to "see with their eyes, and hear with their ears, and understand with their heart, and should be converted...." A man who does not learn the Gospel of the Son of God by reading with his eyes and by hearing with his ears cannot understand what the will of the Lord is. And a man who does not understand the will of the Lord cannot be converted. Conversion, or bringing a man to righteousness, or saving his soul, is not then an unintelligible process. It is not some mysterious experience that is better felt than told and one only knows when it has happened by the way he *feels*.

That is not what the Bible describes as conversion. The Bible describes conversion as the process of *learning* what the will of the Lord is, coming to *an understanding* of it in our hearts, in order that we might *believe* it. Jesus definitely described the function of intellect in ability to "understand" as the function of the heart of a man. So, the intelligence and the heart are at least in these functions the same. But, let us look at another.

In Romans 10:10, the Apostle Paul said, "If a man believes with his heart that Jesus is Lord and that God has raised him from the dead, he shall be saved." Here is at least a part of what man must believe in order to be saved. God requires the *believing* of the fact that Christ is Lord, and the believing of His resurrection from the dead. Also, *confessing* Him as Lord and the resurrected Savior is essential to our conversion, to our salvation. But faith in Christ must be "with the heart." "If a man believes with the heart"—so the heart functions in the exercising of faith. Faith belongs to the Bible heart! It is a function of the heart!

One could sum up these points by saying, then, that the Bible heart *thinks* and the Bible heart *reasons*. The Bible heart—the scriptural heart of man, the heart that is to be purified or that needs to be cleansed—also is able "to understand" what the will of the Lord is, and it accepts the will of the Lord in faith. In faith! So the function of the heart is the function of intelligence. When a man talks about his heart, from a Bible point of view, he is talking about his intellect. Now, leaving that fixed in our minds, let us look at another part of the heart of man.

The Bible teaches that *"with the heart" man loves*. Jesus said in Matthew 22:37 that the great commandment of the law is that "thou shalt love the Lord thy God, with all thy heart, with all thy soul, and with all thy strength and with all thy mind." Thou shalt love the Lord thy God with all thy heart! And so, with the heart, man loves. That is emotional nature; our emotional ability is a function of the heart of man from the viewpoint of the teaching of God's Word. Peter said, "Love one another from a pure heart fervently" (1 Pet. 1:22). Then, I learn in 2 Samuel 6:16 that the heart of man despises evil ways. The heart's function is *to despise*, to hate, to abhor, as well as to love. In Acts 2:26, we are taught that men "rejoice in their hearts." The heart is capable of *rejoicing*, as well as despising and as well as loving.

In John 16:6, Jesus said to His disciples that "your hearts are full of sorrow," because of these things that I have said unto you. So, the heart can *sorrow*. In John 14, Jesus said, "Let not your hearts be troubled: ye believe in God, believe also in me." In Isaiah 61:1, the prophet talked about the heart's being broken. So, the heart of man can be *grieved*. The heart of man can be *troubled*. The heart of man can be full of sorrow. The heart of man can rejoice and be glad. The heart of man can despise. And, the heart of man can love. These are functions of the heart, according to the Word of God. That simply means that the heart is capable of emotional ability, of emotional functions. So, the heart of a man is a man's intellect, and the heart, from a Bible point of view, is a man's emotions.

But look at another truth concerning the heart of man and its nature. The Word of God teaches that the heart of man *devises evil ways* (Prov. 16:9). And then we are taught by the Bible, in Daniel 1:8, that Daniel "purposed in his heart." The heart not only devises, plans, or schemes, but the heart *performs purposes and determinations*. In 2 Corinthians 9:7, Paul taught that a man in his giving to the Lord of his money ought to give as he has "purposed in his heart," according to the purpose that we have formed in our hearts, and out of that purpose. So, the heart purposes.

Not only that, the heart *desires*. Paul said, "Brethren my heart's desire and prayer to God for Israel is that they might be saved" (Rom. 10:1). "My heart's desire"—so, the heart is capable of desiring. Also, the heart is capable of *willing*. In Exodus 35:5, we are taught that it is the "will of the heart" that men must submit to God, and unto God's Word and way. So, the heart is willpower. That, of course, is what purposing, devising, planning, or aiming all mean.

There are three things one learns about the heart of man from a spiritual point of view. It is not this physical heart. It is the heart that is made up of intellect or intelligence—the ability to think, reason, understand, and believe. It is the *emotional nature*: the ability to sorrow, the ability to despise, the ability to love, the ability to rejoice. This is the heart of man and its function of emotional nature. And then, it is made up of the ability to *will*, or to purpose to do a thing. The heart is intelligence, the heart is emotion, and the heart is willpower. That serves our purpose at this time in defining what the Bible heart is. We will add another function of the heart, another part of the heart, from a scriptural point of view, in a later part of the lesson.

Purifying the Heart

But remember, when the Bible talks about *the heart's being purified*, when the Bible talks about the heart of man being cleansed by the blood of Christ, it is not talking about the physical heart. But it is talking about *the intellect, the emotion, and the will*. This is the heart that is purified "by faith." Somebody might say, *"But how does faith purify the intellect of man?"* Well, I think that is not difficult for us to understand when we get in our minds the fact that the heart is intellect, and we know what the function of intelligence is. The heart has to surrender its trust in man's wisdom and man's way to the wisdom of God and God's way. Until faith brings one to put his faith in God's wisdom, in God's Word, and in God's way, faith cannot purify his heart!

I would call your attention to the fact that this word, "purify"—and Peter used it ("that God purified their hearts by faith")—is a word that does not mean just to "make clean," like you might wash something and make it clean. But it means to "filter out the dross"; it means to purge and purify in the sense that the thing which is defiled and that which is evil is eliminated. Now, one of the things that is evil in the sight of God is for man to trust in his own wisdom. When a man trusts in his own wisdom, or in human wisdom, God resents it and God rejects it, because that is evidence of a man's failure to trust in God and in the provisions of God's grace.

The Bible, in Romans 1, talks about the Gentiles, who rejected the knowledge which had been given them of God. What they knew about God, they rejected. They refused to trust in it; they refused to rely upon it; they refused to be guided by it. In the vanity and the conceit of their own minds, they walked after their own way. They trusted in their own wisdom and refused to recognize God, and to put their trust in God, and the record says, "God gave them up."

You remember that when the Ethiopian eunuch raised the question, "Why can't I be baptized?" Philip said to him—and Philip was an inspired preacher—that if you want to be baptized, you must believe with "all of your heart." With _all_ of your heart! Faith with _all_ of the heart means faith that has surrendered the intellect of man to trust in the wisdom of God, and not in the wisdom of man. To refuse to trust in man's wisdom, even his own, and to put his trust in the wisdom of God, is the way faith purifies that kind of trust which is offensive to God and which means a rejection of God and a rebellion against His will.

But the intellect is not all that God must purify. _Faith must purify the whole heart of man_, and the second thing that the heart is made up of is _emotional nature_. An emotional nature is the ability to love, to desire, to despise, and to hate. Now faith in God and in God's Word will not only lead a man to God, but it will lead him to _despise sin_. The Bible teaches that we are to love God with all of our hearts and we are to abhor that which is evil. We are to despise and hate that which is wrong in God's sight, and our affections are to be centered upon God.

All of the affections of our hearts must give God first place in our affections, in our emotional beings. God demands and requires it! He shall be exalted in our love to a position of primacy! If I allow anything to stand before me and the God who is able alone to save my soul, that thing becomes an idol that is offensive to God, and God rejects me because I have served an idol rather than serving Him. So, my love must be centered upon the Lord.

Paul told us where to center, set, or "place the affections of your heart": "upon things above, where Christ is seated at the right hand of God," and not upon the things of this world (Col. 3:1-2). John said, "If any man love the world, the love of the Father is not in him" (1 Jn. 2:15-17). This is a good way to find out how real and how genuine your Christianity is. What value do you place upon the things that this world is able to give? How much do these mean to you: knowledge and wisdom of a human nature, power and authority, worldly influence and popularity, the possessions of this world from the viewpoint of wealth that it has to offer, and the satisfaction of fleshly desires by the pleasures that the world can offer? Have you withdrawn your affection for them? If you have the kind of faith you ought to have, you will. We are to cleave to that which is good, and we are to abhor that which is evil! Our affections are to be centered and set, *fixed*, upon the things that are above!

Paul said that we are to look at that the things that are not seen, "for the things that are seen are temporal, but the things that are not seen are eternal" (2 Cor. 4:18). This is one of the great points at which the faith of so many people fails. We put the value upon the things that are physical and material, upon the things that have to do with time, on the things that belong to this world. All such things are unsatisfying in their nature and uncertain in their attainment. If we had them all, they would merely cost our souls and we would have made a very bad bargain. The value needs to be put upon the soul—the inner man, *not* the outer man! The things of Heaven and the things that are eternal are not the things that can be seen with the physical eye.

It would have been better for you to have been born blind, and never to have beheld the sunlight of God's day, than for you not to perceive and not to understand what the will of the Lord is and not to know the truth. It would be better for you to starve to death for something to eat, than it is for you to dwarf your spirit and starve your soul for the bread of life, which the Word of God alone is able to give. It would be better for you to suffer death a thousand times over physically, than to die spiritually and to be separated from God for all eternity. And the sentence of spiritual death rests upon the soul of a man who is guilty of his sins. Jesus said, "If you die in your sin, where I am, there you cannot come" (Jn. 8:21-24).

I need, then, to recognize the importance of putting the value where it belongs and placing my affections upon the things above, where Christ is seated at the right hand of God. And I can do so only by faith. It is faith alone that will help me to see, not the things that are of this world. I should put my trust in the things that are eternal: the hope of Heaven, the value of the soul, pardon for the guilt of sin, my need of salvation, the saving power of the blood of Jesus Christ, faith in God's Word and in the promises and the provisions of God's grace. That alone can cleanse one's emotional nature and being from the love of the world! Paul says that faith must work "by love"; it must "beget love"; and through love, faith must accomplish the purpose in our hearts that God would have it to accomplish.

Surrender of the Will

But look at the third point. The heart of man is made up not only of intellect and emotions. Faith must conquer our intellect that we might place our trust in God rather than in the wisdom of man. Our emotions must center our love and affections upon God and not upon the things of this world. But, in addition to that, *the will power has to be cleansed and purified by faith.* A man wills to do his own will. One reason why so many people are not the children of God is that they have not been able to crucify their own desires and their own wills. We are too strong-minded, too stubborn in heart and soul, too selfish in our thoughts, too self-centered to be concerned about doing the will of the Lord.

But the Bible teaches that the very essence of being a disciple of Christ is to surrender the will, by faith, in obedience to Him. Jesus said, "If any man would be my disciple, let him deny himself" (Lk. 9:23). Let him crucify self! Let him put self to death! When he crucifies self and puts down his own selfish ambitions and desires and purposes, and makes the will of God the purpose of his life, then he can be my disciple. Then he can take up his cross and follow me! But as long as a man follows after his own will, does what he pleases, rejecting what God would have him to do, that man is lost and his heart is impure. The blood of Christ has not redeemed him from the guilt of sin, and faith has not purified his heart.

So, faith must surrender the will or the purpose of man. It means complete surrender unto the Lord, to do his will. To be able to say, "Not my will but thine be done"—that is what Jesus said as he gave himself for our salvation (Matt. 26:36-44). This is what he taught his disciples to pray in Matthew 6:10: "Thy will, Father, be done on earth, even as it is in heaven." And, this is the sort of an attitude that faith plants in the heart of a man.

Paul said, "I have been crucified with Christ, so that it is no longer I that live" (Gal. 2:20). He was not any longer concerned with Paul's will and doing what Paul wanted to do. I hear him saying later on, when writing to the Philippians, that he had a difficult choice to make. He said that he was in a strait betwixt two; he knew not whether to depart and be with Christ or whether to remain. He said, for me "to live is Christ." He valued life, estimated life, and defined life in terms of the will of the Lord, and doing it in the life of the individual (Phil. 1:21-24).

"To live is Christ!" Not to serve Paul, but to serve Christ! That is what life is! And that is what the life of the Christian has to be. Until faith in one's heart grows strong enough that it will surrender his will in complete submission to the will of the Lord—to do *whatever* the Lord would have him to do, to be *whatever* the Lord wants him to be—and until faith is strong enough to conquer and purge one's will of selfishness, self will, self desire, the love and esteem of self, faith will not purify one's heart. It cannot do so. It has to purify our intellects of trusting in the wisdom of man and ourselves and our own way, and to place our trust in God. It has to be strong enough to purify our emotions and set our affections upon the things that are above, not upon the things of this world. It has to be strong enough to conquer our wills and to surrender us and our all in complete submission and obedience to the will of the Lord.

Faith purifies the heart to obedience to the truth. Peter said, "Faith purifies the heart of both Jew and Gentile alike," and God bore witness to that fact in the conversion of Cornelius when He gave to Cornelius the Holy Spirit, even as He had unto the Jews on the day of Pentecost in the city of Jerusalem (Acts 15:7-11).

Purified Through Obedience
But Peter said, "Seeing ye have purified your souls, through your obedience to the truth" (1 Pet. 1:22). Now, I ask you, is there any difference between and is there any conflict between *faith's purifying the heart of man* and the doctrine of *obedience's purifying the heart of man?* Well, certainly not. Why wouldn't there be? There are a lot of people in the world who want to pit and array the doctrine of justification by faith against the doctrine of the necessity of obedience. And they claim, "If one has to do anything to be saved, even in obedience to the will of God, then he is not saved by faith." Now, a more erroneous concept never filled the heart of any individual than that.

That just is not so, because one of the requisites of faith's purifying the heart is that faith must conquer the will of man and must surrender that man's will in *submission* — or you could say—in *obedience* to the will of God. They mean exactly the same thing. My faith must bring me to fall at the feet of the Son of God, and say, "Lord, what wilt thou have me to do to be saved?" So, that is what men who were brought to believe asked in the New Testament day.

When the Philippian jailor of Acts 16 thought that Paul and Silas had escaped, and was about to take his life, Paul cried out, "Do thyself no harm, we are all here." He came trembling in before them and fell down at their feet, and said, "What must I do to be saved?" And Paul said, "Believe on the Lord Jesus Christ and thou shalt be saved and thine house." I heard a preacher one time say, "That's all Paul told him to do." He had not even read the next verse. The next verse says that they preached unto him Jesus. They preached unto him a whole sermon after Paul said that.

A whole sermon was preached. And in the preaching of that sermon, what effect and what reaction was produced? It produced faith in the heart of that man. The record says, later on, that he returned to his house, "having believed." Where did he get his faith? From the Gospel that Paul preached. Well, what did faith cause him to do? I will tell you. It caused him in the same hour of the night to submit himself to the will of the Lord by being baptized, in obedience to the commandment of Christ. That is what faith did! Faith conquered his willpower, and caused him to obey the Son of God! It always does, when it saves!

When faith purifies our hearts, when our hearts are cleansed and purged and refined by faith, then our own will is put to death. We make the will of the Lord the objective of our lives and we begin our obedience to Him at the very point that He requires. Turning away from our sins, and hence, repenting, confessing with the mouth that which we believe in our hearts, that Jesus Christ is Lord, we then submit ourselves by the act of baptism because Christ commanded it, because it is the will of God. And it is addressed to every human being on earth.

I cannot do the will of the Lord without being baptized. And, I would impress you with the fact that if you have never been baptized into Christ, in obedience to the will of God, if you have never submitted yourself to be buried with him by baptism into death to be raised up to walk in newness of life, through faith in the working of God who raised him up from the dead, then your heart never has been purified, because your faith has never led you to submit your will to the will of Christ. It is the will of Christ that *all* men obey the Gospel! That *all* men be baptized!

But somebody said, "Now, preacher, I can't see the connection between faith conquering the *intelligence*, the *emotions*, and the *will*, and man's being willing to submit himself to the Lord rather than to do his own will—I can't see the connection between that and *being baptized*." Well, let me just show it you you. In language plain and clear we will read it from the will of God, and if you have a Bible handy, you turn and read it with us.

The Conscience Cleansed By Christ's Blood
When We Are Baptized

First of all, the only thing that can purge and purify the heart is the *blood of the Son of God* and the Bible makes that abundantly clear. In Hebrews 9:13-14, Paul said that the ashes of a red heifer and the blood of bulls and of goats could sanctify unto the cleansing of the flesh—unto the purifying of the flesh, ceremonially, that is. Back under the Law of Moses, there was the water of cleansing, and the ashes of a heifer, with water and scarlet wool and hyssop sprinkled upon that which was defiled to cleanse and purify it, ceremonially, or outwardly, according to "the flesh." That is the thing Paul refers to in Hebrews 9:13 (cf. Num. 19).

Then, there was the blood of bulls and goats offered as sacrifices; two he-goats and a ram died for the sins of all Israel on the day of atonement every year, as often as it came, in accordance with the commandments of God under the Law of Moses. But Paul said in Hebrews 9:14, if the blood of those animals back there, and if water of cleansing under the Old Law, under Judaism, could sanctify unto the cleansing or the purifying of the flesh, "How much more shall the blood of Christ, who through the eternal Spirit offered Himself without spot to God, purge your conscience from dead works to serve the living God?"

Now, here comes another part of the heart. The heart is made up not only of intellect and emotion and will power, but it is also made up of *conscience*. The conscience of the heart is simply the ability of the heart to remind us to do our duty and to leave off that which is wrong. Two things, the conscience does. The conscience smites one if he does not do what he knows to be his duty, because that is sinful. In the first place, it will destroy his own self-respect, and conscience preserves self-respect. A man that does not act, when he knows that he ought to act, has a sense of guilt in his own mind, and is condemned by his own conscience for his failure, until his conscience becomes so hardened that it is insensitive to man's duty and to the will of God and to man's good.

But the conscience not only reminds us to do what we ought to do, our duty, the conscience also reminds us and pricks us and punishes us when we do that which we know to be wrong. When we sin, we also violate our conscience. So, the conscience reminds me to do what I know to be right, what I understand to be my duty. And, the conscience reminds me to leave off that which I know to be contrary to the will of God, that which I know to be wrong or understand to be wrong. The conscience is not the intellect. It does not tell me *what* is right or wrong. It is not the function of the conscience to understand. The conscience is not the emotional nature. It is not the function of the conscience to love. The conscience is not the will power. It is not the function of the conscience to form the purpose and the determination of a man's heart. But the conscience is that constant reminder in our hearts to do that which we understand to be right and to leave off that which we understand to be wrong.

Well, suppose I violate my conscience and engage in something that is contrary to the will of God and I know it. Whatever sin it may be, it does not matter. One sin separates from God as well as any of the rest. What is the result? Well, the result is guilt, and as long as my conscience has guilt upon it, I cannot be at peace with God. Faith has to purify the conscience also, and the only thing that can purify the conscience is the blood of Christ. The blood of Christ! "How much more shall the blood of Christ, who through the eternal Spirit offered himself without spot to God, purge your conscience from dead works to serve the living God?"

What is it that purges a man's conscience? It is the blood of Christ, by faith of course. And there is not any conflict between *faith's doing it* and *the blood of Christ doing it*. It is "by faith" in the blood of Christ that purging of a man's conscience is made possible. Paul said in Romans 3:25 that God sent forth His Son to be a propitiation for the sins that are passed, through faith in his blood. I have to have faith enough in the ability and power of the blood of Christ to purge my conscience from the guilt of sin in order to surrender myself in obedience and to render my will in complete submission to the will of the Lord. When I do that, and I am baptized into Christ, the blood of Jesus Christ will remove—it will cleanse and purge from my heart—the guilt of sin.

And we know how faith leads us to the blood of Christ. We learned that in the lesson last night: by the cross the blood was shed, upon the cross the sacrifice was made. Paul went out and preached the Gospel; and when he went out and preached the Gospel, he preached the death and the burial and the resurrection of Christ. When the Romans obeyed it—when they, by faith, trusted in the Lord and learned to love the Lord, and surrendered themselves to the Lord, and obeyed from the heart that pattern or that form of doctrine— they were buried with Christ by baptism into death, "that like as Christ was raised from the dead by the Father, even so they also might walk in newness of life" (Rom. 6:4). And this was when they "obeyed from the heart that form of doctrine," in the act of baptism.

Paul said, "We were buried with him." Therefore baptism is a burial. That disqualifies sprinkling and pouring, doesn't it? For certain! But not only is it a burial, it is "into" or in order to "die unto sin," to have our guilt of sin removed by the blood of Christ. Paul said, "When you were baptized into Christ, you were baptized into his death." That is where his blood is.

So, it is *by faith, through obedience,* in the act of baptism, that we reach the death of Christ and the blood of Christ and thus we *die unto sin!* Are justified from sin! Separated from sin! And then, the old body of sin having been circumcised or cut off from our hearts by the Lord, we are able to walk in a *new life* as new creatures in Christ Jesus! Raised up into newness of life! We are made free from sin, Paul said in Romans 6:17-18, and become the servants of righteousness.

Cleansing the Heart Discussed In Hebrews 10:10
Now, that is not the only passage that tells us how faith reaches the blood of Christ, or how we can reach the blood of Christ by faith. It takes the blood of Christ to purge our hearts. Our hearts cannot be refined by faith except through and in the blood of Jesus Christ. Let us look at another passage. Turn right on over to the tenth chapter of the book of Hebrews, and let us read again. Paul,

talking about the new will that Christ had sanctified by the offering of His own body, said,

> By the which will we are sanctified through the offering of the body of Jesus Christ once for all. And every priest standeth daily ministering and offering oftentimes the same sacrifices, which can never take away sins: but this man [talking about Christ, R.E.C.] after he had offered one sacrifice for sins forever, sat down on the right hand of God; from henceforth expecting till his enemies be made his footstool. For by one offering he hath perfected for ever them that are sanctified. Whereof the Holy Ghost also is a witness to us: for after that he had said before, This is the covenant that I will make with them after those days, saith the Lord, [God had promised this, R.E.C.] I will put my laws into their hearts and in their minds will I write them; and their sins and iniquities will I remember no more (Heb. 10:10-17).

The law of God in the heart! Taking possession of the heart! The will of God written upon the mind and in the heart of man, and received by faith, brings all this about!

But what is the consummating act that cleanses the conscience? Read right on with me: "I will put my laws into their hearts, and in their minds will I write them; and their sins and iniquities will I remember no more." That is the kind of purging. The guilt of sin is cleansed and purged away, and we are loosed from it. Washed from it! Purified from it! Never to have it remembered against us any more forever!

Back under the Old Covenant, the Jewish Covenant, God remembered their sins every year. Under the New Covenant, sanctified by the body and the blood of the Son of God, our sins are forgiven and forgotten, never to be remembered against us. That is the kind of forgiveness God offers. How a man can reject it, I cannot understand. God offers by the blood of Christ to wipe the slate clean, to give us a fresh and a new page upon which to continue our lives in holiness and in righteousness and in obedience to His will.

I read a little poem one time that I never fail to think of when I read about the blood of Christ purifying and cleansing the heart. One part of it ran like this: "I wish there were some wonderful place called the Land of Beginning Again, where all of our mistakes and all our heartaches and all our poor selfish grief, could be dropped like a shabby old coat at the door, and never put on again." Well, I have longed for that time, haven't you? I have wished that I could call back some of the mistakes, or all of the mistakes that I have recognized in my own life, and some of the blunders that I have made that have been so disastrous to me, and do it all over again. I think that I could eliminate them the next time.

But I cannot call my mistakes back and undo them. I do not even have the chance to avoid them any more. That chance has flown. It is gone. What I can do is claim the cleansing power of the blood of the Son of God that is able to erase all of them, to purge me completely from all of them and from their guilt and from their consciousness of guilt, that I might be at peace with God, and that I might have the assurance that I am justified before God and allowed to enjoy the freedom that is in Christ Jesus.

We still have not found the consummating act that cleanses the conscience, but read right on down with me. God said, "Their sins and their iniquities will I remember no more. Now where remission of these is, there is no more offering for sin. Having therefore, brethren, boldness to enter into the holiest by the blood of Jesus, by a new and living way, which he hath consecrated for us, through the veil, that is to say, his flesh; and having a high priest over the house of God";—*with all these provisions now having been made and these promises having been offered, what can we do about it?*— "let us draw near with a true heart in full assurance of faith...."

How? By "having our hearts sprinkled from an evil conscience." What does that? The blood of Christ! What is it that is sprinkled upon the heart? Remember that it is upon the heart and not upon the head or face, and remember that it is the blood of Christ that is sprinkled upon the heart to purify and purge the heart from an evil conscience. It is the sprinkling of the blood upon the heart of a man that does that.

You and I can learn from the next part of that sentence *how and when we claim this promise for our own*: "Having our hearts sprinkled from an evil conscience," by the blood of Christ, that is. "And our bodies washed with pure water." Baptism is a washing. It is described in Titus 3:5 as the "washing of regeneration and the renewing of the Holy Spirit." Here, baptism is described as the "washing of the body in pure water." He meant plain, unmixed water—water unmixed with anything else. Not the water of cleansing in the Old Testament. It is when I wash my body in unmixed water, *in the act of baptism*, being buried in the water and raised up out of it, thus having washed my body in the act of baptism by water, that the *blood of Christ sprinkles my heart from an evil conscience.*

How much clearer could God have made it than that? *I* did not say it. *I* am not responsible for it. It is not what some preacher thinks or what some creed teaches. You can read that for yourself in Hebrews 10. That we draw near unto God. How? "With a true heart." How can I draw near unto God with a true heart? "In the full assurance of faith." And this is what faith does for you! And when I draw near unto God with a true heart in the full assurance of faith, I will have my body washed in plain, unmixed water in the act of baptism, and God will have cleansed and purified my heart from an evil conscience, from the consciousness of the guilt of sin, by sprinkling the blood of Christ upon it.

This sprinkling of Jesus' blood is evidently an allusion to the sprinkling of the blood of the Passover lamb in Egypt, isn't it? Israel, on the night that they went up out of Egypt, was commanded to slay a lamb and the blood of that lamb was to be sprinkled upon the lintel and upon the doorpost. Wherever it was in evidence, wherever they sprinkled the blood of that lamb and as God told them to do it, death passed over that house. They escaped death; the firstborn of all who were in it was allowed to live. But where the blood was not sprinkled, the firstborn of everything in that household died. What is the consequence of not having the blood sprinkled? Death!

Well, Christ is our Passover! Paul said so in 1 Corinthians 5. It is his blood that must be sprinkled upon our hearts, and when the blood of Christ is sprinkled upon our hearts, God passes over the sentence of death as the penalty for sin. You escape the sentence of spiritual death by the sprinkling of the blood of Christ upon your heart! But when is the blood of Christ sprinkled upon my heart? When my body is washed with pure water. That is what baptism is in action. Its action is a burial and a resurrection. Its action is a washing of the body with pure water.

Cleansing the Soul, Not the Body

Somebody said, "Well, what on earth would just dipping one's body and washing one's body as one is baptized have to do with salvation anyway, and with the remission of sins?" Well, it is not just in order to make the body clean that you wash it. It is an act of faith and of obedience to God. By faith, the body is washed in the action of baptism. In action, it is a washing; but the purpose of it is not the cleansing of the body.

Let me read it to you, and 1 Peter 3:20-21 again tells us that it is connected with the cleansing of the conscience, the purifying of the heart. Talking about Noah and his salvation by water in the Ark, Peter said, "Noah and eight souls were saved by water." By the agency of water, they were transported out of the old world of sin into a new world cleansed and purified—purged and made clean by the agency of the water that came when the flood came. Noah was transported out of the old world where God repented that He had even made man and put him in it. And the world was cleansed and purified by the flood from the evil that characterized it; Noah was transported into a new world, or a fresh world, a refined world, a world cleansed from the evil that had formerly characterized it.

Now that is a figure. "...the like figure whereunto..." It is a figure of a fact. Sometimes people say there are two figures in this verse. You cannot have a figure of a figure. That would be like a shadow casting a shadow. That does not happen. It takes substance to cast a shadow and it takes a type or a figure to produce the antitype of the fact presented to us in this passage.

Noah saved by the waters of the flood—that's the type or figure. A sinner saved by the waters of baptism—that's the antitype or the fact established by the gospel. Sinners are saved by the agency of water in the act of baptism in fulfillment of the type seen in Noah's salvation. "Not the putting away of the filth of the flesh"; baptism is not simply a bath to cleanse the outside of the man; but rather it is the answer of a good conscience toward God. It is the answer of the man who seeks to have a good conscience, purified before God. That's what the act of baptism is, and that is what it is for.

Do not rob yourself of the only hope God offers you for eternity. You can be purified by faith in the blood of Christ, this very hour. When an individual goes down into the waters of baptism and there washes his body by being baptized in pure, unmixed water in obedience to the will of Christ, he is raised up, having come into cleansing or saving contact with the blood of Christ. He is raised up cleansed and purified. That is the reason Peter said we are redeemed by the blood of Christ "in obeying the truth" (1 Pet. 1:18-22).

It is baptism, a washing of the body in pure water, that brings us into contact with the blood of Christ. His blood can be reached in no other way at all. There is no substitute. We are hoping you are ready to come now, as we stand to sing for your encouragement, that you might truly embrace the promises and rejoice in the hope of the gospel.

Further Study On Chapter Six

1. A pre-assigned student should read 3 review questions on chapter 5, give the class a few moments to write answers, then announce correct answers. Assign someone to prepare 3 review questions on chapter 6 for the next class.

2. Memorize Acts 15:8-9, Hebrews 9:13-14, or 1 Peter 2:22-23 and be ready to quote it. (Give the class 1-2 minutes to write down their passage, then call on a few to recite.)

3. Outline chapter 6 at home (main points and scriptures). The teacher will call on class members to briefly explain what each heading means (such as "Faith in The Faith Purifies") and how some passage was used to support the heading.

4. Write a brief commentary on or explanation of one of the passages in question 2 or 1 Peter 3:20-21. Tell in your own words what each verse means. The teacher may call upon several students to read all or part of what they have written.

5. Explain the circumcision of Colossians 2:11-12. What is it and when does it occur? What are the results?

6. Each student should have prepared a list of questions and answers on chapter 5 (5 true-false; 3 brief answer; 2 asking, "What passage teaches us that. . .?"). The teacher should ask students to read some of their questions for the class to discuss.

7. What are some functions of the heart? What does it mean to cleanse the heart?

8. What are some functions of the conscience? Is the conscience alone a safe guide? In what sense is the conscience cleansed by obedience to the gospel?

9. Compare washing in the Old and New Testaments. Compare sprinkling. Use Hebrews 10 and find Old Testament passages.

10. How would you answer these arguments: "I know baptism does not save because while praying I got a strange feeling from God in my heart" (speaker puts hand on chest over physical heart).

"If one has to do anything to be saved, even in obedience to the will of God, then he is not saved by faith."

(If possible, the teacher may break the class into smaller groups of 3-5 for about 5-7 minutes of discussion; then let each group leader tell the whole class one or two important points developed by the group.)

CHAPTER SEVEN

Walking By Faith

We have a good audience tonight, perhaps the best one we have had since the meeting began, and that is a source of encouragement. Our audiences, of course, have been fine all week. The interest has been very encouraging. Association in these services has been very, very pleasant to me, indeed. I could go into a long speech telling you how much it means to me to be with the good friends that I have in San Antonio and in this congregation, and to have the encouragement of brethren from so many different places outside of San Antonio, as well as the congregations within it, as you have attended these services and listened so patiently to the lessons that we have tried to present. It is not only *always* a greatly pleasant experience to me to be associated with the Highland Avenue church, but also I have enjoyed that experience through the years *since 1924.* That is a long time, and it has grown more pleasant as the years have gone along.

But it is a real pleasure to be associated with the preachers that work with this congregation. I know of no church that is more favored with fine Gospel preachers than you have here. Certainly, association with them is to me a personal pleasure of the very highest sort. For all three of them I have the very highest regard, and I reciprocate fully in the personal expressions of regards that Brother Wharton has made on more than one occasion during this meeting. They are very encouraging to me and I fully appreciate them, and certainly reciprocate in the feeling expressed.

I have the very highest regard for him and have had all through the years of association with him. The first time I met him, we slept on the ground when it was raining, on a deer hunt; and he had to cover up his bald head with a tarpaulin. But I have known him through years, and he has preached where I have labored, and I have preached where he has worked. We have crossed paths, back and forth across the country, many, many times, and I have for him the highest personal regard and the warmest personal feelings, and regard his ability and devotion to the truth in the utmost.

It has been good to be with all three of these fine preachers. Brother John Witt I do not know as well, and have not known as well through the years as I have Stanley Lovett and W.L. Wharton. Both of them have been very close personal friends of mine for a long time, and it has been a pleasure to me to know Brother Witt better. He has done a very fine job in many regards during this meeting, and not the least of them is the good singing in which he has directed us in these services. And so, for it all we are very grateful, and certainly, it has been in every way a wonderfully pleasant experience to me.

We have in the audience tonight a large number of people from many different places. Among them, a number of mighty close personal friends from the West Avenue congregation. We have had several here, several different nights of the meeting. We have a good number here tonight, and it is always a joy to me to see them.

The Text: 2 Corinthians 4:13-5:9

I want to talk to you tonight about a passage of Scripture in the fifth chapter of Paul's second letter to the church at Corinth. I want, however, to begin reading with a few verses in the latter part of chapter four that need to be in our thoughts and in our consideration with the part that we shall read from chapter five. I think if I were to name this section in the Second Corinthian letter, I would call it, "The Proper Perspective In Life." Paul had the right attitude toward life; he had the right estimate of it. The right estimate of life or the right understanding of its values, is, of course, essential to a proper attitude toward it.

Paul begins in the fourth chapter by saying in verse thirteen:

> We having the same spirit of faith, according as it is written, I believed, and therefore have I spoken; we also believe, and therefore speak; knowing that he which raised up the Lord Jesus shall raise up us also by Jesus, and shall present us with you. For all things are for your sakes, that the abundant grace might through the thanksgiving of many redound to the glory of God. For which cause we faint not; but though our outward man perish, yet the inward man is renewed day by day. For our light affliction, which

is but for a moment, worketh for us a far more exceeding and eternal weight of glory; while we look not at the things which are seen, but at the things which are not seen; for the things which are seen are temporal; but the things which are not seen are eternal. For we know that if our earthly house of this tabernacle were dissolved, we have a building of God, a house not made with hands, eternal in the heavens. For in this we groan, earnestly desiring to be clothed upon with our house which is from heaven: if so be that being clothed we shall not be found naked. For we that are in this tabernacle do groan, being burdened: not for that we would be unclothed, but clothed upon, that mortality might be swallowed up of life. Now he that hath wrought us for the selfsame thing is God, who also hath given unto us the earnest of the Spirit. Therefore we are always confident, knowing that, whilst we are at home in the body, we are absent from the Lord: (for we walk by faith, not by sight:) we are confident, I say, and willing rather to be absent from the body, and to be present with the Lord. Wherefore we labor [make it our aim, R.E.C.] that, whether present or absent, we may be accepted of him.

To please God ought to be the primary desire of the heart of every individual. The man who properly has the right attitude toward life always makes it his *aim* and his *purpose* in all that he does and in every relationship *to be pleasing unto God.* The basic consideration in this particular place is the eternal nature of man's soul and his need for salvation. God has provided our salvation. Our hope of it is based upon His promises and we walk in order that we may attain it, so that we may be pleasing in His sight. Our footsteps are directed by *faith* in *the faith*!

"Walking" By Faith

The term "walk" simply denotes a course of conduct. The Bible talks about "walking" in many different ways. Paul talks in Romans eight about "walking after the Spirit," and in Galatians five, being led by the Spirit and "walking after the Spirit." It is that course of conduct in life which the Holy Spirit directs, which God has revealed as His will, and in which the Holy Spirit directs our footsteps in all of our efforts to do the will of God. That is being led by the Spirit, or walking as the Spirit directs us to walk.

John said in First John, chapter one, "If we say we have fellowship with God and walk in darkness, we lie and do not the truth, but if we walk in the light...." The glorious light of the Gospel of Christ is what he was talking about, contrasted with the darkness of error and sin. If we walk, if we live in the light, as the light of the Gospel directs us to live and to walk, if our conduct is so directed, then we can have fellowship with God, and the blood of Jesus, His Son, will cleanse us from all unrighteousness. So, the expression "walk" simply means the way a man lives, how he serves God, how in his mind and in his heart he directs his footsteps, by faith. And that means "walking by faith."

Living by faith is "walking by faith." A similar expression is that the just shall "live by faith." If a man is to enjoy justification in the sight of God, it must be as the result of his faith in *the faith!* And if he has faith in the faith of the gospel, the word of God, and walks according to it and lives by it, then he can enjoy righteousness and justification in the sight of God Almighty. But, in order to understand what it means to have our course of life conducted "by faith," we want to eliminate from our consideration some things that are not embraced, in fact, some things that are ruled out by that expression.

Walking "By Faith"
First of all, if a man walks by faith, if he lives by faith, then he is not living according to, or by the standard of, human reasoning. His conduct is neither according to his own reasoning and rationalizing, nor according to reliance upon any other human's reasoning. He recognizes that the way of man is not in himself.

Back in Deuteronomy 12:8 God condemned Israel because they were walking every man according to that which was right in his own eyes. Somehow or other, people have gotten the idea that in the matter of religion, they ought to be allowed to practice what they please, to do whatever seems good to them—to believe, and to obey, and to live in whatever way their own judgment may dictate or demand, or whatever way they think to be right. And somehow or other, we feel that when we do what we believe to be right, or when we do that which we consider to be in harmony with the will of God, that which is right in our own eyes, that God ought to be willing to accept it and that God is under obligation to save us as the result of it. Especially do people think God is obligated if what we believe is sincerely believed, and if what we do is sincerely done.

Well, Paul was living in all sincerity; he was striving with all the sincerity of his heart and with good conscience to please God. He was not an ignorant man; he had been educated; he had the benefit of all the wisdom of his day. He had sat at the feet of Gamaliel, and had enjoyed, perhaps, the very best of instruction that his day afforded. He was an intelligent individual, and certainly, very well educated; but all that he knew, and all in which he had learned to trust, was misleading and misguiding him.

There is not any force or any factor in the lives of men and women in this age of the world that is any more misleading than human philosophy and human wisdom. Reliance upon it means to desert the ground of faith! To rely upon human wisdom means to lay the way of God aside, to get away from it, and to walk after man's own will and man's own way, rather than by faith in the Word of God. This, of course, will not bring anybody to justification. One cannot be righteous in the sight of God and walk in harmony with human wisdom or in harmony with human reasoning.

In the next place I would like to suggest that *if a man walks by faith, he cannot follow the popular conception that in numbers is safety from a religious point of view.* The standard by which a lot of people like to determine their conduct is what the multitude of people accept as right and whatever has popular approval. If it is the popular opinion of the day, then we do not want to go against it. Rather, we want to go along with the tide. It is easier for us; we do not have to think for ourselves. We can simply let somebody else's judgment and the judgment of the multitude be our standard and our guide. And, sometimes, we want to prove that we are right by how many agree with us. But, you know, Jesus upset that idea when he said that those who enter in "at the strait gate" and who travel the narrow way that leads to eternal life are *few*. But, those who enter "the broad gate" and travel upon the broad way that leads to eternal torment are *many*. You cannot afford to get along with the crowd!

In multitudes and in numbers there is no safety, from the viewpoint of religion. It is a false standard indeed! Rather than that, we need to walk by faith in or by reverence for God's will, by an understanding of what the Lord would have us to understand and be, with complete confidence in it and commitment unto it.

Now, a lot of people want to be governed in matters religious by established practices, but that is not walking by faith. I hear so often the argument, "Well, look how long we have done it; just think about how many generations have so believed, and think about how long this thing has been practiced." Sometimes when one objects to something upon the ground that it is not in harmony with what the Bible teaches, even brethren want to justify it because "we have done it so long." The fact of the matter is that if they would look at a little religious history, many times it would correct that idea and that impression. But, even if it has been done from the beginning and has had its origin in human will and in human wisdom and rested upon judgment and opinion, it would not be walking by faith. It does not matter how long a thing may have been done. The question is: where did it *originate?* Where did it come from? Is it Divine, or is it human in its origin?

Upon one occasion, you remember, the Pharisees came to Jesus and they said to Him, "By what authority doest thou these things?" And Jesus said, "If you are interested in authority, let me ask you a question. The baptism of John, is it from God or is it from man?" This is the issue. Does it originate with God, or does it originate with man? And in Matthew 15, as we pointed out in a former lesson in this meeting on "Faith," Jesus drew the line between human traditions and the commandments of God. He said human traditions violate, make void, and nullify the commandments of God. So, when we walk by customary, long established practices, we do *not* have any assurance of Divine sanction; we have no assurance of Divine approval. There is not any promise that God will accept our practice upon any such basis.

I do not know how long the Jews by human tradition had practiced the washing of the hands; maybe, for generations. When it originated, I have never been able to find out. They thought that it was necessary. The tradition of the Elders bound it upon Israel. Jesus rejected it and refused to be bound by it. He refused either to keep their human traditions or to teach them to his disciples, and he taught, "Your human traditions make void the commandments of God." It does not matter how long you may have observed them. It does not make any difference how many generations may have practiced it. So, inherited traditions in religion that have been handed down to us by our fathers have no promise of Divine approval and no ground of Divine authority upon which to stand!

In the next place I would suggest to you that Paul was calling our attention to the fact that it is our obligation in all of the affairs of life to please God. Not ourselves! Not to pursue the course of least resistance! You know it is easy for us to want to be at peace with others, to want to stand in agreement and in harmony with them. To go contrary to what our friends believe, and to teach contrary to what brethren have accepted, is not an easy matter. And sometimes, the temptation and the disposition of a lot of people is to take the path of least resistance.

Back in the Old Testament, there was a demonstration of that. A man wanted to go along with the crowd and please the crowd and this was his excuse. When he failed to do the will of God and when the prophet of God called it to his attenton, his excuse was that the voice of the people demanded it. His name was Saul; he was King of Israel. God had given him the task of utterly annihilating the Amalekites, of the land of Amalek, ruled by King Agag. And God had sent him down with the Army of Israel to utterly destroy those people.

He failed to carry out God's instructions because the voice of the people wanted to keep the best of the sheep and the oxen, that they might offer them as a sacrifice unto God. And you remember that God told him through the prophet, "Behold to obey is better than to sacrifice" (1 Sam. 15:22). To do the will of God is better than to follow the path of least resistance — no matter how much effort you exert in it, how much sacrifice you may offer, or how much good you may seem to accomplish.

What If God Does Not Specifically Forbid A Thing?
Another false standard along this line is that I can practice a thing because God has not specifically forbidden it. One of the misconceptions concerning Divine authority is that we have the privilege of doing whatever God has not told us *not* to do. If God has not prohibited it in so many words, then the attitude of a lot of people in the world is that it is permissible. The permissibility of a thing! The doctrine of *permissiveness* is a doctrine that has taken hold in the world. The idea of the new morality is the idea of leading a life of permissiveness.

Just anything goes that one may think or believe to be right. *Existentialism*, with its concept that what is right for one person to do may be wrong for another and what is wrong for one may be right for another, is another one of the modern attitudes in the world of religion today. It, likewise, is a doctrine of permissiveness. Whatever I may be constrained to do under the circumstance, or whatever may seem to me to be the appropriate thing to do, is as much service to God as if God had authorized it, whether God has said anything about it or whether the will of God approves it or not.

Well, that idea is not a new one. It is finding new expression in the fields of existentialism and casuistry [resolving ethical questions on the basis of sophistry, R.H.] and the new morality. These concepts have gained a great hold in the religious world. In all of them the idea of permissiveness is present.

The thought is that if God has not specifically prohibited it, if there is not some law that says, "Thou shalt not do it," then it is all right to practice it in religion. So often people want to put a premium on the silence of the Bible. Now, walking by faith is not walking by what God has not said. "Faith comes by hearing and hearing by the Word of God," and a man cannot be governed by the silence of Almighty God—by what God has *not* said—and at the same time walk by faith! Faith founded upon the Word of God and emanating from it means that I must rely upon that which God has revealed to be His will.

I cannot believe a thing if God has not said it. So often people use the expression, "I believe," in a very unscriptural manner and, certainly, in a very incorrect way. I hear people saying everywhere I go, "I believe this or I believe that," and God never said anything that sounded like it. There is not anything in the Bible that even indicates it—nothing in the Word of God that even hints at it. And yet, we talk about "believing." Well, Paul says, "Faith comes by hearing and hearing by the Word of God." If the Word of God does not teach it, then one cannot hear it from God; and if one does not hear it from God, there is no proper way of believing it, beccuse one believes in God.

God's Revelation, Not His Silence, Authorizes A Thing

I remember in First Corinthians 2, Paul laid down the principle that that *which is the Word of God has been revealed by the Holy Spirit.* All I know about God's mind and God's will is that which the Spirit has made known. I hear him saying, "We have received the Spirit, not of the world, but the Spirit which is of God that we might *know*." The Holy Spirit came into the world, Paul said. God sent the Spirit. Jesus fulfilled His promise of the Spirit.

The Spirit came *"that we might know the things freely given us of God."* The very purpose of the Holy Spirit was not to speak something wholly apart from what God willed, or from what God said—not to make known something foreign to God's word. But the Spirit came "that we might know the things given to us of God." That was the mission of the Holy Spirit! And the Holy Spirit does not reveal to anybody anything that is not in God's Word or in harmony with the Word of God. The Spirit reveals God's mind through God's words! Paul told us that in First Corinthians 2.

He even reasons it out for us like this: "Who among men knoweth the things of a man save the Spirit of man which is in him." Now, nobody knows what is in your mind except as you reveal it. Oh, I know there are a lot of people who claim to be mind readers. But after all, they have to detect from you in some way, by some means or manner, what you are thinking about and what you know. Usually they pick it out of us with questions whenever they undertake to tell us something about what we have in our minds and our hearts.

I had one lady one time offer to tell my fortune and I told her I did not believe she could. And she said, "I'll demonstrate it to you, if you'll just show me your hand." I stuck my hand out. She began to look at my palm, and started asking me questions. And I said, "Now wait a minute. You were going to tell me. I am not telling you anything. Just leave off your questions. I am giving you no information. You give me the information if you are able to see it in my hand and know what is in my life and in my mind." Paul said that no man knows what is in another's heart. "Only the Spirit of the man that is in him."

Now, notice his application of it. "Even so the things of God none knoweth save the Spirit which is of God." Now, that passage simply means that the Holy Spirit is the only one who knows what the will of God is. The Holy Spirit is the only one who can reveal God's mind and God's will to you and me. If the Holy Spirit has not said anything about it, if there is a doctrine or a practice about which the Spirit has offered no testimony in the Word of God, that is, the Spirit has been perfectly silent concerning it, that is prima facie evidence that it is not God's mind or God's will. This is clear evidence that He does not approve it and that it does *not* please Him.

You and I need to know that all that we can find out about what pleases God Almighty is by the testimony of the Holy Spirit. So, we are under obligation to read it in the testimony and the language of the Holy Spirit, or else to know and to recognize that it is *not* the will of God. We have no right to draw the conclusion that anything pleases God unless we can find the testimony of the will of God to that effect. The Spirit has revealed unto us, and *He alone* can reveal unto us, what is the mind of God.

And Paul goes on to tell us how it was revealed. "We have received the Spirit that we might know the things freely given to us of God, which things also," he said, "we speak, not in words which man's wisdom chooseth, but in words which the Spirit chooseth, combining spiritual thoughts with spiritual words." We are guided into a knowledge of God's mind by the revelation of the Holy Spirit. By the inspiration of the Spirit, we speak God's mind in *words which the Holy Spirit himself chooses*. Now, that is what the Bible is. It is God's mind revealed in words of God's own choosing, and it is the only source we have by which to know what the will of God is.

One cannot walk *by faith* in regard to anything unless he is able to put his finger on the passage in the Holy Spirit's revelation that teaches it! That is the only way we can have faith in God—*by faith in the Word of God!* And when we practice such things simply upon the grounds of their being permissible in our judgment and estimate because God has not specifically condemned them, we are approaching it altogether from the wrong angle.

I remember the scriptures talking about the priesthood of Christ and the tribe from which He came. Paul in the Hebrew letter said concerning Jesus' lineage from Judah, "Of which tribe Moses spake nothing concerning a priest" (Heb. 7:14). There is nothing in the Word of God about a man from the tribe of Judah ever being the priest over God's people. Not a word on earth about it! And so, the Levitical priesthood, which had been ordained by God under the Law of Moses, had to come to an end in order for Christ to be priest. The Law did not provide for anybody from the tribe of Judah serving as priest of Israel. The Law said the tribe of Levi shall be the ones who shall be chosen as priests. It did not say, "and not the tribe of Judah"—that no man from Judah can be priest. God did not prohibit it *specifically*. He just told them where to get their priests and from which tribe the priests would come.

Hence, under the Law of Moses, Jesus could not be a priest on earth. He could not be for the reason that He was not of the tribe that was ordained by the Law. The Law of Moses spake nothing concerning a man from Judah serving as priest. There was no authority for anybody's being a priest over the people of God from the tribe of Judah. Now, that is our attitude toward the silence of the scriptures!

Another example of it is in Acts 15. Certain men were going around over the country among the Gentiles preaching that the Gentiles had to receive Jewish circumcision, fleshly circumcision, in order to become Christians. False teachers were making Jewish circumcision a condition of salvation. Remember that the question was brought to the Apostles at Jerusalem, and that they rendered a decision guided by the Holy Spirit. They based their judgment upon "it seemeth good unto the Holy Spirit," and because it seemed good to the Holy Spirit, it seemed good to them.

Concerning these men who were preaching circumcision, they said, "They have no such commandment from us." We gave them no commandment to preach the doctrine. They did not receive it from the Apostles of our Lord. It was not a part of the Gospel revealed through the Apostles by the Spirit of God, and hence, the Jews who required circumcision had no right to preach it. Paul said, "If any man preach unto you any gospel other than that which we have preached unto you, let him be anathema" (Gal. 1:8-9). Let him be *anathema!*

So, one of the extreme attitudes in the world is, if the Bible does not specifically prohibit it—if God does not say, "Thou shalt *not* do it"—that means it is all right. That would let in a floodtide of things that we never have even thought of in connection with religion, wouldn't it? It would destroy any authority in the Word of God at all. It puts a premium upon the silence of God rather than expressing reverence for the Word of God.

Something Can Be Authorized Without Being Specified
But may I suggest to you that there is an opposite extreme to that.

From the viewpoint of trying to establish authority in the realm of religion, the concept that a lot of people have when it comes to walking by faith is the idea that if the Bible does not specifically mention it, if specific authority does not justify it by name, then it cannot be done. Well, that of course is the opposite extreme. There is no merit in the fact that the Bible does not say it and offers no testimony about it. There is not any authority in that for a practice. Neither is there any prohibition in the fact that you cannot find authority for it in the form of specific mention. There are some things for which we have specific authority. There are other things that are essential and even necessary in carrying out the law of God, about which He has not legislated specifically.

Every once in a while I hear somebody say that we do not have any authority for a meeting house. If you talk about Bible authority and say, "We have no authority for a Church building or a meeting house," you are just as wrong about that as you can be. That is ridiculously absurd when you stop even to think about it reasonably for a moment.

In the first place, God has commanded the Church to assemble, hasn't He? In the very next place, anybody ought to know that we cannot assemble without a place of assembly. Now, God did not tell us what kind of a place it had to be. But in *the very command to assemble* there is authority for *the necessary place of assembly.* We cannot assemble without a place. It may be in a tent, it may be under an oak tree, it may be in a rented hall, it may be in somebody's house or home, it may be in some public building, it may be in a building which the brethren have provided out of their resources to furnish the facilities to carry on the work of the Lord. God has not said how to do it. God just commands us to do it and some place to carry it out is essential in obedience to the command.

So, one test of authority from the point of view as to whether or not we could practice it by faith would be, *is it necessary in carrying out God's commandments; is it essential for fulfillment of the commandment; is it included in and a necessary part of the commandment itself and of the authority that it carries?*

The Realm of Expediency
Then sometimes a commandment will include something that is not specifically essential and necessary, but which *aids or expedites*

in carrying out the will of God. Again, God has given us a test by which we might determine whether or not an expedient can be used by faith. What is the test? Paul said, "All things are lawful, but for me all things are not expedient" (1 Cor. 6:12; 10:23). He simply meant by that to lay down the rule that for a thing to be expedient, *it first of all has to be lawful.* It has to be authorized. It has to be within the realm of that which is taught. It has to be included in the law of God or else it cannot be expedient.

In the next place, I would suggest that *it cannot be specifically commanded* and be a matter of expediency. When God specifically commands, we do not have any choice to make, except to do or not to do. Man is a free moral agent. He can obey God's command-ment, or he can rebel against it and not do it. But when God specifically commands a thing, that is the only choice he has.

For instance, on the Lord's table we have the unleavened loaf as a memorial to the body of Christ, and we have the fruit of the vine as a memorial of his blood, commemorating his death in the institu-tion that we refer to as the Lord's Supper. Now, Jesus specified what would be an emblem of his body. It is the unleavened loaf. He specified what would be an emblem of his blood. It is the fruit of the vine. That does not mean orange juice. Orange juice does not grow on vines, does it? Certainly not. It was the juice of the grape that Jesus had in mind. And the fruit of the vine is the emblem that Jesus selected for the memorial of his blood, in commemorating (remembering or memorializing) the observance of his death upon the Cross.

So, he specified the emblems. Now, *add* to that, and one has disobeyed God if in any sense he substitutes anything for it. Sup-pose somebody decides graham crackers and Coca Cola would be just as good as unleavened bread and the fruit of the vine. Well, he does not have any right to make such a decision. The Lord specified, and when the Lord specifies, man does not have any choice. He can do what he says do or not do it; but if man does what he says do, he's made the choice and man has to do it exactly like the Lord chooses for him to do it. And, that is the only way faith can express itself.

Where God has exercised specific authority, there is no human choice or opinion to be expressed in matters concerning what we might consider to be expedient. We simply have to do it like God said to do it, or we are disobedient. So, a thing that expedites cannot be specifically commanded. If it is, then it becomes a matter of Divine requirement and there is not any human judgment to be exercised in connection with it, except to do that obediently which God commands.

In the next place I would suggest to you that in matters of expediency in the Church, in order for a thing to be by faith, *it cannot be an offense to the conscience of a brother—it cannot cause him to sin against his own conscience.* Paul taught this not only with reference to our concurrent action in the worship and the service of the Lord, but he taught it to be a matter of personal consideration for one another even in our private lives. If eating meat causes my brother to offend his conscience, I will eat no more meat forever. I have not the liberty simply to consult my own conscience about the matter; I must keep in mind the conscience of my brethren.

If I encourage my brother, even in matters in private living, *to do a thing in violation of his conscience,* I have encouraged him to sin. To violate your own conscience is always sin. The rule with reference to the conscience is, "If a man knoweth to do good and doeth it not, to him it is sin" (Jas. 4:17). If man does a thing that is not done by faith, then it is sinful. "Whatsoever is not of faith is sin" (Rom. 14:23). Those are the two rules that govern the exercise of my conscience. I cannot violate my conscience by doing that which God has not authorized or which God has condemned, and I cannot violate my conscience by leaving undone that which the Lord has said for me to do, without sinning in the sight of God. But we are discussing here another sort of sin. When I, by the exercise of my own personal rights or liberties in the matter of personal conviction and conscience, cause my brother to offend or sin against his conscience, I have led him to sin before God. And that is wrong for me to do.

Then, the next part of the rule is that in order for a matter to be expedient and, therefore, possibly be done within the realm of faith, *it has to edify.* It has to be something that instead of destroying and tearing down, creating dissension and strife, will build up and edify and strengthen the souls of Christian individuals, as well as extending the boundaries and increasing the strength of the Kingdom of

God and its influence in the world.

Now, let us summarize the principles which govern expediency. Nothing can be classified as being expedient in the service of God, unless first of all it is within the realm of authority either as a matter of that specifically required or as a matter of that which expedites the doing of that which God teaches and commands. It is then lawful. Then, I must remember that it cannot be specified. There is no question in matters specifically commanded, for they are matters only of obedience.

Another point to remember is that expediencies may be authorized without being spelled out, named, or specified. So, we ought not to think that because the Bible does not specifically authorize a thing by name (although the Bible may include within the scope of the thing taught and commanded what we are practicing and what we believe), that it therefore is unlawful because it is not specifically commanded. Nor should we think because God has not specifically condemned it that it is permissible. This is a misunderstanding of Bible authority or the way Bible authority works.

A practice may be authorized or permissible, it may be lawful, and still be inexpedient. It must not only be within the law and it must not only be within compliance with the will of God, but also, as we have suggested, it must not be offensive to the conscience of others or lead them to offend or violate their conscience. It must be edifying in the body of Christ. It must be productive of good. These are the rules that the scriptures lay down concerning matters of expedience in the service of God.

Old Testament Illustrations

As we further our lesson along the line of how Bible authority works, we are to understand that the Old Testament lays down for us the principle of what it means to walk by faith. In a number of illustrations I would like to get the point clarified in our minds. When the Bible says, we "walk by faith" or "the just shall live by faith," what is included? What are the principles that ought to be applied that are to guide us in doing so?

Well, I would suggest to you in the first place that it means there are *no substitutes for what God has said*. Cain demonstrates that. You know, Paul teaches that the principles of God's righteousness are laid down in the Old Testament scriptures. I hear him saying that, as he reviewed Old Testament history in Hebrews 11. From righteous Abel on down through the Old Testament period of history, Paul reviewed God's dealings with His people. From Abel he came down to Enoch, and to Noah, and to Abraham and Isaac, and to Jacob and Joseph, and to Moses and Aaron, and to Joshua and Caleb. Finally he said, "What more shall I say? The time would fail me if I should tell you the whole story" (paraphrasing it).

But, in the twelfth chapter, after this rapid review of all the Old Testament period and the "worthies" of the Old Testament period, he said, "Seeing we also are compassed about with so great a cloud of witnesses." Who are these witnesses? These characters in Old Testament history. Of what do they testify? The principles of the righteousness of God. You think about the meekness of Moses, the faith of Abraham, the patience of Job, the virtue of Daniel, the perseverance of Nehemiah, and other qualities of all the Old Testament characters that the history of God's people contains. Among the examples that we are able to find coming from these many characters in Old Testament history, and as a demonstration of the principles of God's righteousness, is the example of Cain and Abel.

Abel offered unto God a sacrifice by faith. By faith! Now we discussed the other night what faith means. It means that God says it; or else, it cannot be done by faith. It means that the thing done is the thing that God said do. Not some substitute. That was the mistake that Cain made. He was offering a sacrifice and he thought that faith prompted that sacrifice, but he substituted the fruit from the field for a sheep from the flock and God would not have it. God would *not* have it!

"By faith" means that God not only commanded the *action*, but it means He also commanded the nature of that action and gave the definition of it. One cannot offer a human substitute for what God says and obey God. Sprinkling is an example of it. There is not a passage in the Old or New Testament that commands plain water to be sprinkled upon anybody for any purpose. If you know where one is, you bring it to me and I will preach it. That is as fair as I know how to be, and I will preach it one time right here in this pulpit, if I have to close the meeting and go home when I get through. Try me and see. It *is not* in the Bible—Old or New Testament.

God *never* commanded plain, unmixed water to be sprinkled on anybody for any purpose. It did not originate with God! The first case of it in religious history was about the year 250 A.D. in the instance of Novation. It was not given general acceptance, even by the Catholic Church, until about the year 1311 at the Council of Ravenna, when it was authorized as a general substitute for immersion. Protestant denominationalism has borrowed it as a practice from the Roman Catholic institution. There is no authority in the Word of God for it! Baptism does not include it! It is not an act of baptism! Not in the Bible!

The act of baptism means to dip, not to sprinkle. The action of it is a burial and a resurrection, a washing of the body, a planting of the body, and a coming forth up out of the place where the body was planted. That is the Bible description of the action. That is the meaning of the word. In the New Testament, it means that the person who was baptized was always in the water when he was baptized. That is not so in sprinkling. Sprinkling is a substitute for immersion. It is a human substitute for the thing that God commands. When we substitute something that God does not say for what God does say, we are not walking by faith. And we can see that demonstrated in Cain and Abel.

On the other hand, Abel offered his sacrifice by faith. God accepted it. It was not only what God said do, it was also done like God said do it, and it was prompted only by faith in God and in God's Word. Cain, on the other hand, reasoned with himself that the fruit from the field would be just as acceptable with God as a sheep from the flock, and this was false reasoning. God had not said it! It was not included in what God did say! It was a substitute! A substitutionary action for that which God had ordained! So, we need to remember that God will not permit that because it is *not* walking by faith.

Lessons From King Saul

Then, I would come back to the example of Saul in the Old Testament. God sent him down to take the land of Amalek, and to destroy the Amalekites who had harrassed the people of God and lived in rebellion against God's will in all of their generations. God's wrath, His righteous judgment, was to be visited upon them by their being utterly annihilated, and He commanded Saul, the King of Israel, to go down and do it. But Saul saved old King Agag. Instead of killing every living thing in the land of Amalek, he spared the best of the sheep and of the oxen.

Why? Because he and the people thought they would do good with them. What good did they think could be done with them? We will offer them as a sacrifice to God and God will be pleased with our sacrificing to him. God commands us to offer sheep and God commands us to offer bullocks, and so we will just offer the sheep and we will just offer the bullocks. We will save these and we will make a sacrifice to God. This is the thing that God has commanded us to do. Not when they come from Amalek!

God said kill those in the land of Amalek. Kill them! Destroy *every living thing!* And, when they saved the sheep and the goats from the Amalekites to try to please and to honor God by offering them as a *living* sacrifice, and when they reasoned in their hearts that we thus will be within the thing that God has commanded and we will do good in God's sight by offering such a sacrifice, they had reasoned falsely. They had reasoned falsely and they were disobedient. And, Samuel, the prophet, came to Saul and laid down the principle that you and I need to fix in our hearts: "Behold, to obey"—to respect God's will, to act by Divine sanction and by Divine authority, to carry out that which God tells us to do—is better than any sacrifice that one can offer at any time. God prefers obedience!

Obedience is the ground upon which sacrifice can acceptably be offered to God! We want to measure sometimes what we do because we think it will be doing a lot of good. Just look at how much good it is doing. Well, God is the judge as to whether or not it is good and the good works of the New Testament are the good works that God has ordained. Paul said, "You are saved by grace through faith and that not of yourselves, it is the gift of God. Not of works, lest any man should boast, for we are His workmanship, created in Christ Jesus unto good works" (Eph. 2:8-10). What are good works? The good works of the Christian life, "which God hath before ordained—planned, arranged—that we might walk in them." So the good works of the Christian life are the works that God has arranged, *not* works of our own that might seem to be good unto us. We are walking *not* by the way things seem unto us, but we are walking by faith. And "faith comes by hearing and hearing by the Word of God.''

Saul's case is an example demonstrating another principle also: *there is not anything just as good as what God says!* We must learn that we cannot substitute something else or fail to do what God commands, because of good intentions. Man's good intentions will *not* take the place of obedience. God is not bound to accept something just because we judge that good is to be done! We cannot justify doing evil just because we claim good will come from it. Paul said, ''Shall we do evil that good may come?'' And the answer was, ''God forbid'' (Rom. 3:8). The end does *not* justify the means! That is what we need to learn.

But look at a third example. This time we turn to Nadab and Abihu. God had commanded the priests of the seed of Aaron to get fire for the burning of incense in the tabernacle in honor and in worship to God from the altar upon which fire was kept burning perpetually day and night. God did not say, *''Do not* get it here,'' and, ''Do *not* get it there,'' and *''I prohibit* you from getting it over here.'' But God said, *''You get it here!''* He told them where to get it. That limited the matter. That certainly precluded their obtaining it anywhere else, *if* they respected the Word of God. If they wanted to obey God, then they ought to get the fire where God said for them to get it.

But, do you know how they reasoned? They said, ''What God wants done is incense to be burned. He wants us to burn incense, and the fire which we put upon the altar with which to burn it is of no importance. I cannot see how that would affect the burning of incense in worship to God.'' And these two sons of Aaron went over to another source and obtained a strange fire. It was not from the altar which was kept burning perpetually, but from another source, and therefore *strange* fire. They brought it back and tried to burn incense with it. You remember that when they sought to burn incense with that strange fire, that the fire flamed up and licked out its angry tongue in God's judgment upon them and burned them to death. Instantly they perished in the fire that they had put upon the altar of incense, fire which did not come from the place *God said* to get it.

Do you learn anything by that? The principle that is demonstrated in it is this: because a thing is not prohibited specifically does not

necessarily mean that it is permissible in the sight of God! That is
the point we were talking about just a few moments ago.

But another Bible demonstration or illustration. God set up a
government over Israel. You remember that He had the whole congregation of Israel which was delivered from Egypt numbered. He
set them in certain companies, arranged the camp, told them where
each tribe and each company was to be placed when they camped,
and appointed how and what the order of march was to be as they
marched through the wilderness on the way to the land of Caanan.

God arranged for their government and it was His right to do so.
He put Moses over them to be His speaker, to be His communication with Israel as the lawgiver of God unto His people. He set Aaron
over them to be their means of communication with God. The priest
represented the link of the people with God Almighty. God spoke
through Moses, and the priest went to God in behalf of the people;
and He appointed Aaron and Moses to fill these offices.

But when Moses came down from the mountain and the congregation of Israel found out that God had given such authority to Moses
and to Aaron, you remember from Numbers 15 that Korah, Dathan,
Abiram, and certain princes of Israel rebelled against God's government. This was God's arrangement. It was a very specific and a
detailed one, as you can find easily by reading the Old Testament,
and yet they claimed the right to challenge and to change God's appointed ordinance.

The Lord in His righteous anger opened the earth and swallowed
these rebels. Selfish ambition and gullible indifference have often
caused men to propose alterations in the organizational features of
the work appointed by Jehovah God. Destruction awaits all men who
dare to tamper with God's appointments and who dare to presume
upon His authority. The authority of God's Word must be respected
in all things and that is the lesson we must learn if we are to walk
by faith today.

Are You Walking By Faith?
If you are not "walking by faith" tonight, not pardoned by God's
gracious provision in His Son, not faithfully abiding in the light of
His Word, then you are under the terrible curse of sin. We cannot
live in sin and expect to die in the Lord or to spend eternity with

Him in heaven. We cannot go beyond the perimeters of the faith—failing to walk by faith in the faith once revealed—and truly embrace the gracious promises of the gospel. But God is ready this moment to receive and forgive every sinner who will come to Him tonight. All the prayers, sacrifices, and worship of a false religion will avail you nothing. Any attempt to save yourself would reflect on God's all-sufficient plan.

Come tonight by faith in the crucified and risen Savior, not by faith in yourself or in any other man or in any human system or in any earthly philosophy. By faith repent of your sins, confess and acknowledge Jesus Christ as Lord, and then by faith submit yourself to baptism in water that you might accept God's terms and conditions of pardon. If you once made that commitment in the past but have fallen back into negligence, carelessness, and unfaithfulness, God is ready yet to forgive every failure and every sin. If you desire to walk by faith in God, the Lord's invitation is extended to you this hour as we stand to sing.

Further Study On Chapter Seven

1. A pre-assigned student should read 3 review questions on chapter 6, give the class a few moments to write answers, then announce correct answers. Assign someone to prepare 3 review questions on chapter 7 for the next class.

2. Memorize 2 Corinthians 5:6-7 and be ready to quote it. (Give the class 1-2 minutes to write it down, then call on a few to recite.)

3. Outline chapter 7 at home (main points and scriptures). The teacher will call on class members to briefly explain what each heading means (such as "Walking By Faith") and how some passage was used to support the heading.

4. Write a brief commentary on or explanation of 2 Corinthians 5:6-7. Tell in your own words what each verse means. The teacher may call upon several students to read all or part of what they have written.

5. Explain the opposite ways of walking in Romans 8:1-4; Galatians 5:16-26; and 1 John 1:5-2:2.

6. Each student should have prepared a list of questions and answers on chapter 7 (5 true-false; 3 brief answer; 2 asking, "What passage teaches us that...?"). The teacher should ask students to read some of their questions for the class to discuss.

7. Explain the difference between walking by faith and the ways of walking found in Deuteronomy 12:8 and 1 Samuel 15:22-23.

8. We can do anything in religion which God does not specifically forbid by name. True or false? Defend your answer.

9. We have no authority in the Bible for a church building or meeting house. True or false? Defend your answer.

10. What lessons can we learn about walking by faith from Cain and Abel; King Saul; Nadab and Abihu; and Korah, Dathan, and Abiram? Apply some of these lessons to modern problems. (If possible, the teacher may break the class into smaller groups of 3-5 for about 5-7 minutes of discussion; then let each group leader tell the whole class one or two important points developed by the group.)

CHAPTER EIGHT

The Failure of Faith

I would like to join very heartily with Brother W.L. Wharton in expressing our appreciation for those of you who have been in attendance at these services from the other congregations of this city and places around and about. You have added a great deal to the meeting by coming and certainly have been a great encouragement to us, not only by your presence, but by your interest, and by the very fine way in which you have listened to these lessons. For all that, I am just as grateful as I know how to be.

It is fine to have visitors even in our audience tonight. Here are Brother and Sister Earl Hart from Denton, and Brother James Yates, who led our prayer, and his good wife, and Karen their daughter, from the Spring Branch church in Houston, Texas. And I might just tell you, while I am talking about that, that the Lord willing, I will be moving to the Spring Branch congregation in Houston around the first of June, to work with them. I have been away from Texas for about eight years, and that is just about as long as one can ordinarily take it, after he has lived there as long as I did. So, I will be glad to be coming back. We are happy to have you, whoever you are, and wherever you are from, in the services tonight. We trust that it will be of benefit to us.

We have been talking and studying in this meeting on the theme of faith. Sometimes when I preach a series of sermons on one subject, it causes me to remember a story they tell about an old preacher who went to a place and preached thirteen sermons on repentance, in sequence, without interruption. One of the brethren asked him one day, "When on earth are you going to quit preaching on repentance." And he said, "When you fellows repent." And so, perhaps it is a good thing for us to emphasize a particular theme in a series of sermons in a meeting.

I believe, as much as I believe anything as far as my own judgment is concerned, that we need to understand more of the theme of faith than, perhaps, any other theme in the Bible. People sometimes get the impression that because we preach on baptism and we preach on the Church that we do not believe in the necessity of faith, and that we do not believe in the necessity of repentance, and that we do not believe in the blood of Christ. Our religious neighbors sometimes have such an impression of us and perhaps, to some degree, *we* have been responsible for leaving that impression, by putting the emphasis so much on some Bible doctrines and studying maybe so little on others.

We have stressed the importance of faith by emphasizing the fact that a man cannot come to God without it, and by emphasizing the fact that the provisions of God's grace can be enjoyed only in and through it. Paul says, "By faith we have access into this grace wherein ye stand" (Rom. 5:2). So the provisions of God's grace are available to any individual in the world only upon the conditions and terms of acceptable and saving faith exercised in his heart. This faith must motivate his life and be manifested in it. We have talked about the "spirit of faith" and the "hearing of faith," and we have talked about the "obedience of faith," and "walking by faith," and the "law of faith," and I want to talk to those of us who are God's children about the "failure of faith."

Faith Necessary In All Of Our Service To God

Understanding what faith is, and what its necessity and importance is in the Christian life, impresses us with the fact that *our entire lives in God's service depend upon it*. We cannot live acceptably in the sight of God without faith. There is not any service that we can perform, there is not any act of obedience that we can render, there is not any sacrifice that we can make, there is not any act of worship in which we can engage, except as we are prompted and guided by faith in the Son of God and in the Word of God. For example, in the Lord's Supper, unless a man has faith enough to discern in the emblems on the Lord's Table—in the unleavened bread and the fruit of the vine—the significance that they have as emblems of the body and the blood of the Lord, he partakes of it in condemnation rather than in God's acceptance and in God's approval.

The same thing exactly is true in all else that we do. James 5:15 talks about the prayer of faith: "the prayer of faith shall save the sick." He said, "If any man lack wisdom, let him ask of God who giveth to all men liberally and upbraideth not." But he goes on to say, "Let him ask in faith, for he that doubteth is like the surge of the sea driven by the wind and tossed" (Jas. 1:5-6). We pray by faith. We worship by faith. *By our faith*, we must enter heartily into the sentiment of the songs that we sing and make them the sentiment, the adornation, and the expression of reverence that actually is in our hearts. Paul wrote to Timothy and said that the end of the charge is love out of a pure heart, "faith unfeigned," and a good conscience (1 Tim. 1:5). These ought to be the very objectives of the Christian life.

In the first chapter of the Roman letter, I hear the Apostle Paul saying,

> For I am not ashamed of the gospel of Christ: for it is the power of God unto salvation unto everyone that believeth; to the Jew first and also to the Greek. For therein is the righteousness of God revealed from faith unto faith: as it is written, The just shall live by faith.

Paul said, "I have been crucified with Christ. The life that I now live, I live by the faith of the Son of God." He added, "It is no longer I that live, but Christ that liveth in me" (Gal. 2:20). So, the only life that a Christian can live acceptably before God, even after having his soul pardoned and his sins forgiven, is a life that is motivated by or directed by his individual, personal faith—genuine and sincere and wholehearted—in that which God in His Word has taught. And the minute that that faith falters, and the minute that it begins to fail, I begin to fail to live as God would have me to live.

Every step of the way is a step that requires *faith in the Son of God and in the teaching of His Word*. Paul said that "the righteousness of God has been revealed" in order that we might have faith in it. It has been revealed in the Gospel, in the faith of the Gospel, in the system of faith of which Christ is the author, in order that we might exercise faith in it. Only as I walk in the faith of the Gospel can I expect to attain unto the justification and the righteousness that God has offered unto me. The just, the righteous, necessarily have to live and continue to live by faith. The direct promise of a reward is promised only unto those who are faithful.

I remember that the Apostle Paul said in chapter one of First Peter, verses three to five:

> Blessed be the God and Father of our Lord Jesus Christ, which
> according to his abundant mercy hath begotten us again unto a
> lively hope by the resurrection of Jesus Christ from the dead, to
> an inheritance incorruptible, and undefiled, and that fadeth not
> away, reserved in heaven for you, who are kept by the power of
> God through faith unto salvation ready to be revealed in the last
> time.

I must be "kept by faith." I not only must be kept by faith, but
also I must keep "the faith," as Paul expressed it in writing the second letter to Timothy—"I have kept the faith." I am to receive
the crown of righteousness which is "laid up for me and for all those
who love his appearing," and which will be bestowed in the last day,
only if I have kept the faith.

Once Saved Always Saved? (Heb. 3:12)

So many people in the world have the concept—and I think that
it is true in the minds and the hearts of some of us who profess to
be Christians—that because we *once became believers*, and because
we *once were moved by faith to begin* a life of submission and obedience to the will of the Lord, that this is the essential and the fundamental thing, that this guarantees a mansion in the skies, that it
gives us an abstracted and guaranteed title to Heaven. Oh, I believe
that Jesus Christ is the Son of God. I even have been baptized for
the remission of my sins. I am a child, therefore, in Christ Jesus—a
member of the Church of the Lord. I am bound to go to Heaven
after a while. Well, friend, it depends.

My good brother, it depends upon your faithfulness in the Lord.
Jesus said, "Be thou faithful unto death and I will give unto thee
the crown of life." It is faithfulness, continuing in the faith—not
allowing our faith to fail—that is the important consideration and
the challenge before every one of us as the children of God. So often
it has happened, and Divine history has recorded as we shall see in
the course of our lesson, many, many instances wherein men have
failed, or allowed their faith to fail, and through the failure of faith
have forfeited the hope of eternal life. *The failure of faith simply
means to fall again into condemnation.*

Oh, I know there is the very popular doctrine in the minds of a
great many people (and in denominationalism and many religious

bodies it is a fundamental consideration and premise in much of what they believe and teach), that once a man is saved he can never be lost. The Bible does not teach this. One can readily see what difficulties it would involve. They tell us that a man is saved by faith alone, at the moment of faith, at the very minute that he gives assent to the fact that Jesus Christ is the Son of God, that he is saved and saved eternally, and hence, can never again come into condemnation. They tell us that no sin that he can commit will condemn his soul or keep him out of Heaven or cause him to lose the favor and the approval of Almighty God so as to be lost.

When we ask the question, "Is a man saved and saved eternally at the moment of faith alone?" we need to follow that with another question: "Can a man's faith fail, and is he saved eternally and will he never be lost because he once believed?" If so, then there will be eternally saved *unbelievers* in Heaven.

You look at that a moment as a consequence for such a doctrine. If a man is saved at the moment he believes and can never so sin as to be finally lost, and after once believing and being saved he allows his faith to fail, he is still eternally saved and will go to Heaven in spite of unbelief. So the doctrine simply necessitates the acceptance of the premise that if a man's faith fails, he will be saved anyhow; that it is not necessary to continue in the faith—to be faithful unto death or to be kept by faith—but that a man can allow his faith to fail and even as an unbeliever he will still be eternally saved in Heaven. And that is a rather unthinkable conclusion.

The Bible teaches that a *man's faith can fail*. There are many instances of it. The fact of the matter is that much of what Paul wrote in the New Testament was concerned with apostasy. He wrote, for example, to the Hebrews to keep them from turning away from the Gospel and from Jesus Christ and the religion of Christ and going back to Judaism. He pointed out throughout the entire Hebrew letter the superiority of the New Covenant over the Old; that Christ is superior to Moses; that Christ is superior to Aaron; that the Word of Christ is superior to the Old Covenant; that the Church of our Lord, the New Tabernacle, the new and living way dedicated by His blood is superior to the Old Jewish Tabernacle; that all of the New Covenant, in its sacrifices, in its provisions, in all that is connected with it and related to it, is superior to the Old.

What was he doing this for? For the purpose of persuading the Jews not to turn their backs upon Christ, Christianity, and the Gospel, to go back to Judaism. Well, why was he interested in that? In order to prevent their apostasy and to insure their salvation. I hear him talking about falling away from the living God, through and by the sin of unbelief. He said in Hebrews 3:12, "Let no one of us" (it can happen to any one of us) "depart from the living God" (as the result of unbelief) "in falling away from the living God." It is possible for a man, therefore, to have a failure of faith.

Paul pointed out in Hebrews 3 and 4 the failure of faith upon the part of the Jews. They were delivered from Egyptian bondage. They were baptized unto Moses in the cloud and the sea (as he related to us in First Corinthians 10). They were saved from Egypt! They started on their way to the land of Canaan, to the final rest at the end of their journey. God assured them that they would enter into His rest.

But, God's promise to them of a final rest was a conditional promise. When they became unfaithful, when they displeased God, when their faith failed, they perished in the wilderness and did not enter into the land of Canaan. God swore that because of their sin and their unfaithfulness, that *they would not enter into His rest*. Now, there was no unfaithfulness upon God's part.

The first promise of a conditional rest at the end of the journey was a conditional promise. God had prepared it for them. He would deliver it into their hands, but upon the condition of faithfulness that one can find repeated often both in the book of Exodus and in the book of Deuteronomy. God reminded them of the necessity of their choosing to walk in obedience to His will. They became disobedient in the wilderness. They were unhappy in the provisions that God made for them and they murmured against Him. They sat down to eat and drink and rose up to play. They made pleasure, their own pleasure, their god. They committed fornication, and perished in one day 23,000 of them. With them God was not well pleased.

Paul explains in Hebrews 3-4 that the real trouble was not just the sin of fornication itself. This was a manifestation of the *failure of faith*. The real problem was not their seeking pleasure and forgetting God. This was true only because their faith had failed. That is why God destroyed them. It was not because they simply wanted to murmur and complain against God and about the provisions that He had made for them, but it was because of a failure of faith. Their sin was fundamentally the sin of unbelief. And so, Paul said, "Let not an evil heart of unbelief enter into your heart" lest you might fall away from the living God (Heb. 3:12). This is the warning that the Bible sounds out to us over, and over, and over again!

Paul, you remember, in addressing the Ephesian elders in chapter 20 in the book of Acts, as he had called them to him at the town of Miletus, warned them against impending apostasy. He said, "After my departure grievious wolves shall enter in not sparing the flock, and from among your own selves shall men arise speaking perverse things and drawing away disciples after them." False doctrines will be taught. Men will be led astray from the truth. The obligation of the Elders of the congregation is to guard and protect the souls of those who have been entrusted to their care, who are their responsibility, and for whom they shall answer to God in the last day. The Elders are to guard the flock against any corruption of their faith—guard them against being led astray from the faith by false doctrine.

Can Faith In Christ Be Separated From Faith In His Word?

Men sometimes say that if a man continues to believe that Jesus Christ is the Son of God it does not matter whether he believes the rest of the Gospel that Jesus taught or not. One can depart from the Gospel, in one way or another. One can leave and turn his back upon it, just so he continued to believe that Jesus is the Christ. This, again, is *not so*.

Were we to turn to First Timothy—and remember that First Timothy was written to Timothy while he was at Ephesus—all the way through we read about the failure of faith. The fact of the business is, that this is the *very theme* of the letter. It talks more about that than it does about any other one thing: *that faith can fail, and that in many instances it will fail, and does fail.* "Faith unfeigned," is the very end of the charge!

But in the first chapter of the First Epistle, I hear the Apostle Paul saying in verses 5-6, "Now the end of the commandment is charity out of a pure heart, and of a good conscience, and of faith unfeigned: from which some having swerved have turned aside unto vain jangling; desiring to be teachers of the law; understanding neither what they say, nor whereof they affirm." Back up in the third verse, "As I besought thee to abide still at Ephesus, when I went into Macedonia, that thou mightest charge some that they teach no other doctrine"—that they teach "*no other doctrine.*" So, the Bible then warns against some "other doctrine" than the Gospel of Christ because all such false doctrine corrupts our faith and leads us away from the Lord.

This business of separating faith in Christ from faith in what Jesus teaches has always been, to me, rather ridiculously absurd. Suppose one talks about believing in somebody, but he is not willing to believe what they say. Suppose I say to you, "I believe in W.L. Wharton." Then somebody tells what W.L. Wharton says, and I say, "Well, maybe he said it, but I do not believe it." "Well, I thought you said you believed in him?" "I do." "I believe there is such an individual, but I do not believe in him to the point that I am willing to take his word for anything."

That would be faith, wouldn't it? *Is that the kind of faith in Christ that saves?* "Oh, I believe in Christ, but I do not believe in what Christ teaches. I believe in Christ, but I do not have enough confidence in him to believe and accept his Word and be governed by it and to be satisfied with it." *What would faith in Christ mean without faith in the doctrine of Christ?*

John was discussing this in 2 John, verses 9-11, when he said, "Whosoever transgresseth, and abideth not in the doctrine of Christ, hath not God. He that abideth in the doctrine of Christ, he hath both the Father and the Son." This is not just the doctrine of the teaching of the Deity of Jesus, but it is faith in the Deity of Christ to the extent that we will abide in what Christ teaches, in the Word of the Gospel of Christ. That is the faith by which the just must live! *We must live by our faith in Christ and in the Gospel which he has revealed*! So the Apostle is emphasizing the importance and the necessity of believing in the Gospel of Christ. Not only that Jesus Christ is God's Son, but believing the doctrine that has emanated from and that is based upon his Deity!

Paul said, "I was determined to know nothing among you save Jesus Christ and him crucified, when I came unto you to preach the Gospel" (1 Cor. 2:2). What did he mean? Did he mean that he was determined to preach nothing else except the crucifixion of Jesus? Did he mean that he did not discuss anything else connected with the Lord but the crucifixion? Is that what that verse teaches? Certainly not!

It means that he came determined to preach nothing but the Gospel that had emanated from and been authorized by a crucified Christ— *all* of the Gospel that had come from the Christ who was crucified! That is what gives the Gospel acceptance. That is what makes us willing and ready to abide by it. It is because we believe in him who was crucified for us and who made possible for us the Gospel that is able to direct our footsteps aright.

So, John said if a man does not abide in the doctrine of Christ, he cannot have God. He cannot have Christ. If he goes beyond the doctrine of Christ, he cannot have God. He cannot have Christ. If he goes beyond the doctrine of Christ, he has neither the Father nor the Son. Then, he added another statement: "If there come any unto you and bring not this doctrine, receive him not into your house, neither bid him God speed; for he that biddeth him God speed is partaker of his evil deeds."

A man who does not preach what Jesus taught stands condemned not only because he *does not believe it*, but also because he *preaches a gospel that he has no right to preach.* Paul said, "If any man, or even an angel from heaven should preach unto you any other gospel than that which we have preached unto you, let him be anathema." And he said, "If any man preach unto you any other gospel than that which you have received, let him be anathema" (Gal. 1:8-9). The curse of God rests upon a man that teaches something that Christ has not taught! And the only way spiritual life has been promised to you and me, either here or hereafter, is to follow in the teachings of Christ!

In First Timothy 4:8, I hear the Apostle Paul talking like this: "For bodily exercise profiteth little: but godliness is profitable unto all things, having promise of the life"—*look at it now*—"the life that now is and of that which is to come." Two kinds of life are mentioned in the passage. The promise of the Gospel in its provisions of God's grace is spiritual life in Christ—freedom from condemnation. And the promise for faithfully following the Gospel of Christ is that we will enjoy eternal life in the world to come. But when a man does not exercise himself unto godliness by faith, when he does not walk in faithful obedience to the will of God, when he allows his faith to fail or falter, *then* he ceases to live by faith, or to walk by faith. His faith fails! And he stands condemned again as an unbeliever!

To the Jews who were in covenant relationship with the Lord in His own generation, but who had become unbelievers, who would not believe in Him, Jesus said; "You are of your father, the Devil" (Jn. 8:44). Who were they? They were the children of God, born of the family of Abraham, circumcised on the eighth day. They were Jews, who were partakers of covenant relationship by virtue of being the seed of Abraham. They were, therefore, God's children under the Old Covenant, but they were guilty of unbelief! They rejected the Lord! And they rebelled against the will of God! And to them, Jesus said, "You are the children of the Devil." God would not accept them. God would not recognize them. Rather than that, God had rejected them and they were the children of the Devil!

A Major Theme In 1 Timothy: Faith Can Fail
If one follows the whole course of the teaching of First Timothy, he will find not only the positive exhortation that pleads with brethren to be faithful and to hold fast to the Word of God and the faithful doctrine, to turn away from all things that would detract from it, but he will find *warning after warning*, and *instance after instance*, where *faith did fail*. Let us just look at some of them. Then we will analyze why there was and what caused a failure of faith, and we will take warning from them.

In the last part of the first chapter of First Timothy, I remember the Apostle Paul was talking about the matter after this fashion (verse 18): "This charge I commit unto thee, that thou by them mightest war a good warfare; holding faith"—*notice now, not allowing it to fail, not allowing it to slip away from you, not allowing it to falter, but* — "holding faith, and a good conscience; which some having put away concerning faith have made shipwreck."

Now we know what happens when a ship wrecks. The cargo is lost. The ship goes down, and the cargo is lost. He even gives an example: "Of whom is Hymenaeus and Alexander, whom I have delivered unto Satan." He had turned them over unto the Devil. God no longer recognized them. Paul was inspired! He knew what the attitude of God was! Paul was caused to express it by the Holy Spirit! He was not mistaken in this matter! It was not personal judgment that he was passing! Well, why had they been delivered unto the Devil and rejected as children of God? Because they made shipwreck of the faith. "Concerning faith they have made shipwreck," and they have been "delivered unto Satan, that they may learn not to blaspheme."

But, let us look at another passage in the same first letter to Timothy, in chapter four: "Now the Spirit speaketh expressly, that in the latter times some shall depart from the faith" (v. 1). What did the Holy Spirit say? That "some shall depart from the faith." Will they go to Heaven anyhow? Will they be eternally saved even though they depart from the faith of the Gospel? Even though they cease to live by faith and walk by faith? "The just shall live by faith!"

Well, suppose they cease to live by faith, and depart from the faith? Will they still be just? If so, what God says does not mean anything. The Holy Spirit prophesied that "in latter times some shall depart from the faith." What caused it? "Giving heed to seducing spirits, and doctrines of devils; speaking lies in hypocrisy; having their conscience seared with a hot iron." They were led away from the faith—*departing from the faith* — because they gave "heed to the doctrines" of those who had no respect for God, and who preached their own commandments—the doctrines and the commandments of men—rather than those of the Lord.

Turn on to chapter five and read with me again. In the eighth verse of chapter five, Paul said, "But if any provide not for his own, specially for those of his own house, he hath denied the faith, and is worse than an infidel." Now, here is a man who had "denied the faith." That meant that he once embraced it. One cannot deny what he has not embraced or affirmed. He was irresponsible in the fact that he would not provide for his own family. He did not fulfill his obligation. He did not live by faith. He was not just before God, because he was too lazy, or too sorry, or too irresponsible to provide for those who had the right to depend upon him. He failed to fulfill that obligation which belongs to every man who walks by faith. It is the Word of God! And it is imposed upon us as God's will! If we walk by faith we will perform it. We will do it.

But what has happened to the man who does not do it? He has

denied the faith in failing to do his duty. What is the result of it? Having denied the faith, he is worse than an infidel. Will he be saved anyhow? He once was a believer. He once was saved by faith. He was justified by faith and had peace with God through our Lord Jesus Christ. But now his faith has faltered, his faith has been weakened and has failed to the point that he has denied it; he is worse than an infidel.

A man like that cannot go to Heaven. The idea that an unbeliever can be eternally saved anyway is an idea that denies everything on earth that God in His Word affirms and that the Bible teaches. *Faith can fail!* And when faith fails, one is not *kept by faith;* and if one is not kept by faith, the salvation "ready to be revealed in the last day" will not be his!

But, this is not the end of the matter. Turn in that same fifth chapter, and you hear him saying in verse eleven: "But the younger widows refuse: for when they have begun to wax wanton against Christ, they will marry; having damnation." Saved? No. They were damned. They were now lost. Why? Because they have cast off their first faith." *Their faith had failed!*

Here now are some younger women. The church was not to accept the responsibility of enrolling them for regular sustenance, for regular benevolence, help, or maintenance. They were to be refused. Well, why? Because, Paul said that "they will wax wanton against Christ"—and they will have "damnation, because they have cast off their first faith." The man who casts off his first faith, or the woman—widow or widower—in fact, *any Christian* that casts or throws away his faith in the Gospel of the Son of God, is no longer living by faith or walking by faith. The just, those who are justified before God, *must live by faith!* When we cast off our faith, we are no longer justified. We lose our acceptability before God and we have damnation as the result. "They have cast off their first faith."

Well, not only that, I remember in verse ten of chapter six, that the Apostle Paul says: "For the love of money is the root of all evil: which while some coveted after, they have erred from the faith." The word, "err"—E-R-R—means to go astray from. It means to take the wrong road, to get off in the wrong direction. And so, here are some people who love and covet money. They are enticed by what they will be able to do with it—enticed by inordinate desire in their hearts for money that they might misuse it in serving their own appetites and their own desires and their own ambitions. As a result, *they have erred from the faith, gone astray from the faith, "and pierced themselves through with many sorrows."* They have brought upon themselves a very dire or a very sad result or consequence. It is the condemnation of their souls.

"But thou, O man of God, flee these things; and follow after righteousness, godliness, faith, love, patience, meekness. Fight the good fight of faith." And what will be the result of that? "Lay hold on eternal life, whereunto thou art also called and hath professed a good profession before many witnesses." *"Fight the good fight of faith!"*

But, this is not all. The Bible teaches that those who are minded to be rich shall "pierce themselves through with many sorrows. Charge them that are rich in this present world, that they be not high-minded, nor trust in uncertain riches, but in the living God." Jesus says that the man who trusts in riches cannot enter into the Kingdom of God (Matt. 19:23-26). It would be like trying to put a camel through a needle's eye, and there was not any possibility of doing that. That is what the Lord meant. It would be impossible to put a camel through a needle's eye from a human point of view. That simply cannot be attained. Jesus said that, though all things are possible with God, it is just as impossible for a camel to pass through a needle's eye as it is for a man who trusts in riches to enter the Kingdom of Heaven. The man who has his heart centered upon the uncertainty of the things of this world, and who longs for and covets after the things of this life and the material possessions of this world, that man, that individual, *cannot* inherit the Kingdom of Heaven. Covetousness is one thing that will keep a man out of Heaven just like anything else will.

Well, when we have begun to sum up all the story, the failure of faith is made possible by what?

Faith Fails Because of False Doctrine

Well, it is made possible first of all by *false doctrines that deceive us.* We need to try and prove everything by the Word of God. Paul said, "Holding the form of faithful words, which thou hast received from me" (2 Tim. 2:13). Holding *fast* unto them! Paul wrote his letter to Titus, and the exhortation that is common to it all the way through is this: *Hold fast the form of sound words, or sound doctrine.* This is the obligation of faith! My faith must not separate itself from the pattern of truth. My faith must not be corrupted by, must not in any sense be undermined by, the doctrines and the commandments of men — those things which are not in harmony with what God has taught. I need carefully to "prove all things and to hold fast unto that which is good."

Paul warned the Colossians in chapter two that they were to continue to walk in Christ as they had received Him. "As you have received Christ Jesus the Lord, so walk in him." Then he said in verse eight, "Beware lest any man make spoil of you." Hymenaeus and Alexander were made spoil of. They allowed their faith to be shipwrecked and they even became blasphemous as the result of it, and they were delivered unto Satan. Paul warned the Colossians against it. He said, "Beware, lest any man make spoil of you through his philosophy and vain deceit after the traditions of men and rudiments of the world, and not after Christ."

One is going to have to walk in accordance with the will of Christ — as Christ teaches! One must walk in harmony with the teachings of *his Truth!* One must faithfully do *his will,* and serve *his purpose,* and not allow his faith to fail, if he is going to lay hold upon eternal life in the world to come. False doctrine and the teaching of error leads us astray from the truth. It causes us to turn away from Christ and what he taught. It is not the only cost.

Faith Fails Because of the Cares of This World
Faith is destroyed by *the cares of this world*, as we have seen in our discussion of men trusting in riches. A wanton disposition leads us to abandon our care and our concern for spiritual things. We get to the point where we are no longer concerned about going to Heaven and about our eternal salvation. One of the gravest dangers we face is that of becoming overly concerned about fulfilling our own appetites and fulfilling our ambitions and achieving our desires from a worldly point of view. These young widows that Paul warned about became so wanton they utterly abandoned the meaning of things spiritual and the hope of eternal life for the sake of what the world had to give (1 Tim. 5:11-12).

The love of this world becomes so important to us that it may lead us away from the Lord. Remember that Paul sorrowfully and sadly said, "Demas hath forsaken me, having loved this present world" (2 Tim. 4:10). Speaking of the work of Christ in connection with the things of this present world and the evil things that are in it, Paul said in Galatians 1:4, "that he might deliver us." Jesus died to deliver us from this present evil world. When we abandon our pursuit of our eternal life, abandon our desire and our effort to attain unto life and incorruption in the sight of the Lord, and abandon our determination to gain eternal life in the world to come, and when we "wax wanton" after the things of the world, then we have allowed our faith to fail and our souls stand alienated from God. Sin always does that! It does not matter whether it is upon the part of a child of God or anybody else.

Sin separates men from God! It did Simon, the sorcerer. You remember that when the Gospel was preached in Samaria, Acts 8:12 says: "But when they believed Philip preaching good tidings concerning the kingdom of God and the name of Jesus Christ, they were baptized both men and women." Then it says that Simon also believed, and having been baptized, he continued with them. The Samaritans believed and were baptized. Jesus said, "He that believeth and is baptized shall be saved" (Mk. 16:16). They were *saved*, if the Lord kept his promise.

Simon, the sorcerer, believed and was baptized. Jesus said, "He that believeth and is baptized shall be saved." And so, Simon was *saved*, if the Lord kept his promise. But then Simon insulted Heaven when he tried to buy the power of God—the gift of God—with money. He offered Peter money, and said, "Give me the power that upon whomsoever I lay my hands, I may confer upon him these gifts." Peter said, "You have neither lot nor part in this matter. Thy heart is not right before God. Thou art in the gall of bitterness and the bond of iniquity." That does not mean that he had always been that way. He did not say, "You are *yet* in the gall of bitterness and the bond of iniquity," or "Your heart has *never* been right." It once had been right; the Bible said he believed and was baptized.

Somebody said, "But he did not genuinely believe." Well, if *he* did not genuinely believe, then the Samaritans did not genuinely believe. If one is going to tear the case of Simon out as a case of conversion, he will have to tear out the case of the conversion of the Samartians—rid his Bible of the whole eighth chapter of Acts.

And if he is going to tear out the eighth chapter, he would just as well throw the rest of it away. They believed and they were baptized; Simon believed and he was baptized; but now he insults God by offering Heaven money for the power that he saw Peter and the Apostles exercising.

Peter said, "Thy money perish with thee. . . . for thou art in the gall of bitterness and the bond of iniquity." He was not saved *at that time*, was he? He had been saved, if Jesus kept his promise, and I believe he did. He did what Jesus told him to do in order to be saved, and the Holy Spirit records it. But then he became a sinner. He had sinned before God, and sin alienates from God, either the child of God or anybody else. If one is guilty of sin, in or out of the Church, the guilt of his sin keeps him separated from God until the blood of Jesus Christ takes it away and his soul is purged of it. So, Peter said to him, "Repent therefore of this thy wickedness."

Of *this*, thy wickedness! *Just one sin had been committed.* Sometimes people say to me, "Well, will one sin separate you from God?" The Bible says that it did Simon. "Repent of *this* thy wickedness, and pray God if perhaps the thought of thine heart may be forgiven thee." Sin alienates! When men wax wanton, when they get to the place where they abandon all care and all concern for the salvation of their souls, and when they turn after the world to walk as the world walks, they stand alienated from God. They are *no longer just* in God's sight, and they are not living by faith.

Faith Fails Because of An Unstable Heart
Not only false doctrine and the cares of the world choke out the influence of the Word of God, keep it from bearing fruit in our hearts, and destroy our faith, but more than that so will *fickleness and shallowness of soul*. A lack of depth of character can cause a man's faith to fail. His determination is not strong enough simply because his willpower is not strong enough. His purpose does not abide because his will falters. He is represented by the shallow soil that Jesus said good seed was sown into; it brought forth no harvest (Matt. 13:20-21). Oh, it sprang up. It came up all right. But it soon withered and died because there was no depth of soil.

There are a great many people who are so unstable and so fickle in disposition and so unstedfast in heart and in purpose that they simply cannot remain or do not remain because of their unstedfast characters. They fall away because they have not cultivated stability of heart and soul, and because their faith has not firmly enough anchored their hearts and their souls to the Rock of Ages. They simply cannot abide faithful in the service of God and soon they fall away. Jesus said they believed for a while. That means after a while they do *not* believe.

So the message is that the believer can become an unbeliever. His faith *can* fail! While one's faith is the means that must motivate his heart in submission to the will of the Lord to be obedient to him, and while a person's faith brings him to the cleansing power of Christ's blood, and while a man's heart is purified by faith, this does not guarantee the eternal salvation of his soul. The fact that a person once has believed and has been saved, does *not* mean that he will be admitted into the Grace of the City and allowed, necessarily, to live with God forever.

What does it depend upon? Revelation 2:10 says, "Be thou faithful unto death!" Somebody said, "Well, that means to the point of dying." It means as long as one lives anyway, doesn't it? It would mean that even indirectly. It means just as long as one lives, he is under obligation to pray that his faith may grow, to study that his faith may grow, to work that his faith may grow and be strengthened.

The faith of the Hebrews faltered because they did not exercise their senses to discern between good and evil. Paul said, "When some of you by reason of time ought to be teachers you need to be taught again" (Heb. 5:12). You have made no progress. You have not grown. You have not developed. You have not matured. Your faith has not been increased, and you need to be instructed all over again.

Some of us are still "babes in Christ." Though we have been members of the Church for many, many years, we have not studied our Bibles. Our faith has not had the food to feed upon that it might grow strong. We have not prayed to God for a greater faith. We have not exercised our senses in discerning between good and evil. As the result, our souls are in jeopardy because of an immature character and unfinished service upon our part. An unfinished work is always a very sad thing, isn't it?

Paul admonished the Philippians that they might work out their own salvation, carry through to a successful conclusion that which they had begun (Phil. 2:12). This is what we need to set our hearts upon. It is one thing to be saved. It is another thing to remain saved. It is one thing to become a child of God and to begin to walk by faith. It is another thing to continue to live and to walk by the faith of the Son of God.

Receive Pardon By Faith

I want to propose to you that if *once you began such a course*, if faith in your heart in the Lord caused you to yield yourself in submission to his will and to be buried with him by baptism, to become a child of God (Paul said, "You are all the children of God by faith in Christ Jesus, for as many of you as have been baptized into Christ, have put on Christ," Gal. 3:26-27); and if once you did that, *but you have allowed your faith to weaken*, then you need to see your true condition. You have made *shipwreck* of the faith; you have *denied* the faith; you have *erred* concerning the faith; you have *strayed away* from the faith, or fallen away from it; you have *cast away* your first faith; you have not grown in faith stronger and stronger as the days have gone by. Rather than that, you have allowed your faith to be shipwrecked.

You need now to renew your faith and ask God's mercy and pardon as your faith leads you to repent of your wrongs and your unfaithfulness. You need to ask God to forgive them and to reinstate you in His favor, pardoning your soul from the guilt of sin through the blood of Christ, and to acknowledge and recognize you once again as one of His own, that the hope of Heaven may once again be planted in your heart upon the promises of God's Word. If you have been unfaithful as a child of God, remember that God offers to pardon, *if* we confess our faults, repent of them, and seek His mercy and His pardon in prayer. We can even pray for one another that we might be forgiven.

But if you have *never become a child of God*, if you are not a simple Christian—only that and nothing else—because you have not put your faith in the Lord and not rendered obedience to his will, *you need tonight to become one*. You need to turn away from everything else, from all other considerations. Simply by faith surrender yourself to Christ, turning away from your former manner of life and repenting of it, confessing and acknowledging that you do believe in him with all of your heart. Be buried by baptism into his death, into your death to sin; reach the cleansing power of his blood that your heart may be purified by your faith from the guilt of every sin, through that atoning power of the blood of the Lord. Then be raised up and walk in newness of life. This is God's offer. It is the invitation of Jesus Christ, our Lord, who died for us.

And we would like to plead with you with all the earnestness of our hearts, if you have not begun a life of faith, *this* is the time to do it. If you have once begun it and you have failed or fallen, *this* is the time to renew it, and to reestablish yourself in God's favor, by claiming once again His Divine grace. We urge you to come in obedience to the will of the Lord while we stand and sing the song of invitation.

Further Study On Chapter Eight

1. A pre-assigned student should read 3 review questions on chapter 7, give the class a few moments to write answers, then announce correct answers. Assign someone to prepare 3 review questions on chapter 8 for the next class.

2. Memorize 1 Peter 1:3-5 or Hebrews 3:12-14 and be ready to quote it. (Give the class 1-2 minutes to write down their passage, then call on a few to recite.)

3. Outline chapter 8 at home (main points and scriptures). The teacher will call on class members to briefly explain what each heading means (such as "Once Saved Always Saved") and how some passage was used to support the heading.

4. Write a brief commentary on or explanation of 1 Peter 1:3-5 or Hebrews 3:12-14. Tell in your own words what each verse means. The teacher may call upon several students to read all or part of what they have written.

5. What sins of Israel are mentioned in 1 Corinthians 10:1-12? What underlying cause is recorded in Hebrews 3-4? How can we apply this lesson today?

6. Each student should have prepared a list of questions and answers on chapter 8 (5 true-false; 3 brief answer; 2 asking, "What passage teaches us that...?"). The teacher should ask students to read some

of their questions for the class to discuss.

7. A fundamental theme of 1 Timothy is that faith can fail. Read it and list as many passages as you can which point up that theme. Discuss some in class.

8. We may believe in Christ and be saved in heaven, even if we reject some things which He taught. True or false? Use passages to defend your answer.

9. Discuss the case of Simon in Acts 8 as an example of the failure of faith.

10. What are some signs and causes of failing faith? What can we do to overcome each of these? (If possible, the teacher may break the class into smaller groups of 3-5 for about 5-7 minutes of discussion; then let each group leader tell the whole class one or two important points developed by the group.)

CHAPTER NINE

Measuring The Temple

I appreciate more than I am able to express the very kind words that have been spoken in introduction of me this morning by Brother Roy D. Spears, who serves as an elder here. All of my life it has been an ambition that I might live to be worthy, and that I might serve God in such a manner that I could be worthy, of the confidence and love of the many good people with whom I have been associated in the work of the Lord. That is a pretty big job for any Gospel preacher. The association that I have enjoyed in this meeting with all of you has been very pleasant indeed. My association with this congregation has always been that way through many years.

Brother Graves, one of your elders, is enjoying this morning his ninety-second birthday. I told him a little while ago that I had known him nearly all that almost-100 years—more of it, perhaps, than we like to have to acknowledge.

There are many others in this congregation who have been counted by me among my very close personal friends for all of the years since I first attended a service and had a part in a service over at the old Denver Heights church here in San Antonio. There is none whom I have been more closely associated with than Brother Spears and his good wife, and their family, and none whom I have any higher regard for, nor any greater personal love and appreciation for. I think I know him and I know his love for the truth and for the Lord. I know that he uses himself and what he has to try to honor, to glorify, and to serve God, and it is to me an ambition to try to be worthy of the love and the confidence of men like that in the service of God. I fully reciprocate all of the very warm personal regard that he expressed concerning me and also the expression of pleasure that this week has brought. It has added a great deal of pleasure to the meeting to me to be in his home and to be associated with him and his wife and with Brother and Sister Roy Crawford (Roy Crawford of West

Yellowstone, Montana, was a brother to Sister Spears, R.H.), as they also have stayed in the home during this meeting. We have had a very pleasant time and a very fine week in every way, and for it I am very grateful.

But we are interested in the service this morning in the accomplishment of all possible good, as we will be in the service again this evening, and even until the very last song has been sung and the very last prayer has been prayed. We could say a lot of things about the good things we have enjoyed together personally. The association with the preachers of this congregtion is, and always has been through the years, uplifting and encouraging to me and as pleasant as it could possibly be. And that goes for all three of them. I am glad that it has been my privilege to be associated with them, as well as with you, in the work of the Lord.

The Text: Revelation 11:1

I want to read a passage of Scripture from the eleventh chapter of the book of Revelation, beginning with verse one: "And there was given me a reed like unto a rod: and the angel stood, saying, Rise, and measure the temple of God, the altar, and them that worship therein." Arise and measure the temple of God, the altar, and them that worship therein! There is a scene similar to this back in the Old Testament from the vision that Ezekiel had of a wonderful city. In that wonderful city was a wonderful temple. While he looked upon that scene, as God gave the vision to him, there was one who took a reed and measured the Temple.

I wonder sometimes if we recognize the standard by which our measuring is to be done. Our appraisal, our judgment, our decision, our attitudes, our approval or disapproval, is to rest not upon some personal peculiarity that we may have, or some personal judgment that we may render, or some personal conviction, even, that dwells in our hearts (except as it involves our own conscience). But, we are to be measured, and the Church of God is to be measured, always by one standard alone—not by the wisdom of man, not by the decision and judgment of any man in his own mind and his own intellect. It is to be measured by the truth of Almighty God as it has been revealed in His Word. *That* is the measuring reed!

This congregaton, and any other congregation, stands approved by the Lord only to the degree that it measures up to what God in

His Word has set for it as a standard of righteousness and holiness. So, we want to take the suggestion of the lesson this morning and simply apply it in a practical way to our own situation.

Measure The Church

First of all, there is to be measured by the measuring reed, the Church. The Church is the Temple. It is God's dwelling place. It was back in the Old Testament and it is now. His dwelling place is not the physical building or the physical house in which we may worship, but the spiritual house of God made of spiritual stones, in which spiritual sacrifices are to be offered unto God acceptably through Jesus Christ, our Lord. The Church is God's Temple.

In Ephesians 2, the Apostle Paul said, "Now therefore, ye are no more strangers and foreigners, but fellow citizens with the saints, and of the household of God." And then in the next verse or so, he said: "You are built together...an holy temple in the Lord...for a habitation of God through the Spirit." Ye are built together for a holy Temple in the Lord for a habitation of God in the Spirit!

Back in the Old Testament, when God spoke to Moses in the Mountain and commanded him to build a tabernacle and gave to him the pattern for it, God charged him: "See that you build all things according to the pattern" (Ex. 25:9,40). That simply meant that his obligation was not to use his own wisdom or judgment, not to use what might appeal to him or what his preference might be, or to take a vote of the people to decide upon how the tabernacle should be built. But, it was his obligation to obey the charge that God delivered unto him that he build it according to the pattern. God had given that pattern.

The same thing exactly was true when Solomon built the Temple. The record says that God gave the pattern of the Temple of Solomon to his father, David, and Solomon built it according to all the things which God had shown in the pattern and the plan of it to his father, David. David delivered it to Solomon. Solomon was charged to build it according to the pattern (1 Chron. 28:11-12,19). When Moses built the tabernacle according to the pattern, God filled it with His Spirit and Israel gathered before it to be in the presence of Jehovah. And Solomon built a Temple according to the pattern that God had given his father, David. The record says that God met Solomon in it and spoke to him. And God said to him: "If my people who are called by my name will turn away from their sins and seek my face, I will hear their prayers" (2 Chron. 7:14).

He said also, "I have chosen this place in which to cause my name to dwell" (2 Chron. 7:12). It was a place designated by the God of Heaven as His dwelling place among His people. His name was inscribed or written there, engraved there upon the altar, and the sacrifices that God wanted them to offer were acceptable unto God when they were brought to the place God had ordained. The sacrifices that God had said should be offered in Jerusalem, upon the altar upon which was written the name of Jehovah in the house in which God dwelt, *could not be offered anywhere else.*

If one were to turn back to Deuteronomy, chapters twelve and sixteen, he would find God prohibiting that. He prohibited them from offering their sacrifices, as sometimes they were wont to do, upon every green hill or under every tree and in its shade. Rather, they are to bring their sacrifices that God had ordained that should be offered to Jerusalem, His chosen city, and offer them upon the altar where His name was inscribed, and in the house that He had designed and where He chose to dwell among His people.

The same thing exactly is true of the Church of God. Our sacrifices are to be offered in the Church of God, in God's Temple now. God's Temple is God's Church—God's tabernacle. It is the house in which God dwells, where the presence of God can be enjoyed and where spiritual sacrifices can be offered unto God acceptably in His service. In order that we may know of our acceptability in the sight of God, we need to measure that Temple by the measuring reed.

Every congregation ought to look at itself, examine itself, look into its own affairs, and be certain that it measures up to what God in His Word has revealed to be His will. That is what it takes to constitute the Church of our Lord. We may *call* it the Church of Christ, but it is not that unless it measures up, at least to the point of God's approval in His mercy and by His grace, to that which God has set as the standard. It is that standard by which the very identity and the existence of the Church is to be determined and to be made known. The pattern is revealed by the Holy Spirit in the Word of God! We do not have to guess about it.

The Church's Organization
We do not have to guess about *the pattern of the organization*

of the Church. It has an organization that is Divine in its design. God is the author and the architect of it! The organization of the local Church, which is made up of saints, has Deacons to serve and Elders or Bishops to oversee. This is what every Church of Christ ought to be from the viewpoint of organization and what it must be if it is organized in a fashion that God will approve, if spiritual maturity has been reached, and if proper service unto God is to be offered. Acts 14:23 says, "They" (that is, the Apostles, Paul and Barnabas, and those who had a part in it), "appointed for them" (as their agents to provide the leadership God ordained), "elders in every church." That is God's plan! And in every Church, not only Elders (Bishops or Pastors) oversee the work and are responsible for carrying it out in harmony with the will of the Lord, but also in addition to that, Deacons are to serve in assisting the Elders in doing the work that needs to be done, and Saints are to live and serve in harmony with God's will. That is the organization or structure of the Church as one reads about it in the Word of God.

The Church's Work

But in another matter, we need to measure the Church. That is *in the work that it does.* Now, many times congregations go far astray. They mix into their work a little bit of nearly everything. There are churches which have a recreational program—a program of athletic activity—for the recreation of its members. There are churches that have turned more into social clubs than they are spiritual bodies, and who function in the realm of dining, in playing, and in enjoying social activity. There are churches that are teaching in the realm of homemaking, and in the realm of leather tooling, and in the realm of wood carving, and in various other trades and various other arts. There are churches that are engaging in the realm of secular education and supporting institutions whose work is 95% secular education, which is not the business of the Church at all. We have corrupted the work of the Church. We have adulterated it, and we have prostituted the Church in many instances to serve our own aims and our own purposes, rather than the will of Almighty God. But God has been *very* specific, not only about the organization of the Church, but *very* specific about the work.

The work of the Church is the work of evangelism—to preach the Gospel of Jesus Christ—to tell the good news of the plan of redemption, and to proclaim the possibility of redemption as God has offered it by grace and mercy to the souls of men and women. The Church is God's agency for teaching the truth — both to save the lost and to edify the saved!

And then, it is the business of the Church, and certainly a part of its mission, to minister unto its own needy—to needy saints who are worthy of being cared for, who are in need, and who are destitute and unable to provide for themselves. The needy saints become the obligation of the other saints of God (to share with the needy the abundance that some have) and become the objects of help to have their needs ministered unto. And some of them at least, although *that some* has been limited in Divine wisdom, can become and should become the charge of the Church insofar as caring for them is concerned.

So, the Church has three obligations: the obligation *to preach the Gospel to the lost*; the obligation *to minister unto the needs of those who are saints of God*; and the obligation *to edify the saints and to build up, or edify, the body of Christ*. This is the work of the Church! And this is what the Lord's money and the efforts of the Church ought to go for! We cannot spend the money that Christians give into the treasury of the Lord on the first day of the week for just anything that might suit us. We cannot spend it for just anything that even the Elders might approve. It is under Apostolic Authority! It has to be used in harmony with that which the Apostles have authorized.

We have no right in the teaching of the Church or the work of the Church, or in any other of its activities, in worship or in anything else, to engage in anything unless we have received commandment from the Lord through His Apostles, recorded by the Holy Spirit in the Gospel of God's Son. The Church is to be measured in its organization, in its work, and in its worship. It is to be measured by the measuring reed of the Word of God.

The Church's Worship
That worship must be "in spirit and in truth" (Jn. 4:24). It must be from the heart, sincerely and earnestly offered, if it is to be accepted in the sight of God. But, sincerity is not enough! It must be in harmony with the truth! According to the standard! The sacrifices that are to be made, the service that is to be rendered, and the praise that is to be given has been prescribed by the Lord, and His Church

has no right to depart from it! It has a pattern of worship, just like it has a pattern of organization. It has a pattern of worship, just like it has a pattern of work. And those patterns are Divinely prescribed. They are set forth in the Word of God. And what Divine authority has set forth to constitute them, and to make them up, and to be a part of them, is *all* that any man has any right to inject into them!

We cannot put into the work of the Church and the worship of the Church just whatever may suit us. We could not add ice cream and cake to the Lord's Table—not even to get a crowd. We could not spread a sumptuous banquet for the purpose of attracting people by the loaves and the fishes. This is *not* what God has ordained! We are to assemble on the first day of the week to break the unleavened loaf and to drink the cup of the fruit of the vine in memory of the body and the blood of the Son of God and to commemorate his death until he comes again. This is of what the Lord's Supper consists.

When the Corinthian Church began to observe their so-called "love feasts" and to so corrupt the assembly of the Church that they were actually so glutted with food and wine that they could not properly partake of the Lord's Supper, Paul condemned them for their activity in that regard, and reminded them that they had houses to eat and to drink in. We need then to keep the work of the Church and the worship of the Church free from any human innovation, including the modern "love feasts" called "fellowship meals."

I have no right to add to the work of God's Church a single, solitary thing, or to add to the worship of the Church a single thing that God has not provided. The Lord needs to say it to teach it. The Apostles need to preach it. I need to be able to find it upon the pages of New Testament teaching, or it does not belong in the program or the worship of the Church of the Lord.

That is the reason why we do not have instrumental music. The Lord said nothing about it. No Apostle ever preached it. No New Testament Church ever used it in worship to God. There is not any pattern that includes it. There is not any authority for it. Instrumental music in the worship is a departure from the pattern of worship that God has prescribed and we cannot measure the Temple of God and its worship and find any approval for the instrument if the Word of God is the measuring reed. The same thing is true of a multitude of other things.

That which is human needs to be left out—such as the observance of religious days and holy weeks. Where does one read in the Word of God about Holy Week? Ash Wednesday? Maunby Thursday? Good Friday? Where does one read in the Word of God about Easter Sunday? Or Christ Mass? You will not find it. It is not God's will, because the Holy Spirit has not revealed it. Only the Spirit can reveal the mind of God, and that has been revealed in the Word of God, through the Apostles and prophets, by the Holy Spirit.

I need to be satisfied with the pattern of worship that God has set for His Church, and I must be unwilling to add aught to it. I would just as soon add to the Word of God itself as to add to the organization and the work and the worship that God has prescribed for His Church to engage in. I had as soon add a chapter to the Bible and make it a part of what is considered the Word of God as to build a human organization onto the Church and try to make it serve God's purposes and do the work that God built His Church to do. I would just as soon do either one of them, as to add a single, solitary act by human authority and human wisdom to the worship of the Church of God.

Measure The Sacrifice

But I want you to notice that John was told to take the measuring reed and measure another thing, and that is, the altar. This of course suggests *sacrifice*. The altar is to be measured to determine whether or not the sacrifice is in harmony with the will of the Lord. I think that we need to look into this carefully, individually or personally, as well as congregationally. We need to look a lot more carefully and prayerfully than most of us have. How does *your* sacrifice unto God measure up? Go back to the book of Leviticus in chapters 21 and 22 and we will have a principle laid down.

Back in that book, which had to do with the priesthood and the law of the priesthood, God said to the priests that they were not to take a lamb, or bullock, or any other animal that is to be offered as a sacrifice ordained of the Lord, that is crooked backed or that has a broken leg, or that is scurvied or scabbed, or that in any way is deficient. No such animal will God accept. When they went out to select a lamb to offer, they were to pick the firstling and the fatling of the flock. When they selected a bullock to offer upon the altar, they not only had to offer it upon the altar where the name of God was written, upon the altar where the name of the Lord had been inscribed, but they had to offer the kind of sacrifice that God said He had commanded.

And that bullock had to be perfect in all of its parts. It had to be "the firstling and the fatling." They could not take an old, sick one that was going to die anyhow and offer it to God. God would not have it! They could not take one that is of no market value and offer it to the Lord. The Lord would not accept it! But they had to bring the best that they had.

The same thing was true of the sacrifice of the wave offering before the Lord. Of their harvest, God demanded the first fruits. He would not take what was left over! When they had garnered all that they could and went back to pick up a few scattered heads from the ground that they might have a wave offering unto God, that would not be acceptable in God's sight. God said it had to be the first fruits of the harvest.

I need to measure *the sacrifice and the devotion of my time, my ability, my possessions, and whatever else I have* with which I serve God according to *the principle of whether or not I consecrate unto God first*. Before any other consideration is given to any other duty or obligation, I consecrate what belongs to God unto Him first! To Him belong the first fruits of the harvest!

Most of us go into debt for everything on earth that we can buy on credit. We pay installments until there is scarcely anything left to live on. And when we get all of our installments paid, and all of our bills met that we can possibly provide for, we give God a little bit of what is left over that He blesses us with. We have not consecrated out of the purpose of our hearts to God the first fruits of the harvest. Why, *we* made that. *We* worked for that. *We* earned what we have. God did not give us anything.

I met a man one time who was a very wealthy farmer; he had been a very successful farmer. He had moved into town and lived in a beautiful home; and he made a big speech about being a self-made man, that he had worked hard for everything that he had. Nobody had given him anything. He had worked for it. He had earned it.

It belonged to him. And I raised with him a question. He never did invite me back for dinner any more. In fact, he did not the first time. His wife did that. But, I raised with him the question: Who put the soil there for you to farm? Who gave it the fertility that it had? Who caused the sun to warm it and the rain to fall upon it? Who put the life into the seed that you planted and made it germinate and bring forth a harvest?

You say God has not done anything for you. That is utter nonsense! You are what you are and you have what you have by the grace and the mercy of God, and you ought to devote the first fruits of it to the honor and to the glory of God and to the accomplishment of His purposes and the furtherance of His cause! As long as one lets his "sacrifice" be a little of what is left over when he gets through with it—just as long as one puts serving God upon that basis—his service is not acceptable. It will not meet the standard! Measure it by the Word of the Lord!

You know, Paul talked about the grace of Christian liberality—a grace that most of us have forgotten, or never did know about. The grace of Christian liberality! And he said, "As you abound in other graces, see that you abound in this one also" (2 Cor. 8:7). Well, Paul, what is liberality? Is it seeing how little I can give and get by with? *Oh, no, no, no!* Liberality is exactly the opposite of that! Instead of seeing how *little* I can do and ease my conscience, liberality sees how much I can do that will be to the honor and the glory of God and in harmony with His will. God gave us an example of it. In fact, he gave more than one.

The best example that He gave was the giving of Christ himself. "Though he was God and was on an equality with God, he emptied himself" (Phil. 2:5-7). He gave up all that he had, came into the world and became a man, was found in fashion as a man, and suffered as a man, dying finally, in order that you and I might be saved. I hear Him saying, "Christ was rich and yet he became poor that we through him might be made rich" (2 Cor. 8:9).

There is not any danger of one's doing too much for the Lord, financially or otherwise! We are not going to *work too hard* in his service! We are not going to *devote too much* time to his honor and glory! And we are not going to *give too much* of our money! What we need to learn is that we will not be any poorer when we give it! If we had the kind of faith we ought to have we would know that.

Paul said concerning the Macedonians that "in the deepness of their poverty..." (2 Cor. 8:2). That would hardly characterize a description of any of us, would it? Adversity had beset them. They were deeply poor, but, "In the deepness of their poverty they abounded in the riches of their liberality." And he said, "I bear them record that of their own accord they had given themselves first unto God, not because we commanded them to do it" (vv. 3-5). That is the secret of Christian liberality! When a man gives himself to God, he is not going to rob Him of anything else he ought to give Him. He is not going to short the Lord at any time of any service or any sacrifice that he is able to make.

I suggest that you take the Word of God and study it carefully, and measure your sacrifice by it. Study not only the altar upon which it is offered, where the name of God is inscribed, but also the sacrifice that is offered upon the altar. Be certain, if you want your soul to be saved in eternity, that you are dedicating unto God the kind of a sacrifice in your life that will be pleasing to Him, that will honor Him, and that will be a blessing to you.

Measure the Worshippers

But I would like to suggest in the lesson again, as a third point, that he said to arise and measure the temple, and measure the altar, and "measure them that worship therein." Measure the worshippers! That is, *measure the individuals who come to offer their sacrifices*. Not just anybody can offer a sacrifice unto God acceptably. Had you ever thought about that? It does not do a man any good to give of his money and his time if he is not going to give himself, and be in heart and life what he ought to be! There is not any part in the service to God that one can have until he gives *himself* unto Him. This is the first demand that Christianity makes.

Paul said, "Whose I am" (Acts 27:23). I belong unto God. By the grace of God and through the blood of Christ, I have been purchased and bought and redeemed. The life that I have and the freedom from condemnation that is mine in Christ have been granted to me by God. I belong to God; I am a bondservant to God, a slave of the Lord. This, Paul counted himself to be. He had no rights. He had no privileges. He had no desires and no ambitions for Paul.

All of these he had forsaken. Everything that was advantage to him according to the flesh, he had counted loss for Christ (Phil. 3:8). The same ratio still exists! The same truth is still applicable!

When you and I serve our own selfish purposes, we are always—*always*—failing to serve God as we ought to serve Him. Now, that does not mean that God has not ordained some obligations of a personal nature in our lives that we ought to take care of. Sure, a man is responsible for providing for his family. Sure, he is responsible for helping his neighbor when he is in need. Sure, he is responsible for dividing his goods with his brethren whom he loves, when they are in need. Sure, he is responsible for doing the will of God in any avenue and in every relationship in life.

But, let me tell you something: *one* duty is no more important than the rest. There is not any way to graduate or to classify the will of God and the commandments of God Almighty! There is not any way that I know anything about. They are *all* essential and I have to do my best to fulfill *all* of these obligations!

Only, in the fulfilling of my duties, *I must not allow* any obligation that God has put upon me to take precedence over my duty and responsibility to *honor* and *glorify* God, in my life, in the worship, in the sacrifice, in the service that God *expects* me to render unto Him. *Nothing* is any more obligatory than that! I cannot excuse myself from my obligations to honor God with my time, my substance, and my ability, and to put God at first place in my life, as a worshipper of God. I cannot afford to fail to give God preeminence over every other consideration. That will not prevent me from doing my duty otherwise. It will help me to do it. It will help me to fulfill my obligations.

Let me read you a passage on it. In Second Corinthians, chapter nine, the Apostle Paul, talking about the contribution that was to be made and sent for the relief of the poor saints in Jerusalem, had this to say concerning it: "Let each man give according as he hath purposed in his heart: not grudgingly, or of necessity: for God loveth a cheerful giver" (2 Cor. 9:7). It is out of the love that we have in our hearts that we need to serve God with our substance as well as with ourselves. We need to serve God with our whole bodies and with our whole lives, without any reservation and without any kind of exception. The greatest commandment is the giving of oneself without reservation, as he lives in this world, to the service and the glory of Almighty God.

Paul went on to say: "For he that supplieth seed for the sower and bread for food, shall supply and multiply your seed for sowing" (2 Cor. 9:10). What are you talking about, Paul? Well, the seed for sowing in this case was the ability to serve the need of indigent, destitute saints. And as one responds to *this* obligation, and does so liberally, God will enable him to do *still more!* That is the reason I said a little while ago that when a man gives to the cause of the Son of God, it does not make him any poorer. Paul said, "And God is able to make all grace abound unto you; that ye having always *all* sufficiency in *everything*, may abound unto every good work" (2 Cor. 9:8).

I have heard people say, "Well, that just does not mean *everything.*" Well, that is what it says! "That does not mean every good work—that I will be ready to help in every good work." That is *what* it *says!* "That does not mean that God is going to bless me financially if I use what He gives me as I ought to use it, or that He enables me to do more." *That is what it says!*

One cannot limit *that* passage! It has five universal terms in it. God is able to make *all* grace abound unto you, abound unto you *always, so that having all* sufficiency in *everything*, you may be prepared unto *every* good work! Do not tell me one can limit it. One denies it when he does. Now, what *I need to do* is believe it! I need to believe that God's blessings will be mine, when *I give myself* wholly and entirely unto Him.

But, I want you to notice that when the priest back in the Old Testament offered his sacrifice, God laid down some requirements about him too. God said that not only must your sacrifice be the firstling and the fatling of the flock (go back to Leviticus 21 and 22), but also He said concerning the priest that the priest must be a perfect specimen physically. If he is going to officiate at the altar, if he is going to offer sacrifices acceptable unto God, that priest must be a complete man, a whole man, without any deficiencies. He cannot be an individual that is deficient in any part of his body. He has to be a perfect specimen physically. If there is anything wrong with his body, he cannot offer bread upon the altar of God. That is what God said about it.

I wonder what that means? What possible significance could that have? Well, one can find its spiritual counterpart in the New Testament very easily—*very easily*!

In the obligation that God puts upon us to give ourselves wholeheartedly, full-handedly, and unreservedly to Him and to the doing of His will, there is not any corner of my life that I can keep back from the Lord to serve my own purposes or to gratify my own appetites and desires. There is not any exception that I can make. There is not any sort or kind of reservation that I can have about it.

The word "consecrate" comes from a word that means literally, "full-handed." To be consecrated is to be full-handed. What does it mean? Did you ever say: "I have my hands full"? That is what it means. It means that one is fully employed. There is not any left over space. There is not any place where it is vacant and it is empty. There is not anything kept back! Full-handed, wholehearted consecration unto God! That is what it means to give yourself. And, we know what was said of Caleb in the Old Testament—that he wholly, *w-h-o-l-l-y*—followed the Lord, his God (Num. 32:12). Do you do it?

You need to measure *yourself*. Paul said to the Corinthians: "Examine yourselves whether or not you are in the faith" (2 Cor. 13:5). We had better apply the measuring reed to our own lives. Do not take your salvation for granted. *Do not* take it for granted that God is pleased to acknowledge you as one of His own! *Do not* take it for granted that His approval rests upon you just because you have gone through some acts of obedience or submission to His will! You had better take the measuring reed and measure yourself by it! Lay it down to see just exactly what the dimensions are from a spiritual point of view! This is the lesson.

If You Have Not Complied With God's Word
If you have not complied with it, if you have not given yourself wholly unto the Lord, *full-handedly and wholeheartedly*, to do what the Lord commands us to do, to serve his will and his purposes in your life, now is the time to act. You must come unto him in obedience to his will, do what he commands you to do, and give yourself to him without reservation, that your life may be spent in pleasing him, doing his will, and serving his purposes. And you can have the assurance that his promises will be yours when such you do.

If there is a subject to the Gospel invitation in the audience today, if you have not believed with all of your heart, if you have not confessed your sins to the Lord by being buried with him in baptism, if you have not been raised up to walk in newness of life, *you need to do so.* This is the beginning. This is the way to start. This is the way to resign your will to his, and to begin to give your life to his service for the accomplishment of his purposes. It is only the beginning, but it is the only way you can begin. One cannot *begin* to serve God any other way! And you have not begun until you do it.

If you have started but have fallen by the wayside, having become unfaithful, having not carried out your duty, having alienated yourself from God, and having separated yourself from Him by sin, you no longer belong to Him. No more does your life honor and glorify Him. You need to come back repenting and turning away from your wrongs, from the things that have separated you from your hope of eternal life. Determine that you will not be guilty of them anymore, asking God's mercy and pardon, and brethren can pray with you and for you.

If you want to be identified with this congregation, if you want this to be your home from a spiritual point of view, your place of work and worship, you may come. Come to work with the other members of this church in accomplishing the program that it has set before it in harmony with the will of God, under the supervision of its Elders, so as to serve God's will in a congregation of God's people. You ought to come and let it be known, that the brethren may know to count upon you, and that you may be identified as one of them. We invite you whatever may be your need to come at this very time, this very moment that God gives you by His mercy and through His grace, and while you have the opportunity. May God help you to come while we stand and sing.

Further Study On Chapter Nine

1. A pre-assigned student should read 3 review questions on chapter 8, give the class a few moments to write answers, then announce correct answers. Assign someone to prepare 3 review questions on chapter 9 for the next class.

2. Memorize Exodus 25:8-9 and be ready to quote it. (Give the class 1-2 minutes to write down their passage, then call on a few to recite.)

3. Outline chapter 9 at home (main points and scriptures). The teacher will call on class members to briefly explain what each heading means (such as "Measure the Church") and how some passage was used to support the heading.

4. Write a brief commentary on or explanation of Exodus 25:8-9 or 2 Corinthians 9:7-8. Tell in your own words what each verse means. The teacher may call upon several students to read all or part of what they have written.

5. What use did God and Israel make of the tabernacle or Temple? Explain how the same purposes are served by God's Temple today.

6. Each student should have prepared a list of questions and answers on chapter 9 (5 true-false; 3 brief answer; 2 asking, "What passage teaches us that...?"). The teacher should ask students to read some of their questions for the class to discuss.

7. What is the local Church's proper organization? How have men changed and perverted it?

8. What work or mission has God given the local Church? How have men changed and perverted it?

9. What is the pattern for acceptable worship? How have men changed and perverted it?

10. Explain how God measures the sacrifice and the worshipper. What will He accept? What will He reject? (If possible, the teacher may break the class into smaller groups of 3-5 for about 5-7 minutes of discussion; then let each group leader tell the whole class one or two important points developed by the group.)

CHAPTER TEN

The Victory Of Faith

I had a good deal to say at the beginning of the service this morning concerning the real personal pleasure that has been mine this week in this meeting. I shall not say a great deal again about it tonight, but I do want you to know, from the very depth of my heart, that I am grateful for the opportunity that I have had to be with you in these services and to study God's Word with you once again. I trust that God will continue to bless your work in His kingdom, and to bless all who are engaged in it here at Highland, to the accomplishment of the greatest amount of good. Many of you, as you know, hold a very warm place in my heart. I have always been interested in the work of this congregation. I shall continue to be, and I ask a continued interest in your prayers.

It was a genuine delight, let me say once again, to be with Brother and Sister Wharton. I reciprocate fully the personal feelings that have been expressed towards me by him. I have a very high regard for him both as an individual and as a Gospel preacher, as a Christian and as a proclaimer of the truth, and it is always a delight to be associated with him. It would have been a delight to me to have sat in these services and heard him preach, as it always has been when I have had that opportunity.

But, all in all, I have enjoyed every single association with every member of this congregation. I have been encouraged by your good fellowship in these services, by the word of personal encouragement that you have spoken to me, and by those who have come from so many different places to be with us during the meeting. To stay in the home of Roy Spears and his good wife, Lola, has been a most enjoyable part of the meeting. So, I am grateful to you in every way that I know how to be, from the very depth of my heart, and I invite all of you, even while we yet remain in Florida, to come and see us—just so all of you do not come at the same time. When we get down to Houston, you will find it perhaps a bit easier, and we will be delighted to have you at the services with us down there, and to visit with us in our home at any time.

The Text: 1 John 5:1-5

In the fifth chapter of the Epistle of First John, and beginning with verse one, we read:

> Whosoever believeth that Jesus is the Christ is born of God: and every one that loveth him that begat loveth him also that is begotten of him. By this we know that we love the children of God, when we love God, and keep his commandments. For this is the love of God, that we keep his commandments: and his commandments are not grievous. For whatsoever is born of God overcometh the world: and this is the victory that overcometh the world, even our faith. Who is he that overcometh the world, but he that believeth that Jesus is the Son of God?

John gives us, in this Epistle, three definitions of *what it means to be born of God*. One of the rules of interpretation is that we allow a writer to define his own terms and to tell us what he means by them. He has the right so to do. Another rule of interpretation, or of understanding language anytime, anywhere, and a rule for treating it fairly, is that we hear all of the testimony. To be born of God, to become a child of God, and to be partaker of the Divine nature through the provisions of God's grace first of all means and requires that we believe in God and that we believe in Jesus Christ as God's Son (1 Jn. 5:1).

But it means more than that. In First John 4:7 John said: "He that loveth is born of God." And then he teaches that "we love him because He first loved us." A man must not only believe in God and in Jesus Christ as the Son of God, but he must love God to be born of God. Then, not only that, an additional bit of testimony was given by the same writer in the same letter, in 2:29, when he said: "He that doeth righteousness is born of God."

To sum up the testimony in this one Epistle, to be born of God requires three things. It means to believe that Jesus Christ is God's Son. It means to love God and love the things that are approved of God, things that are Holy and Divine—truth, righteousness, and all things that are spiritual and eternal. And, it means to do the will of God. "He that doeth righteousness is born of God."

When we are born of God we escape from the pollutions of this world, and the defilements of this world, and the condemnation that rests upon the world as the result of the guilt of sin. This is why Jesus came into the world, that He might deliver us from sin, saving us from our transgressions. Paul said in Galatians 1:4 that he also "gave himself that he might deliver us from this present evil world." The Christian needs to be vitally concerned not with just the fact that he has been born of God and he is a child of God, but with *ultimate* and *eternal* victory.

My faith needs to lead me on in the service of God to *ultimate and eternal victory at the end of the journey*. And, unless it does that, as we pointed out in a previous lesson, if we allow our faith to falter or fail, then we will fall short of the final objective that faith has. The end and the object of faith is the salvation of our souls eternally. Peter puts it like that: "receiving the end of your faith, even the salvation of your soul" (1 Pet. 1:9). If a man misses Heaven after a while, if he falls short of eternal life, then all that faith has meant and all that faith has done for him perishes and is lost. I need then to be interested in the final victory of faith, and the final victory of faith will mean the reward of eternal life.

When Do We Receive Eternal Life?
There are a great many people in the world who do not understand that *we do not have eternal life as a present possession*. They go to passages that you find so frequently in the Gospel of John where Jesus said: "He that believeth on the Son hath everlasting life"—passages like John 3:16, John 3:36, John 5:24, and any number of passages in which John emphasizes eternal life as the reward of the believer. But, John was not talking about an unfaithful believer. He was talking about a believer who triumphs eventually and finally through the growth and development of his faith, and through faithfulness, and receives the final reward that faith has as its goal, the aim that ought to be in the heart of every child of God.

Eternal life is a promise and it is a hope, but it is *not* a present possession! We pointed out last night from 1 Timothy 4:8 that while it is the same *kind* of life, spiritual life, freedom from condemnation, there are two different aspects of spiritual life. One of them is the life that *is now* in Christ Jesus—freedom from condemnation. "Having been dead in sin, we are made alive unto God in Christ

Jesus" (Eph. 2:5-6). That is spiritual life in Christ. That is the life that now is. But, the life that *is to come,* that has not yet come, is *"eternal* life in the world to come," as Jesus expressed it in the tenth chapter of the Gospel of Mark (v. 30).

Eternal life is not granted here, in the sense of eternal salvation. An endless salvation impossible to lose, a saved relationship that will endure for all eternity in its duration, is not our present possession. Paul said, "I have not yet attained. . . I count not myself yet to have apprehended, but this one thing I do, forgetting the things that are behind and stretching myself forward to the things that are before, I press on to the mark of the prize of the high calling of God which is in Christ Jesus" (Phil. 3:12-14). Paul looked upon death, upon the resurrection, and upon the dawning of eternity at the judgment of our Lord as *the time of final reward.*

I can hear Paul saying: "I have fought a good fight, I have finished the course, I have kept the faith; henceforth there is laid up for me"—*he had not received it, but it was deposited for him to his account*—"there is laid up for me a crown of righteousness which the Lord, the righteous Judge will give unto me in that day, and not unto me only, but unto all those that have loved his appearance" (2 Tim. 4:7-8).

The crown of righteousness is simply eternal life. It is the crown that God has promised "to all them that love him," according to James 1:12. Nobody will be saved in eternity after a while *without* receiving the crown of life. It is not an *extra* reward! It is not something in addition to eternal salvation. So many people get that idea of it. They have the old idea that if I excel in righteousness, eventually God will give me a crown, and the more my righteousness exceeds and excels, the more stars the crown will have. We used to sing an old song, "Will There Be Any Stars In My Crown?" I want to suggest to you that everybody that goes to heaven will receive the crown. There will be nobody there without the crown, for God has promised the crown of life to them that love Him. And that means that all those that are saved because they love God, and no man will be saved who does not, will receive the crown of life in the Last Great Day.

Paul tells us when eternal life will be rendered in the second chapter of the Roman letter, verses 6-9.

> God will render unto every man according to his deeds: to them
> who by patient continuance in well doing seek for glory and honor
> and immortality, eternal life: but unto them that are contentious,
> and do not obey the truth, but obey unrighteousness, indignation
> and wrath, tribulation and anguish, upon every soul of man that
> doeth evil.

Just prior to that quotation, he tells us when this rendering will take
place, and he denotes that it will happen in the "day of wrath and
revelation of the righteous judgment of God." When God reveals
His righteous judgment upon all the nations of this earth, through
Jesus Christ, our Lord, it will be *then* that eternal life as a *final*
reward—*eternal salvation*—will be rendered unto those who have
sought for glory and honor and immortality.

The Promise Now, Actual Possession Later
We have the *promise* of it now. John said in 1 John 2:25 that "this
is the promise which he hath promised us, even eternal life." We
have the *hope* of it now. Paul wrote to Titus, in Titus 1:2, and said
that he was a servant of God and an Apostle of Jesus Christ, and
that he was his "hope of eternal life." If Paul had only the hope
of eternal life, and not the possession of it, then I am suggesting
to you that the *hope* is all we have. That is the sense in which the
believer, while he lives here upon this earth, enjoys the promise of
eternal life. He has it in *hope!* He has it in *prospect!* He has the
right to it, and the title to it, but he will *not* attain it in this world!
Not while he lives in the flesh, but in the world to come, and in the
Last Great Day, when the righteous judgment of God is revealed
upon all men!

In Romans 8:24-25 Paul said that what a man hopes for he cannot see or have. You cannot have a thing and hope for it too. Paul
hoped for eternal life; therefore, he did not have it in present possession. Somebody may then raise the question, "Then in what sense
does the Christian have eternal life?" God said, "He that believeth
on the Son hath everlasting life," and He said that "those who believe
have eternal life" (1 Jn. 5:10-12). Eternal life is in God's Son, and
we know that if we are in the Son we have the life. In what sense
do we have it? Well, one can have a thing in more senses than one.
It does not have to be reduced to personal, actual, and immediate
possession. I have a lot of things that I do not have in my immediate
possession, and certainly, eternal life is one of them.

Let me illustrate it. A good many years ago I knew a family down in Houston, Texas, that was very wealthy. A man had grown wealthy by the discovery of oil and by engaging in the oil business. He was not a member of the Church, but his wife was. Their name was Woodard. She attended the Heights congregation in the city of Houston. They had one son, and that son had been killed in an airplane accident on the way back from Ft. Smith, Arkansas. They were making a trip out to a ranch that he owned west of San Antonio and on the way back crossed the Southern Pacific Railroad, just ahead of a fast train, and that train hit their car and both of them were killed in a common accident. They had but one heir.

That heir, at that time, was a nine-year-old boy. By will they left all of their estate, amounting, I understood, to approximately 15 million dollars, to that nine-year-old boy. Now, that belonged to him; it was his; he had every right to it; nobody else had any right to it at all. The right and the title, the sole interest in that estate, had been left to him by will, *but he did not come into immediate possession of it.* He had it by right, by title, in hope, in prospect, in promise. View it from any point that you might want to consider it, but he did not have it in immediate possession.

The courts do not turn over an estate of that kind to a minor. If he had come into immediate possession of that money, there is not any way of telling what all he would have bought with it. Likely, he would have bought all of the popcorn and the ice cream in the United States and tried to eat it all the first week. But the courts simply do not turn money of that sort, or an estate, over to a minor. It belonged to him, but the court held it in trust for him, under the direction of the court, until the time came *when he reached his maturity, when he came of age, and when the terms and the conditions of the will had been met.*

Now, that is when the final victory of faith will be yours and mine. Until the spirits of just men are made perfect, until the Last Great Day when the righteous judgment of God is revealed unto all men, *until that day,* you and I will *wait* upon the fulfillment of the promise and the realization of the hope of eternal salvation. We need to recognize that. And I need to have my mind so fixed upon it and so stirred by it that I will recognize that while I live in this world, my faith is constantly engaged in a struggle in the interest of fulfilling the Word of God and being faithful in His service. By so doing, I, with Paul, might have the hope when death shall approach, of laying hold upon that crown of righteousness which the Lord has laid up in Heaven for those who in love will continue to serve him.

The Victory of Faith Obtained By Faithfulness

Faithfulness! The victory of faith! Faith achieving a victory over this world! This is the only means by which that hope of eternal life in the world to come will ever be entirely a reality to you and to me. I am engaged in a warfare. We are engaged in a war, whether we like to call it that or recognize it as that or not. God declared war upon Satan and sin in the very early morning of time, when God made the promise in the earliest of time "that the seed of the woman shall bruise the serpent's head, and the serpent shall bruise his heel" (Gen. 3:15). This was a declaration of war—enmity between truth and error, warfare between righteousness and unrighteousness, a continuing battle of intense struggle between Christ and Satan, between good and evil, sin and godliness, the church and the world. And you and I are engaged in this warfare.

The weapons of our warfare, Paul tells us, are not carnal (2 Cor. 10:3-5). One cannot conquer them with the sword. We cannot show our strength and demonstrate our courage by the employment of the things of this world. There is just one way *that battle* can be fought, and that is to fight the good fight of faith, as Paul expressed it, and lay hold of eternal life as the result of it (1 Tim. 6:12).

The Bible teaches not only that we are in a warfare, but that *we are all soldiers* in the warfare and that we are to be good soldiers through our faith. We are to be good soldiers, faithful soldiers, in the service, and fighting for righteousness and truth. Not only that, but the Bible teaches us that while we are on duty, and that means while we live in this world, we are *not* to allow ourselves to become *entangled with the affairs of this life*. Paul said no soldier on service, on duty, "entangleth himself in the affairs of this life" (2 Tim. 2:4). Our time and our attention need to be devoted, our efforts and determination need to be directed toward winning the battle in Jesus' name.

We need to win the battle against self; and that can be done only through faith. I can win the battle over my own self and my own weaknesses through faith, the faith that is in Christ Jesus. And, this is one of the great battles that any man has.

One of the great and important things in living the Christian life is for a man to discover himself, not to deceive his own heart, to speak the truth with his heart to himself, to come to a recognition of his own failures and his own faults. The Prodigal Son could not correct his mistake until he "discovered himself." I have often thought that if we had enough faith, individually, to simply stand off from ourselves and to *look at ourselves as God sees us*, objectively, we probably would not like the picture. We probably would not like what we would see, but it would do us good if we could see ourselves as the Scotch poet put it, "as others see us."

Standing ourselves aside without any pretense, stripped of all profession and stripped of all hypocrisy, and seeing ourselves *exactly as we are*, we could know more about our hope of attaining eternal life. We would better understand what our failures and our faults are that we need to correct while we live, in order that that hope might become a reality. It is only through faith in Christ that this victory can be attained.

A man must have faith enough to crucify himself, *to deny himself*, to die so far as his selfish ambitions and purposes are concerned. Paul said, "Ye have died with Christ and your lives are hidden with Christ in God" (Col. 3:3). We need then, with Paul, to say, "It is no longer I that live, but Christ that liveth in me" (Gal. 2:20). And only to the extent that faith enables me to lead a life of self-denial can I faithfully serve the Lord. Only in this way can we obtain the victory that faith is able to give us at last over the world—a victory of eternal life.

But not only am I to win a victory through faith over self. I must *win a victory over sin*. Guilty of sin—"for all have sinned and come short of the glory of God"—under the sentence of spiritual death, men need by faith to be turned away from the love of sin in their hearts. As long as we love sin, the victory cannot be ours. We stand defeated and lost, as long as we entertain in our hearts the love of sin. Any man, whether he is in the Church or out of it, that has in his heart the love of sin, is certain to be lost unless he corrects and controls it, and puts to death his regard for sin. The Bible teaches, "Abhor that which is evil and cleave unto that which is good" (Rom. 12:9). So, by faith, I need to learn to *love* righteousness and truth, the things that are holy and the things that are approved and acceptable in the sight of God, and to *despise* that which is evil and unacceptable to God. Faith alone can give me that victory!

Not only must I conquer the love of sin in my heart, *but also I must conquer by faith the dominion that sin exercises over life.* We are the bondservants of sin—dead in sin—until faith brings us to redemption in Christ Jesus. As surely as a man has not become a child of God, just that surely that man stands guilty of his sin. By his sin, he stands separated from God, and therefore, dead in trespasses and sin. Paul reminded the Ephesian brethren in chapter two that they had been "dead in trespasses and sins" when salvation by the grace of God and through their faith became a reality. God's grace and its provisions found them dead in sin; but when they were delivered from sin through the grace of God, it was by the means of their faith and God's grace that this deliverance came about.

Victory Over Sin In Romans 6

In the sixth chapter of the Roman letter, the Apostle Paul tells us that such a *struggle* all through our lives is *essential*, and that the ultimate victory is necessary if we are to be saved eternally and live with God in the world to come. I hear him saying: "Let not sin therefore reign in your mortal body." He had taught in the previous verses of this chapter about "dying in sin" and about "being justified from sin." They had "cut off" the old sin of which they were guilty, and had been "loosed," and in God's sight they "had been justified and made righteous."

Now, he said, your obligation is not to let sin reign in your physical bodies. Do not let sin have the control over your members "that you should obey it"—that you should do what sin would have you to do, or do what Satan would have you to do—"in the lusts thereof." "Neither yield ye your members as instruments of unrighteousness unto sin: but yield yourselves unto God, as those that are alive from the dead, and your members as instruments of righteousness unto God."

He was talking about the members of the body. Let the mind know, understand, and believe the Word of the Lord. Let the tongue speak it and tell of it. Let the ear gladly hear it whenever and wherever the opportunity presents itself. Let the eyes pursue the study of it by the reading of it in God's own Book. Let the heart—one's love and affection—happily and gladly receive it and rejoice in it, as David did when he sang: *"Oh how love I thy law"* (Psa. 119:97). Let the soul find genuine delight in the truth and in the righteousness of God that has been revealed in His Word. Let the hands serve, as God has directed every member of the body to be yielded in submission to God's will. This is the obligation of the Christian.

This is how much faith is required of us, that we should keep our members back from service to sin, having been made alive unto God, and having become righteous individuals. And, having become justified in God's sight, our members are to be yielded as instruments of righteousness unto the Lord.

But I hear him saying further, "Sin shall not have any dominion over you." If one allows sin to rule in his life, he will lose the battle. That is the way to lose it. Faith must conquer sin. Faith must keep one back from sin. Faith must purge sin from one's life and destroy its power over his heart and in his life. Paul said, "Know ye not that to whom ye yield yourselves servants to obey, his servants ye are to whom ye obey; whether of sin unto death, or of obedience unto righteousness?" It does not matter if one *claims* to be a member of the church, if he *professes* faith in Jesus Christ. If he does the will of the devil, he is a servant of the devil. That is what Paul says about it.

One cannot flatter God, serve the devil, and go to heaven after a while! There is *not* any way to do it. So, faith conquers the love of sin in my heart. It conquers the practice of sin, the dominion of sin in my life.

Paul said, "For when you were servants of sin, you were free in regard to righteousness. What fruit had you then in those things whereof ye are now ashamed? For the end of those things is death." That is the course to pursue to achieve spiritual death. The wages of sin is death, eternal death, or separation from God. The way to get there is to let your body serve sin. Serve the purposes of Satan, that will surely accomplish it.

And Paul went on to say, "But now being made free from sin." They had been made free from the guilt of sin. They had been released from sin's dominion in their lives by rebelling against it, turning away from it, and determining through faith that they would not be guilty of it any more. That is what they accomplished by obeying the form of doctrine that had been delivered unto them in the Gospel. Paul said, "Ye were then made free from sin." That is when they became free from it, and they became "the servants of righteousness." Now, he admonishes: Have enough faith, exercise enough faith, and let your faith be strong enough to keep you back from sin and to present all of the members of your bodies in obedience to God's will. This is the only way that *faith* can lead to *life eternal* in the Last Great Day, and keep us back from sin, for *sin* results in *death*.

It is like Paul teaches in Romans 8:13-14, that as many as are led by the Spirit of God, "these are the sons of God." God recognizes as His children those who have faith enough to walk in harmony with God's will, being led by the Spirit of God to do the will of God and to live as God directs. In that same chapter, he said that if you walk after the flesh to satisfy the desires of the flesh, then "you shall die." Spiritual death is the end of that sort of a course. But if one walks after the Spirit, he shall live not only here with Christ, but eternally after a while. And so, we must be led by the Spirit.

Through our faith in that which the Spirit has revealed, we walk by the Spirit and live by the Spirit. Denying the lusts of the flesh or refusing to yield our members to do the will of Satan and to serve sin, we continue to lead righteous lives. Eternal life in the world to come is the consequence.

But not only must we win a victory over sin, over the love of it, over its dominion and control in our lives, and over the guilt of sin, but *we must win the victory over the world*. You know, a lot of times people think because they have not violated some moral commandment that they are not sinners. Their idea is, "I have not murdered, I have not committed adultery, I am not a drunkard, I am not a liar and I am not a thief; I have not engaged in any of these flagrant violations of God's will. *I have led a good moral life;* therefore, I am all right. I have the hope of heaven in my heart because I have not violated these positive moral commandments that God has given me to govern my conduct."

Well, something more than that is required of a person. John said that if any man is a friend of the world, he is an enemy of God.

Friendship with the world is enmity with God. And the Bible teaches that if a man loves the world, the love of the Father is not in him. You may not yield to it, but what about your *affections?* What about your *desires?* Have you brought them under control? You may not be practicing all the sinful ways of this world, and especially, you may not have violated the moral commandments of God's law. But what about your *attitude* toward what the world has to give? How much do you *love* the things that can be gained only from the world? The world has them to reward you with, if you seek the world and the things that are in it.

John talked about the appeal the world has for us—"the lust of the flesh, the lust of the eyes, and the pride of life" (1 Jn. 2:15). Pride or the vainglory of life is conceit and vanity in our own minds and hearts, and includes the love of the glitter and the gleam of that which the world has to offer. *These are the avenues* through which temptation comes. So, faith must help me to put down the love of the world, for I cannot love the world and love God; and, I cannot gain the crown of Heaven after a while without loving God. A victory over the world can be achieved only by faith.

The Victory of Faith In 1 Peter 1:3-5
But I would like to suggest to you a specific passage of Scripture that outlines the matter plainly enough for us that we can understand exactly that which is essential and necessary in order that we might be eternally saved, that we might gain eternal life through faithfulness in God's service.

In 1 Peter 1:3-5, Peter said, "Blessed be the God and Father of our Lord Jesus Christ, which according to his abundant mercy hath begotten us again unto a lively hope by the resurrection of Jesus Christ from the dead, to an inheritance." I would like for you to notice the description of that inheritance: "incorruptible, and undefiled, and that fadeth not away." It "fadeth not away"—that is, it is not dissipated. We will not fail to find it when we get there. It is an inheritance that is incorruptible, undefiled, and fadeth not away. It is an inheritance that is "reserved in heaven"—deposited in heaven. That is the inheritance that God has for His children! Not a fifteen-million dollar estate here in this world, but an inheritance in the world to come. An inheritance that God has provided for those that love and serve Him!

But Peter says it is reserved in Heaven "for you who are kept." Who will receive that inheritance? Only the "kept." *K-e-p-t!* That inheritance is for only "those who are kept." What are the conditions of that "keeping"? I want you to notice two factors: "kept by" first of all "the power of God," and kept also *by our faith*: "by the power of God through faith." These are the two conditions of the keeping. My salvation, my gaining the inheritance that will come as the final reward for faithfulness in God's service can be attained *only through faith* and *faithfulness!* It depends entirely upon my being *"kept"!*

And one of the two conditions to that "keeping" is *God's power.* Well, *that is not going to fail,* is it? God's power does not fail. I hear preachers preaching about the everlasting arms, the omnipotent hands of God, the shelter that we have under His wing, and the everlasting mercy of His eternal love. They are teaching that God "keeps" us. Their idea is that God is going to keep us in spite of even ourselves. They believe that He will keep us in spite of what we do; God has chosen, God has called, God has elected us into salvation, God in His own time and by His own power will save us. They believe that we are not responsible for any of it. That God will keep us saved in spite of what we do is the culminating doctrine of the system of Calvinism that really underwrites almost all of the doctrines of Protestant Denominationalism.

What does the Bible teach about it? Well, the Bible teaches that since the power of God will not fail, I am not going to be let down in eternity because God failed to keep His promises. He is faithful that has promised. God's power cannot be overcome; God's power will not fail!

But, you know, a covenant has two parties. There are two or more parties to every contract, every agreement, and every covenant. Unless there was a meeting of the minds and agreement upon the terms by two or more competent parties, a contract has not been made and if it has not been made it is not voidable. That is what it takes to make a covenant, and in both instances there must be mutual consideration. A unilateral contract, where consideration flows only in one direction, is not a contract at all. Never is it so. There must be consideration flowing in both directions. God's power is the consideration that God extends to provide for our keeping, but our faith is the consideration that we owe to God to take advantage of the provision of His grace. If we do not keep our part of the contract, the agreement becomes legally void.

The Bible teaches that a man will not be made to suffer beyond that which he is able to bear (1 Cor. 10:13). To the child of God, God makes the promise that with every temptation, He will provide the means of escape. The trouble with most of us is that we are not looking for the way out; we are looking for the way in. We are not searching for that means of escape that God has provided for us, and we are not doing it by faith. The way out is there, if only our faith will lead us to find it and to accept it. But faith is *my part* of the consideration. That is *my part* of the contract!

God's part is to provide for my escape! *My faith* must take advantage of that which God provides! God provides for me the privilege of worship; but if I am unfaithful enough to neglect it, the provision that God has made is of no value. By my own unfaithfulness, I simply condemn myself and lose that which God has provided. God provides the wonderful privileges of prayer to strengthen and to encourage us, but if I do not have faith enough to pray and if I do not pray the prayer of faith, I fail to take advantage of that which God offers. God offers comfort for the hearts that are sorrowed. God offers strength to those that are weak. God offers the means of escape to those who are tempted.

God offers the power, the strength, and the guidance to overcome the obstacles of life. God has put eternal life and eternal inheritance of salvation in the world to come within our reach. But it is only for *"the kept, by the power of God, through faith!"*

Previously we studied the lesson of how it is possible for faith to fail. Now, if faith fails, then I have broken the covenant, and God is released from any promise and from any obligation. When one breaks a contract, he cannot hold the other party responsible for the fulfillment of it. If one breaks the contract, then the other party is released by the breach. When my faith fails, God is released from any obligation to give me that inheritance that is reserved in heaven.

Understanding Eternal Salvation

I want you to notice two things about *eternal salvation—what* and the *when*. Here in 1 Peter, when the Apostle talks about our eternal salvation, he is *not* talking about the salvation of the body from its grave. I remember a number of years ago when I debated Mr. D.N. Jackson, a Baptist preacher, and he affirmed that a child of God is eternally saved and can never sin so as to be finally lost in hell, I pressed him with these questions:

> What is the salvation that you do not have now? If you already have your sins forgiven, and if you enjoy a present saved relationship, and you are in possession of eternal life, what other salvation is there? What is the one that's reserved in Heaven that will be revealed in the Last Day, and that you do not have now? Peter said of this salvation that we must be kept in order to enjoy it, for it is deposited in Heaven. We will not get it here. We will get it in Heaven after a while. It is reserved in Heaven. It will be revealed in the Last Day—not here, and not now. What is that salvation? It is not forgiveness of sin; we already have that. It is not a present saved relationship. If we are in covenant relationship with God now, we already have that; that is a present matter. And if we are in possession of eternal salvation already, then that is not the salvation that Peter is talking about. What is it? (For the original quotes which are paraphrased here, see *The Cogdill-Jackson Debate* [Lufkin, Tex.: Roy E. Cogdill Publ. Co., 1949; reprint Marion, Ind.: Cogdill Foundation Publ., 1977], pp. 139, 145, and 178 for Jackson and pp. 153, 155, and 196-198 for Cogdill. R.H.)

Finally, Jackson said, "It is the redemption of the body from the grave." Well, that means then that only "the kept" will be redeemed from death. The unkept, the lost, will not be raised from the dead. That made a materialist out of him and I told him that we ought to turn him over to the "Watch Tower" folks. That is what they believe and teach. That is their doctrine—that only the righteous will know life after death. The dead will never be raised. The grave is the only Hell to which they will ever be committed. That is the doctrine of our friends who call themselves Jehovah's Witnesses, but it is not God's truth.

The fact of the whole matter is that this *cannot be* the redemption of the body. Now, our bodies will be redeemed, but the bodies of *all* men will be raised from the dead. Jesus said: "The hour is coming in which all that are in their graves shall come forth; they that have done good unto the resurrection of life; they that have done evil unto the resurrection of condemnation" (Jn. 5:28-29).

All men will be raised! But *not all men* are going to *get that in-*

heritance! Not *all* men in that Last Day will receive a *salvation* that has been *deposited in Heaven* for them! Universal salvation is *not* the fact! And it is *not* the truth of God's Word! I want to know, for whom is it? Only for the righteous. When do they receive it? This salvation that I do not get here, it is in Heaven. I do not receive it now. It is in the Last Day. It is insured in Heaven. God insures me that it will be there when I get there.

How can I lay hold upon that final victory? Paul tells us: "I have kept *the faith*" (2 Tim. 4:7). One has to keep *the faith* in order to be *"kept by faith,"* and he has to be "kept by faith" in order to *get the inheritance.* There is only one way on earth that God offers Heaven as our hope, only one way that we have the hope of living with God and dwelling with God in the world to come. The only promise that God has made, in order that we can enjoy the bliss and the beauty of the glory of an Eternal Day in His presence after a while, the only promise that God makes of acceptance, of the crown of righteousness, or of the crown of life in the Last Great Day, *is to those who are faithful in His service.* "Be thou faithful unto death" (Rev. 2:10).

Paul said, "I have kept the faith"—I have been faithful. "I have finished my course"—I did not stop short. I have run the full course, I have kept the faith, I have been valiant and a faithful soldier of the Lord. I have not shirked my duty. I have fought the battle, the good fight of faith, and the result is that there is laid up for me in Heaven after a while a crown of righteousness. It is reserved in Heaven, and the Lord will give it unto me in that day (2 Tim. 4:7-8).

An Invitation to Share the Hope of Eternal Life

Thank God that I have the same promise, if I am faithful, as was given Paul. If I fight the good fight of faith as did he, then that same crown will be mine that belonged to him. There is one for me and there is one for you. But you are not going to get it unless you have faith that leads you to overcome the world. Faith to overcome self! Faith to conquer sin in your life and in your heart, and to yield yourself in obedience to the will of God! And to be *faithful* in doing so!

If you have not begun such a course, we pray that you will have faith enough to do it. The thing that will cause you to come, if you come to do the will of the Lord, will be your faith. Obedience cannot be rendered upon any other basis. You must have *a faith that works by love.* You need enough faith to turn away from every other consideration for the sake of your soul and for the sake of the Son who died to redeem it, and for the sake of having in your heart, based upon the promises of God, the hope of eternal life. You need to come.

You need to have enough faith to come, and you need it now. Saving and justifying faith will not allow you to say, "Tomorrow," or, "Some other time." That is unbelief. Your faith failed. It is not strong enough to save and to justify you, when it puts the matter off. God said, "Now is the time; today is the day" (2 Cor. 6:2).

If there is a subject to the gospel invitation in this audience, your faith is challenged by the invitation that is extended to you by the Lord to come and do his will. The only way that you can evidence that you do believe in him with all of your heart is to turn away from your sins and your own personal will, yield yourself, confess and acknowledge that you believe with all of your heart that he is the Lord, put him on in baptism in obedience to his will, and serve him. And if you faithfully do so the rest of your days, then you will receive that inheritance that is laid up in Heaven for those who are kept by faith through the power of God.

May God help every unsaved person in this audience to consider carefully the invitation of Jesus Christ our Lord, who died that this invitation and this opportunity might be yours. And may God help you to accept it while it is yours, as we stand and sing the song.

Further Study On Chapter Ten

1. A pre-assigned student should read 3 review questions on chapter 9, give the class a few moments to write answers, then announce correct answers. Assign someone to prepare 3 review questions on chapter 10 for the next class.

2. Memorize 1 John 5:4-5 and be ready to quote it. (Give the class 1-2 minutes to write down their passage, then call on a few to recite.)

3. Outline chapter 10 at home (main points and scriptures). The teacher will call on class members to briefly explain what each heading means (such as "When Do We Receive Eternal Life?") and how some passage was used to support the heading.

4. Write a brief commentary on or explanation of 1 John 5:4-5 and Romans 8:24-25. Tell in your own words what each verse means. The teacher may call upon several students to read all or part of what they have written.

5. What does it mean in 1 John to be "born of God" or to be a child of God?

6. Each student should have prepared a list of questions and answers on chapter 10 (5 true-false; 3 brief answer; 2 asking, "What passage teaches us that . . .?"). The teacher should ask students to read some of their questions for the class to discuss.

7. What passages teach that we have eternal life in some sense now? What passages teach that we will receive eternal life on Judgment Day? How do you explain these two points of view?

8. Discuss God's part and man's part in the heavenly hope of 1 Peter 1:3-5. How does Calvinism misuse the idea of God's power to keep us in covenant relationship with Him?

9. Some false teachers claim that the "salvation ready to be revealed in the last time" is only a redemption of the body from the grave. How does the Bible answer such a theory?

10. "If I live a good moral life, I will have the hope of Heaven." Use the Bible to show what is lacking in this view. (If possible, the teacher may break the class into smaller groups of 3-5 for about 5-7 minutes of discussion; then let each group leader tell the whole class one or two important points developed by the group.)

CHAPTER ELEVEN

Christianity Is Undenominational

Part One

(A sermon delivered at the Church of Christ, Lufkin, Texas, on Sunday evening, March 6, 1949, and broadcast over radio station KRBA, Lufkin)

I want to read a selection of scripture from the first chapter of Paul's first letter to the church of God at Corinth, beginning with verse ten.

> Now I beseech you, brethren, through the name of our Lord Jesus Christ, that ye all speak the same thing, and that there be no divisions among you; but that ye be perfected together in the same mind and in the same judgment. For it hath been signified unto me concerning you, my brethren, by them that are of the household of Chloe, that there are contentions among you. Now this I mean, that each one of you saith, I am of Paul; and I of Apollos; and I of Cephas; and I of Christ. Is Christ divided? Was Paul crucified for you? or were ye baptized into the name of Paul? I thank God that I baptized none of you, save Crispus and Gaius; lest any man should say that ye were baptized into my name (1 Cor. 1:10-15).

Those of you who are familiar with Paul's first letter to the church of God at Corinth are acquainted with the fact that the first four chapters are addressed to the Corinthian Christians for the purpose of correcting the division that existed in the church at Corinth. Division was creeping into the body of Christ. Members of the church of the Lord were being divided into factions and into sects. They were following after men rather than after the Lord, calling themselves by human names. If you had approached any one of the members of these various sects in the Corinthian church, and asked him first of all, "What are you religiously?" he likely would have identified himself with a sect before he would have even admitted any relationship with Christ. He would have told you, "I am a

Cephasite." Or, "I am an Apollosite," or, "I am a Paulite." If you
had corrected such use of human names and such sectarianism and
division, *as Paul did,* and if you had condemned that kind of a party
spirit, likely he would have taken offense at it. He would have said,
"That doesn't mean that I am not a Christian. I am a Christian, but
I am a Paulite Christian, or a Cephasite Christian, or an Apollosite
Christian." Thus they claimed that they had the right as Christians,
as members of the body of Christ, to divide themselves into factions
and into sects, and to hold up before the world a divided Christ.

Paul's argument against it was, "Is Christ divided?" That's the
very first argument that he makes. The answer, of course, is in the
negative, for Paul condemns the division that characterized these Corinthian Christians, and pronounces the judgment of God against them.

You have denominationalism as it exists in the world today in its
embryonic form in the Corinthian church. If it had been allowed to
go along without divine condemnation, they would have possibly
parted asunder. The various factions, the different sects, would have
become distinct and separate and apart one from the other and would
have constituted separate and distinct religious bodies. It simply had
not gone that far yet in the Corinthian church. Paul condemned it
by the authority of Christ under the leadership and guidance of the
Holy Spirit of God before it ever got that far.

It is our purpose in this lesson tonight to show you that *such
religious division and denominationalism* as existed then at Corinth,
or a more developed form of it as it exists in the world today, *is contrary to the will of God, contrary to and subversive to the teaching
of God's Word.* No man can be any part of it or in any sense responsible for it and be acceptable and pleasing in the sight of God and
be a Christian. Christianity cannot be denominationalized, it cannot
be sectarianized and remain Christianity. When men corrupt the unity of the Spirit and destroy the bond of peace that makes the unity
of the Spirit possible, God is displeased and God refuses to recognize
those who are responsible for it as His own. Christianity in divine
revelation, the religion of Jesus Christ as it is set forth and revealed
to us in the Word of God is *undenominational.*

Division, A Hindrance To Christianity

Religious division in our present age of the world is possibly the
greatest hindrance to Christianity. It obscures completely the pro-

per conception of the religion of Christ, and confuses the hearts and minds of people who otherwise would be interested in it. Division becomes the hotbed for atheism and infidelity and disinterest in religion and is recognized as the cause of such in the prayer that Jesus prayed in the gospel of John, the seventeenth chapter, concerning unity. I hear the Lord saying, after having offered to his Father a prayer in behalf of his Apostles, "Neither pray I for these alone, but for all them also that shall believe on me through their word; that they may be one in us, even as thou Father art in me and I in Thee, that they may be one in us: that the world may believe that thou didst send me." Even as God the Father and Jesus Christ the Son are one, from every point of view except in person, so those who believe in Christ through the word of the Apostles are to be one in accordance with the prayer of the Lord and therefore the will of the Lord. They are to be one, all believers united in every sense, except in person. One in spirit, one in faith, one in body. From a religious point of view, a complete and a perfect unity among all believers was the thing that Christ was praying for.

To agree or to grant that religious division as it exists in the world tonight is pleasing in the sight of the Son of God, makes ridiculous the prayer that Christ prayed. If unity among all believers in the first age of the world was essential, then unity among all believers in this generation is essential. It was no more important then than it is now. If it was the will of Christ that all believers should be one *then,* even as God the Father and God the Son are one, so it is *today.* The prayer and will of Christ is that all believers now should be one even as God the Father and God the Son are one. Any sort or kind of factionalism, or division, or partyism, or denominationalism that would destroy that unity in the body of Christ among all believers for whom Christ prayed becomes then sinful in the sight of God. I say to you again that the greatest hindrance that Christianity has, the very hindrance that the church of the Lord has today in the world is partyism, factionalism, division, and denominationalism. Looking out upon the religious world, we find a myriad, a host, a vast number of religious bodies, nearly 300 in the United States alone. Each of them claims to be truly representative of the Christ that died to purchase a man's redemption. Each of them claims at least in part to be the body of Christ, the church of the living God, worshipping in different ways, wearing different names, and preaching contrary doctrines.

The religious world is not united in spite of all of the talk about "brotherhood." In spite of all the make-believe fellowship, in spite of all the spirit of tolerance that you hear about in the world, there is neither union nor unity in the religious world tonight. Preachers preach and teach exactly the opposite one to the other. They can put their arms about one another, and yet in faith they are not one, in body they are not one. Neither spiritually nor organically does union or unity in any sense exist among them or between them. And so the brotherhood that is professed is simply a make-believe affair, and the unity that they talk about is a mere profession, and an idle pretense, and does not exist at all.

By their conflicting doctrines and conflicting claims, the only result that could be attained is dissension and confusion in the hearts and minds of people today. Have you ever stopped to ask yourself the question why the majority of the good people of this country are not interested in religion? Why aren't they? The answer is, for the most part, *they have become so confused that they have lost interest by the contrary and confusing claims of denominationalism.* Each church making the claim that it truly represents the Lord, and yet each one of them divided one from another in name, in doctrine, and in many and most instances even in worship. Such of course is not the religion of Christ as it is revealed in the Word of God. Christ prayed for unity among all believers *that the world might believe.* The reason why so many otherwise good people do not believe and have no interest in religion, and attend no service, or take no interest in any kind of religion, is simply because they have become confused and disgusted with the varying and contradictory claims of religious divisions and denominationalism.

When you think then about denominationalism as it compares with Christianity, it is easy to see that the divided condition of so-called Christendom today obscures the true conception of Christianity and of the church of the Lord. It becomes exceedingly difficult for people to get a New Testament idea and conception of the church. It is hard for them to understand and recognize that Christianity ever existed in any other form or in any other way, or without denominationalism and factionalism. They cannot realize that the church of the New Testament existed for several hundred years after its establishment without any human founders recognized in any sense, without any human name, without any human authority, and without any human innovations in its worship, or without human organization.

If you look back at the church as it existed in New Testament history, you cannot find the recognition of any man as the founder of that church in any way or in any sense. Neither did they recognize any human being as its head, nor did they submit to the teachings of any man or group of men. They recognized no human authority, and certainly they engaged in no use of human innovations in their worship. From every thing that was human they turned away and they continued in the Apostles' doctrine as it was revealed by the Holy Spirit and as He made known the will of God. Every such organization then that exists on earth tonight founded by human beings, wearing the name of some human being, or of some human choosing, with a human organization governed by human authority, with a human creed, with human innovations in its worship, *every such organization on the face of the earth represents a departure from the teaching and the authority of God's Word. They all are therefore contrary to God's will and sinful in God's sight.*

Division Is Sinful

This is the proposition, and I invite your careful attention and study of the Word of God on the matter: *Religious division or denominationalism is contrary to the teaching of the Word of God.* Christianity is not only undenominational, but Christianity is also anti-denominational. Not only undenominational, but also anti-denominational! It not only cannot be identified with denominationalism or partyism, but it is contrary to partyism and condemns denominationalism. No one can be a party to it and be a Christian in the true sense of the word or acceptable in the sight of God, because he becomes unfaithful to God, disrespectful toward God's Word, and therefore sinful in God's sight when he takes part in denominationalism or religious division in any sense.

Look at the argument that Paul delivered to the Corinthian church in the first four chapters of that first letter. These first four chapters within themselves are enough to condemn what men today seek to justify, following after men and becoming guilty of factionalism and division in the body of Christ. First of all, Paul said, "I beseech you in the name of the Lord Jesus Christ." That ought to be recognized as good authority. "I beseech you in the name of our

Lord Jesus Christ that ye all speak the same thing."

The common conception in the religious world is that it makes
no difference what men believe, that every man has the right today
to preach what he believes, and believe what he believes. From a
governmental point of view, from a civil point of view that is entirely right. That is exactly right. From the viewpoint of civil liberty, we ought to be willing at the expense of everything that is ours
to uphold the right to worship as we believe, to believe as we think
the Bible teaches, and to practice what we believe to be the will of
God. Surely, that ought to be the privilege and the right of men and
women, the liberty that men and women enjoy.

But from the viewpoint of God, what is our liberty? How does
God feel about the matter and what does God say in His Word about
the right of men to preach different doctrines and to differ in their
faith? Paul said to the Corinthians, "I beseech you," and that word
"beseech" partakes both of the nature of a command and of an en-
treaty. It means simply that I demand of you in the name of the
Lord Jesus Christ, the highest authority and the only authority that
a Christian can recognize, I beseech you in the name of the Lord
Jesus Christ that ye all speak the same thing. There must not be any
variance between you in your speaking.

That is what Paul said to the Corinthians, and I am submitting
to you tonight that if that was necessary in doing the will of God
for the Corinthian church, if it was necessary at Corinth then, then
it is necessary tonight in Lufkin, Texas. If God was not pleased then
when men claimed to be His children and spoke different things,
then God is not pleased tonight. That ought to go without argument
to anybody that believes the Word of God and who has any reverence
for it. In essence Paul said, "In the name of the Lord Jesus Christ
I beseech you to all speak the same thing, preach the same doctrine,
teach the same thing, and believe the same thing." And then I hear
him saying again that there should be no divisions among you. That
was the second demand, that all of you speak the same thing, and
that there be no divisions among you. Do not allow division to come
for personal reasons, or for any other reasons, do not allow division to come. Stand upon the Word of God, and all of you speak
the same thing, and believe the same thing. By the authority of Christ,
Paul demanded that of the church of God at Corinth. Then I hear

him saying, "That ye be perfected together in the same mind and in the same judgment."

Listen to me: Those three rules laid down by the authority of Jesus Christ, the Son of God who died for our redemption, would dissolve and destroy denominationalism and divisions and partyism and strife and factionalism in thirty days time, if you could get people who profess to be Christians in Lufkin, Texas to truly follow Christ. There would not be a single denominational name, organization, or doctrine left. The creeds would be piled on the public square and burned and be forever forgotten if you could get people who profess to believe in Christ and to be followers of Christ to reverence *his* word and to recognize *his* authority enough to all speak the same thing, to refuse to allow division to exist, and to be perfected together in the same mind and in the same judgment.

"Is Christ Divided?"
In condemnation of that division which existed among these Corinthian Christians, Paul raised the question, "Is Christ divided?" Why, they were holding up before the world a divided Christ. They were undertaking to divide and to parcel out the spiritual body of Christ, each of them claiming a part of it, claiming to be a part of it. They were making a Joseph's coat of many colored patches out of the church of the Lord. They were picturing it as that which could be divided and parcelled out. Paul charged them, "You are misrepresenting Christ. With your denominationalism you are misrepresenting the Lord." Christ is not divided. The body of Christ must not be divided. I hear his argument along that line in 1 Corinthians 10. He said that we all partake of "one loaf" and we are therefore "one body." We are one body because we partake of the one loaf. The argument would run like this. Christ had but one physical body to die upon the cross. He has given to us in the Lord's Supper one memorial of that physical body that he sacrificed and of that life that he laid down for us. One body to sacrifice, one loaf to keep in remembrance of that body which was sacrificed. And in the observance of that memorial, unity is brought about so that there is one spiritual body as the result. That is Paul's argument on unity in 1 Corinthians 10.

Here is the demand that God makes of us: That we hold not up before the world a divided Christ. A few years ago I heard a speech over the radio by Dr. E. Stanley Jones, a denominational preacher who had spent thirty years in India in mission work. He was making a plea for union, for federation—not the unity of the Spirit, but for union and federation. His plea was based upon the need in foreign lands of union and federation in order that the natives might not be confused. He said that frequently the natives come to those who are seeking to tell them the story of Christ in those foreign countries and the heathen people ask, "Why do you not all preach the same Christ? Some of you preach a Catholic Christ, and others a Baptist Christ, and others a Presbyterian Christ and a Methodist Christ, and all up and down the line. Why do you not all preach the same Christ?" That man said that what we need in this heathen country is one church of Christ. Well, I thought that sounded fine.

He ruined it in the next sentence. He said, "Of course, it will be all right for us to maintain our separate branches of that church here at home." What he meant was that what we need is a sort of subterfuge, a kind of union or federation that would outwardly appear united and would not be so confusing to the native and heathen, while at the same time we go right along maintaining our division and holding up before the world a divided Christ here at home. Friends, what we need is the kind of unity that will hold up before the world *a united Christ*, not a divided Christ, at home or abroad. But with all denominational lines and parties forgotten, we must endeavor to preserve and promote the unity and the spirit of the bond of peace that would hold up before the world the fulfillment of the prayer that Jesus prayed in John 17.

Division Condemned As Carnality

Not only did Paul condemn and argue against denominationalism and division, but also I hear him pronouncing *severe judgment* upon it. Judgment is pronounced in 1 Corinthians 3, and there is no stronger passage in the New Testament in condemnation of religious division or denominationalism than these verses in 1 Corinthians 3:1-6. He said, "And I, brethren, could not speak unto you as unto spiritual, but as unto carnal, as unto babes in Christ." They were carnal or fleshly in their disposition. What was the indication of that? The division that existed. Their partyism, their following after men rather than after Christ. That is an evidence of carnality, Paul said. It is an evidence of the lack of spirituality, an evidence of the fact that you lack spiritual strength and that you are not spiritually minded, and evidence that you are walking after the flesh. You are exalting men and following men rather than following Christ. He said, "I fed you with milk, not with meat; for ye were not yet able to bear it: nay, not even now are ye able; for ye are yet carnal." Rather than becoming spiritual they had remained carnal and had evidenced that carnality, that fleshly disposition, by creating and making among themselves factional divisions and by drawing party lines.

Then you remember this: That to wear human names and to follow after human leaders and to be members of human organizations and to teach human doctrines, and to engage in human innovations in worship, *is carnality in the sight of God.* It is walking after the flesh and not after the Spirit. "For when one saith, I am of Paul; and another, I am of Apollos; are ye not men? What then is Apollos? and what is Paul? Ministers through whom ye believed; and each as the Lord gave to him. I planted, Apollos watered, but God gave the increase." It is God that must save, and it is God's will that must be done. Do not follow after men, for men are nothing. That was Paul's plea. Do not follow after Paul, for Paul does not amount to anything. Do not become followers of Apollos, for he is not able to save. You will be but blind followers after the blind if you follow men; but rather follow after God and do the will of God.

Suppose that you were to take the names of religious leaders in the world that are prominent, and put them into this passage in the stead of Paul and Apollos. I hear Paul saying in the fourth chapter of this first Corinthian letter that "I transferred these things to myself and to Apollos for your sakes; that in us you might learn not to go beyond the things that are written" (1 Cor. 4:6). Just leave out now the name of Paul, Apollos, Cephas, and in the stead of them put in the name of Luther, Wesley, Campbell, or any other human name. Grant for the moment that they were great men. Grant for a moment that we owe a great debt of gratitude to them for all that they have done. The question is, "What then is Luther, or Wesley, or Campbell, or even John the Baptist, so far as that is concerned? Who are they but men? Are you going to be carnal and walk after men, follow after men rather than the Lord? The challenge is that you should be spiritual and walk after the Lord and not after man!" When men begin to call themselves by human names and divide themselves into factions, divisions, and parties in order that they might walk after men, the condemnation that Paul pronounced upon the church at Corinth is just as applicable now as it was then.

I hear him saying on down in the 16th verse of this same chapter, "Know ye not that ye are the temple of God, and that the Spirit of God dwelleth in you? If any man destroy the temple of God, him shall God destroy, for the temple of God is holy, and such are ye." Paul, what is your argument? Here it is. The church composed of Christians, saved men and women, is the temple of God; the church is God's temple. If any man defiles, destroys, and disrupts the house or the temple of God, God will destroy that man. To defile the temple or the house is to destroy it. It was Jesus who said, "A house divided against itself cannot stand." To divide the house of God is to destroy it, in the sense that Paul uses the term here, and to destroy the house of God is to stand condemned before God. That is the idea. So without any doubt, to those who believe the Word of God, denominationalism or partyism, following after men, is but carnal and God condemns it. It cannot be spiritual. It cannot be Christianity, and God condemns it as sinful in his sight.

Division Condemned In Galatians 5
But I would like to call your attention to another passage of scripture, not only to First Corinthians, chapters one through four, but turn again with me to Galatians 5:16-21. In this passage of scripture Paul is exhorting Christians to walk after the Spirit and not after the flesh. In verse 16 of chapter five, we hear him saying,

> But I say, Walk by the Spirit and ye shall not fulfill the lust of the flesh. For the flesh lusteth against the Spirit, and the Spirit against the flesh; for these are contrary the one to the other; that ye may not do the things that ye would. But if ye are led by the Spirit, ye are not under the law. Now the works of the flesh are manifest, which are these.

Now, I want you to listen to this list of fleshly, carnal, sinful things that God here has listed for us in order that we might know if we are guilty of walking after the flesh and not after the Spirit. No man can be guilty of these sins that are listed in Galatians 5:19 without walking after the flesh. They are the fruits of the flesh. They depict, they identify, they characterize a fleshly course of conduct, and therefore mean that we are walking after the flesh and not after the Spirit. And if we walk after the flesh, Paul said in Romans 8:13 we shall die. Spiritual death is the result of walking after the flesh, and

those who commit these sins that are named in Galatians 5:19 then
have spiritual death pronounced upon them by the authority of
Heaven.

Let us look at them. Now the works of the flesh are manifest.
You could readily divide the sins that are mentioned into four different classes. The *first* class would be the sensual sins that people
are guilty of: fornication, uncleanness, and lasciviousness. These are
sins to which we are led by a sensual spirit, by giving ourselves over
to fleshly desires and fleshly lusts. We are led to such sins by refusing to prohibit and to discipline, and to guide the appetites of the
body. Now the *second* class: that which is idolatry, or false worship. Idolatry and sorcery.

And then a *third* class: A class of sins that have to do with our
relationships toward one another. Here they are: *Enmity*, which
means personal animosty. That comes from a word which means
personal ill-feeling, or a personal animosty. *Strife* — that is rivalry,
or discord, vying one with another, and creating discord as a result
of personal rivalry. It is translated in the King James translation by
the word "debate" in Romans 1:29. But it is not what people call
a debate now, and that word misrepresents the passage. The thing
which he is condemning is not the discussion freely and openly of
whether or not a thing is true. That is not the sense in which the
word is used and it never means that anywhere that it ever occurs
in the New Testament. This word never means an open, free discussion of differences. And any informed man would not undertake
to apply it to that. To undertake to make it condemn an open and
free discusssion of differences, politically, religiously, or otherwise,
is to expose ignorance in the person that thus uses the term. That
is plain speech, but it is so. It does not mean a discussion of religious
or any other kind of differences. It forbids the wrangling which
comes from enmity and bitterness.

And then *jealousy* — that comes from a Greek word which is even
very much like our English word and from which our English word
is derived. Jealousies and *wraths*—bad feelings or malice in the heart
toward one another.

And then *factions*. The word here is *erithia*, which comes from
the simple *erithos*. The word here as it occurs in the New Testament
is defined by Mr. Thayer, the most outstanding scholar on New

Testament Greek in the world, perhaps, that has ever lived, this word is defined by him in this fashion: "A courting distinction, a desire to put one's self forward, a partisan and a factious spirit which does not disdain low arts; partianship, factiousness."

It condemns a party spirit in the heart of the individual and is most frequently translated in the King James Version, and is always rendered in the Revised Version, by the word "faction." The thing that he is condemning is denominationalism, religious division. That is the thing the term applies to, factionalism among those who profess to be Christians, a party spirit. Then the spirit leads to something further, it leads to the reality of open division. *Divisions* is the next word, and that comes from a word which means to split in two. The body of Christ is actually split in two by men who have promoted and who have become guilty of a factional or party spirit. Factionalism and division are degrees of the same sin; the sin in the heart or in the attitude is party ambition and loyalty. And then *heresies* which means personal preferences. To leave the will of God and walk off after your own will is to become a heretic.

Finally, we have the word *envyings,* and then *drunkenness.* These are the sins of the flesh and you can see that Paul puts them right along with this business of partyism, party spirit, sectarianism in heart, denominationalism in reality, right along with the sensual sins of the flesh. I tell you what the Word of God says in so many words when I tell you that *the man tonight who is guilty of religious division is no better in the sight of God than the drunkard, the reviler, the extortioner, the fornicator, or any other man who walks after the flesh.* He is guilty of the sins of the flesh in the sight of God and stands condemned.

But listen further to what Paul says: "I forewarn you, even as I did forewarn you, that they who practice such things shall not inherit the kingdom of God." Friend, do you want to go to heaven when you die? If you are interested in doing the will of God, you better not have the partisan spirit in your heart in religion, better get rid of partisanism and factionalism in religion, better drive out of your heart that spirit of carnality that leads you to be willing to be a party to and to foster and further denominationalism, to walk after men rather than after Christ. God condemns it as a sin of the flesh and God says that they who practice such things shall not inherit the kingdom of God. That is why men should not be willing to walk after the creeds of men, to walk after the doctrines of men, to wear human names, and to be followers of men rather than followers of Christ.

Be Just A Christian

I ask you tonight, *what are you religiously?* Are you just a Christian, simply a Christian, only a Christian, nothing but a Christian? Are you willing to take the Lord at his word, believe what he says, strive to the very best of your ability to do his will, to recognize his word as your only rule of faith and practice, to wear only his name, to be guilty of teaching or practicing nothing whatever that he has not taught, to refuse to be in any sense a party to denominationalism or division, but to plead for and stand upon the unity of the Spirit in the bond of peace? Are you willing to do it?

You can be *just a Christian!* You can be a Christian just like people in the New Testament age were Christians when Christianity existed and when the church of God existed *before denominationalism was ever heard of*, before any or all of *the modern religious bodies had ever come into existence.* The church of God stood and Christianity stood as revealed in the teachings of New Testament History without any partisan spirit at all, or divisions, or denominational differences of any sort or kind — all such tendencies were forbidden and condemned. That is the kind of Christianity that we are interested in tonight. That is the kind of Christian that we would have you to be, simply by believing in the Lord and following the Lord, wearing only his name, marching under his banner, being a member of only his body, doing his will, be what he would have you to be in order that you might be acceptable in the sight of God. Won't you tonight turn away from everything else, from religious error, from the sins of the flesh and everything that God condemns, and be *just a Christian?* We invite you to come in obedience to the will of Christ, that you might be. Jesus said, ''He that believeth and is baptized shall be saved!''

Further Study On Chapter Eleven

1. A pre-assigned student should read 3 review questions on chapter 10, give the class a few moments to write answers, then announce correct answers. Assign someone to prepare 3 review questions on chapter 11 for the next class.

2. Memorize one or more verses used in chapter 11 and be ready to quote it. If the class is large, the teacher may wish to call upon only a few to recite.

3. Each student should have outlined chapter 11 (main point and scriptures). Call on class members to explain what each heading means (such as, "Division — A Hindrance to Christianity") and how some passage was used to support the heading.

4. Each student should write and bring to class a brief "commentary" on every phrase in Jn. 17:20-21. Tell in your own words what each line of the passage means. The teacher can call upon various students to read what they have written.

5. Each student should have prepared a list of questions and answers on chapter 11 (5 true-false; 3 brief answers; 2 asking, "What passage teaches us that...?"). The teacher should ask students to read some of their questions for the class to discuss.

6. Discuss how division creates disrespect, disinterest, and disbelief toward God's Word.

7. Use a dictionary or other aids to define these words: denomination, sect, ecumenical, interdenominational, undenominational, nondenominational, and anti-denominational. Which term(s) apply to the church you can read about in the Bible?

8. Prepare to tell from memory the *passage* (at least Book and chapter) and the *argument* made on unity-division in connection with these key words: "name," "carnality," "temple of God," "the things written," and "the Lord's Supper."

9. With what other sins is denominationalism associated? Define some of them. What will happen to us if we practice such things?

10. What similarities or connections of thought do you see between Jn. 17:20-21 and 1 Cor. 1:10-13? How do these passages clash with denominationalism? (If possible, the teacher may break the class into smaller groups of 3-5 for about 5-7 minutes of discussion; then let each group leader relate to the whole class one or two important points developed by the group.)

CHAPTER TWELVE

Christianity Is Undenominational

(Part Two)

(A sermon delivered at the Church of Christ, Lufkin, Texas, on Sunday evening, March 13, 1949, and broadcast over Radio Station KRBA, Lufkin)

We are grateful for the presence of this fine audience in this service this evening, and we are grateful for your interest and for the good providence of God that makes it possible for you to be here to engage in a service of this kind.

For the benefit of those who have tuned in to the broadcast, we would like to say that this service is being broadcast from the church of Christ, Fourth and Groesbeck, Lufkin, Texas. We are happy to have you listening in, and we would be happy to have you personally present in any of our services at any time. We would be glad to have you take your Bible and study with us the lesson that we have for the service this evening.

Acts 2: The Beginning of Christianity
In the second chapter of the book of Acts of the Apostles we have the record of the beginning of Christianity. The Church of the Lord Jesus Christ was born on the first Pentecost following the resurrection of the Son of God from the grave. That is the beginning of gospel preaching, the beginning of the new dispensation, the beginning of the preaching of Christ, the beginning of the revelation of the Gospel of Christ by the Holy Spirit through the Apostles, the beginning of the Gospel of God. When the Gospel was preached, when repentance and remission of sins began to be preached in the name of Jesus Christ in Jerusalem, as Jesus said it would in Luke 24:47, it was on the day of Pentecost when the Holy Spirit came and when that beginning took place.

When the Gospel was preached under the direction of the Holy

Spirit of God, Christ was set forth as the Son of God and the Savior of men. The sermon that Peter preached upon that occasion is found in Acts 2. He preached the approved life of the Lord, the sacrificial death of Jesus Christ in the interest of the salvation of men, the resurrection of the Son of God from the grave, and his ascension and exaltation to the right hand of God where he has been made both Lord and Christ. He concluded the sermon according to the 36th verse of Acts 2, by saying, "Let all the house of Israel therefore believe beyond a doubt, or know assuredly, that this Jesus hath been made both Lord and Christ." The record tells us,

> Now when they heard this, they were pricked in their heart, and said unto Peter and to the rest of the apostles, Men and brethren, what shall we do? Peter answered and said, Repent, and be baptized every one of you in the name of Jesus Christ unto the remission of your sins, and ye shall receive the gift of the Holy Spirit. For the promise is to you, and to your children, and to all them that are afar off, even as many as the Lord our God shall call unto him. With many other words did he testify and exhort them, saying, Save yourselves from this crooked generation. As many as gladly received the word of the Lord were baptized, and there were added in that day three thousand souls. And they continued stedfastly in the apostles' doctrine and in fellowship and in breaking of bread and in prayers (Acts 2:37-42, KJ, ASV, and some paraphrasing. RH).

There, my friends, you have the beginning of the church of God. The very first congregation or Church of our Lord that was ever in existence upon this earth was in Jerusalem, and it began when the Gospel was preached. When men and women heard the Gospel, when they believed it and obeyed it, they became members of that Church. God added on that occasion three thousand souls. He continued to add to the Church daily such as should be saved, verse 47 of the same second chapter of Acts tells us. So, we can go back to the beginning of the Church, we can see exactly what it was in the beginning.

It isn't necessary for us to rely upon human wisdom, upon what man might say about the Church in order to know exactly what it was then. If you want to know what kind of a Church Jesus built in the world, if you want to know what kind of a Church God planned, if you want to know what kind of a Church the Holy Spirit filled, if you want to know what kind of a Church men and women became members of or were added to when their sins were forgiven, the best way to find out about that is not to consult any preachers.

Even in a town like Lufkin, Texas, they would give very diversified answers. The answers would be very varied indeed. Their ideas and their conceptions of the Church would be denominational and sectarian; and besides that, our faith ought not to be in man, but in God. We are inviting you not to consult preachers or priests, but rather to go with us to the Word of God and see what the Church of God was in the beginning. That is the place to find out about it. Human encyclopedic authorities which can give you the history of movements are certainly not reliable when we want to learn God's will. The Bible is divine history. We had rather rely upon divine history. I had rather take what the Word of the Lord says about the Church, regardless of what any authority human in its nature has said about it from any point of view.

The Inspired Record Perfect

We ought to have exactly the same attitude about the Church and about Christianity that we have about any other matter upon which God has spoken — His Word is final. Men might relate their experiences in conversion and they would be varied, but human testimony is not reliable. When you turn back to the book of Acts, you have *the story of conversion as recorded by the Holy Spirit*. There is not any mistake in it. These cases of conversion passed under the observance of the Holy Spirit when they occurred because the preacher was an inspired preacher, and when they were recorded in the book of Acts they passed again under the observance of the Holy Spirit in the writing of that record. When these men in the book of Acts were converted, the Holy Spirit was present to guide the preacher and tell them what to do, what to believe, and what to become. There was not any mistake in the preaching in those days because the preacher was inspired. He was simply the mouthpiece of the Spirit of God. Then when Luke, an inspired historian, sat down and wrote the record of these conversions in the book of Acts, the Holy Spirit guided him and there is not any mistake in the record. So you have the observance of the Holy Spirit, the guiding of the Holy Spirit in every case recorded.

The same thing is true of the Church. When you go back there to find out what the Church was, you have an inspired record of all the things that occurred and, of course, the Church was guided by the inspired Apostles, by the inspired prophets of the New Testament age. The Holy Spirit was present then to guide the Church by divine inspiration and the Holy Spirit has recorded for us in the word of God the divine history of what the Church was and what it did. So we do not have to depend upon what some preacher says, or what all preachers say. We should not allow our faith to stand in men but in God, and that can be done by simply putting our faith in the record of God's Word and trusting it and relying upon it.

How To Identify the New Testament Church

I am suggesting to you that *the religious body to which men were added when they believed and obeyed the Gospel in New Testament days certainly was not denominational or sectarian in any sense.* It could not be identified with any modern denomination that exists. There is not a single religious sectarian body upon the face of the earth today that can identify itself with the Church of the New Testament, the Church of the book of Acts, and that is the burden of our lesson tonight. We want to show that Christianity then, the Church then, was undenominational, and that the same Church now would have to be undenominational.

We do not believe and have not taught Church perpetuity. I do not believe that the Church can be traced from that day down until now in visible or recorded history. Certainly not. It would be impossible to trace any movement religiously through the Dark Ages when Roman Catholicism held sway over the whole world, not only with religious predominance but with civil power. They enforced the religious decrees of the pope with the sword and put anybody to death who disagreed with Catholicism. I have an idea that they would do the same thing now if they had the power to do it. They cry, "Persecution," when Communism or some other movement arises, but the Catholics in their history have always been persecutors. If they are today persecuted in any sense, surely they are but reaping what they have sown in the ages of the past. For about 1,200 years the Catholic Church exercised civil dominion. So much civil power was within its control that men could not be anything contrary to it. They could not worship in any way except in the way the Church had prescribed. There was not any possibility of being openly identified with any religious movement other than Catholicism itself. I have but embraced in that statement what every informed person should know.

The Dark Ages in the context of our present study means the complete subverting of every man's faith to the dictation of the pope, and the enforcement of those dictations by the sword, if necessary. The time came that spontaneously throughout the world then known, men began to arise and to rebel against Catholicism. Their rebellion was met with the sword and the shedding of blood was the consequence, and the Catholic Church would through its civil power put to death the men of every nation who would not submit to her will. You have but to go to the Spanish and French Inquisition to see the bloody period and the bloody history of a day when men and women paid with their lives in their struggle to break the yoke of Catholic domination.

Now to think that you could trace the visible history of any religious body other than Catholicism back through that period of the Dark Ages when Rome held sway over the world is to be mistaken about the matter. *But how do I know today that we have the Church of the Lord?* There is only one reason for it, that is, when *we can bring into existence by the preaching of the Gospel the same kind of a religious body today that existed in the New Testament age,* then we know that it is what it was then. If the same seed can now be planted that was sown then, if the same Gospel can now be preached that was preached then; if we have the Word of God revealed to us in the Bible, and we can preach the same truth today that they preached then; and if men can believe the same truth now that they believed then, and can obey the same commandments and the same requirements now that they obeyed then, then we can become the same things now that they became then.

And, I am suggesting to you that the preaching of the *same Gospel* now would establish, plant, and perpetuate, as long as the same Gospel is preached, the *same Church* that it established then. The Church continued only as long as the Gospel continued to be faithfully preached. If we want the Church of God in this age, there is only one way to have it. That is to lay aside all human opinions, and all of the doctrines and commandments of men and every human creed, and simply get back to the Gospel as it was preached—free from denominationalism, free from sectarianism—in the New Testament which is God's Word. We need then to study the Church of New Testament history.

The Apostles' Doctrine
First, let us look at its program. In Acts 2:42, the record says that

when those who gladly received the Word of God were baptized, and when three thousand were added together upon that first occassion of the Gospel being preached, the record says that *"they continued stedfastly in the apostles' doctrine, in the fellowship, in the breaking of bread, and in prayers."* Hence the program or activity of that Church in Jerusalem is set forth in the divine record. We ought to compare ours with it then, just like we compare our preaching with the preaching of the New Testament age, just like we would measure our faith by the faith of the New Testament age, just like we must measure our worship by the worship of the New Testament age. We measure the Church now by the Church then and know whether we are members of and identified with the Church that Jesus built. The record says that the Church that Jesus built upon the earth continued stedfastly in the Apostles' teaching, in fellowship, in breaking of bread, and in prayers. That is a general statement concerning the program of the Church, but let's begin to look at it in its particulars.

What was the creed and the message of the Church? Did they have some sort or kind of human creed? Did they get together and formulate a statement of their faith? Did they adopt or publish a Church Manual or Confession of Faith, or Discipline, or some sort or kind of book that would state what they believed? The answer is, "No!" They had no human creed. The Church of God today must not have one. The Church of that day continued stedfastly in the Apostles' doctrine, in the same Gospel preached by the Apostles of Christ. The Word of God condemns men that go beyond that. God not only pronounces condemnation upon denominationalism, God does not only condemn the sin of division, right along with other sins of the flesh, but also God condemns any one who goes beyond what the Apostles taught.

The Authority of Christ and Apostolic Authority
I remember that when Jesus sent these Apostles out into the world, he sent them out into the world with a commission based upon this kind of authority: "All authority is mine. Go ye therefore, and teach all nations." Jesus said, "All authority is mine both in heaven and on earth. Go ye therefore, and teach all nations, baptizing them into the name of the Father, and of the Son, and of the Holy Spirit; teaching them to observe all things whatsoever I have commanded you; and, lo, I am with you always, even to the end of the world."

Upon the basis of his *authority,* and his authority alone, their message was to be preached. They were *not* to preach some message that some Church council had decreed. They were *not* to preach some doctrine that had been adopted by a popular vote of some congregation somewhere. They were *not* to call the Church into convention and decide what they were to believe and what they were to preach, and then go out preaching what the Church decreed.

Jesus said, "All authority is mine, both in heaven and on earth." The authority of the Lord Jesus Christ has been divided with no one. He was delegating the authority to the Apostles to preach that only which he himself had authorized. As his ambassadors, they were given the right to go out and preach only what the Lord himself had made known. I remember that Jesus made this kind of statement concerning his own teaching, "I do not speak of myself. I speak only where my Father has spoken." Again I hear him saying, "I do only those things that please him." When to the Apostles he delivered the message that he had, I hear him saying, "I have given unto them the words that thou, Father, gave unto me." He received the words from the Father, he delivered them to the Apostles, he sent them out to preach it. That is the message that the Apostles were limited to, and they had no right as ambassadors of Christ to preach to the world one single thing that Jesus Christ himself had not authorized.

I hear him saying, "I received the words of the Father. I have delivered them unto you. They are not mine, I do not speak of myself, I speak only where my Father has spoken." Christ limited himself to the message of God the Father. I hear him saying, "I do not speak of myself. He that sent me gave me commandment what I should speak and what I should say, and the words that I spake unto you the same shall judge you in the last day" (John 12:48). And so we are limited to the message that Christ received from God.

Not only did Jesus so limit himself, but the work of the Holy Spirit in his revelation, in his teaching, was thus limited. I hear the Lord saying that when the Spirit is come he shall not speak of himself, but he shall take of mine and shall declare it unto you. He shall declare unto you that which he receives. The Holy Spirit was limited in his message to that which God the Father had made known to him.

So, just look at it. Christ came into the world and limited himself to the message that he received from God. The Holy Spirit came into the world and limited himself to the message that he had received from God. The Apostles were sent out and were limited to the message that they had received from the Lord Jesus Christ. I recall when Paul said in Galatians 1, "I marvel that ye are so quickly removed from him that called you in the grace of Christ unto a different gospel; which is not another gospel: only there are some that trouble you, and would pervert the gospel of Christ. Though we or an angel from heaven should preach unto you any gospel other than that which we preached, let him be accursed." Early Christians were limited in the message preached by the Apostles of Christ. They themselves were limited in the message that Christ had delivered unto them from the Father. John said, in 1 John 4:6, "He that knoweth God heareth us. He that heareth us not, knoweth not God." So we need to recognize that the Apostles exercised the authority of Christ, their preaching rested upon his authority, and they had no right to preach anything or to teach anything that Christ had not authorized. That is what it means to have Christ as our creed.

The word "creed" comes from a Latin word which means, "I believe." Well, a man believes something and we have to believe in order to be Christians. You must believe something. You have a creed if you believe something. *But Christ is your creed only when you believe what Christ has taught.* When we accept Christ, the only authority in religion, when we reject and refuse everything that Christ has not taught, then Christ is our creed. When we accept all that Christ has taught, Christ is our creed. That is exactly what the New Testament Church recognized, and all that it recognized.

No Other Source Of Authority

God's church on the earth today must recognize no other source of authority. There is not any council, there is not any headquarters, there is not any convention, there is not any sort or kind of religious body that can prescribe for the Church of God in this generation one single doctrine, or one single thing that was not originally given by the authority of Christ, and God be pleased. When we go beyond what the Apostles were authorized to preach by Christ, we go beyond the things that are acceptable in God's sight. Paul said, "These things have I transferred to myself and Apollos for your sakes, that in us you might learn not to go beyond the things that are written" (1 Cor. 4:6). And again I hear him saying, "I have believed according to that which is written. Therefore, do I speak" (2 Cor. 4:13). John said, "He that goeth onward and abideth not in the doctrine of Christ, hath not God" (2 Jn. 9).

Friends, when we begin to teach the doctrines and commandments of men, we have sectarianized the Church of the Lord, the Church of which we are members. We have denominationalized, we have sectarianized ourselves by following after men rather than after the Lord. That is the reason that Paul charged the Church at Colosse, "Take heed lest any man should make spoil of you through philosophy and vain deceit, after the traditions of men and the rudiments of the world, and not after Christ" (Col. 2:8). And again, he said, "As ye have received Christ Jesus the Lord, so walk in him" (Col. 2:6). My faith should be prescribed by the authority of Christ. It ought to be found, it must be found within the Gospel preached by the Apostles of Christ if my faith is to be true, genuine, and acceptable to God. It is certain if I go beyond that, I stand condemned.

Exalting One Doctrine Above Another
But there is another point in that: a man might preach the doctrine of Christ, but give some particular doctrine emphasis over and above another, or even to the exclusion of some other doctrine. He might sit in judgment upon the Word of God and magnify one thing that Christ taught to the repudiation and neglect of something else that Christ taught.

For example, suppose that a man should start out in protest against the practice of sprinkling and suppose that he should start in emphasizing the importance of immersion. That one time happened. Out of the Puritan Movement that originated in England, in about 1607 a body of people distinguished themselves by giving particular emphasis to immersion. They were protesting against the unscriptural practice of sprinkling and were making immersion necessary for true baptism (as the Anabaptists had done earlier). They began to emphasize the importance of immersion until they were noted for this doctrine above all else. They became known as "Baptists" as a result of the emphasis that they placed upon immersion. The movement was across to Holland in 1609, and came to the United States in 1639, when Roger Williams baptized himself and others in the state of Rhode Island. That is where the denomination that bears that name today originated, and history definitely establishes that.

You can not read about it in divine history, for it did not exist then. You could not go back to the record of Acts and find out what kind of a church it is, because it is not mentioned there. Its doctrines are not found, its organization is not there, its worship is not prescribed there, it simply was not in existence in the New Testament and was not and cannot be found in divine history. That is not true of that denomination only. It is true of all other human religious institutions on earth.

But when you begin to think upon the emphasis placed upon immersion as against the practice of sprinkling, it is well to remember that while that same body of people emphasizes the scriptural *method* of baptizing, they have *denied and refused the Bible doctrine of the design or the purpose of baptism.* When God mentions salvation and baptism together, He puts baptism first; never does God save in any other way. Not one single time can you find in the New Testament baptism and salvation together with salvation coming *before* baptism. God never did say it in that way. Always, it is *first,* baptism and *then* salvation, *first* baptism and *then* remission of sins, *first* baptism and *then* justification. Never did God mention it in any other order at all. But the same people that gave so much emphasis to the proper method of being baptized (if we can speak of the method of baptism and do it correctly), refused and rejected the emphasis that God placed upon the order of baptism and pardon in the scheme of redemption.

Friends, I am suggesting to you that that very attitude is the cause of denominationalism in the world, exalting one doctrine of Christ, while minimizing or repudiating or rejecting or refusing another thing that Christ has taught. Out of that attitude, division has grown and sectarianism has originated.

Some men have given emphasis to certain forms of church government to the neglect of a great many other things in connection with the church. As they have emphasized these certain forms of church government, they have come to be given and to accept religious names that are descriptive of that particular form of church government. They have taken their name from the emphasis that has been placed on certain methods or forms of church government. When that is true, division, sectarianism, denominationalism is always the outgrowth.

What we need to do is to see that one doctrine of Christ is not to be exalted above another. One is no more important than the other. If God wills it, if it is taught by Christ, and if the Apostles preached it, I do not have the right to label any of that doctrine as non-essential. I have not the right to label any part as *unimportant*. I have not the right to put more importance upon *one* than any of the rest. One promise that God has made is just as precious and just as true as any other promise, and one commandment that God has given is just as binding as any other commandment, because it is all bound by the authority of God.

When men begin to make distinctions where the Bible has not made them, then they are formulating human creeds whether they put them in writing or not. When we begin to teach, and to accept, and to believe human doctrines, we have a human creed, written or unwritten, for a creed does not always have to be written. The Constitution of Great Britain is an unwritten law. Our Constitution is a written law. The thing that makes a human creed is to depart from divine teaching — to teach, to believe, and to accept a thing that was not taught by Christ and was not preached by the Apostles.

The Solution To Religious Division
The Church of the New Testament day limited itself in faith and in teaching to the authority of the Apostles of Christ. Someone raises the question, "When a difficulty arose" — and they had them then just like we have them now—"when division or dissension threatened as the result of some difference about a point of teaching, how did they settle the matter? Who was it that decided what the truth was and legislated what the church ought to believe and what the church ought to teach?" That is not hard to learn.

Turn to Acts 15. Saul of Tarsus, who had become Paul the Apostle to the Gentiles, had gone out on a missionary tour. When he returned from that tour to the city of Antioch from which he had set forth, he made his report to the church there, and he found that the church had been disturbed by false doctrines. Judaizing teachers had crept into the Church and they had taught the people that Christianity was connected with Judaism, that you could not get into Christ and become a Christian without first of all becoming a proselyte to the Jewish religion, that you had to be circumcised in order to get into Christ. You had to accept circumcision in order to become a child of God. Until first of all you subscribed to Judaism by being circumcised, you could not even be a Christian. They were making Judaism the door to the Church of the Lord. They were making it the means of accepting Christianity and therefore salvation. Christianity and salvation became then just a Jewish proposition.

They were wrong about it. It was false doctrine. They began to teach it and it began to disturb the Church. Paul found it out. When he came back to Antioch, the brethren were very much disturbed about it. They wanted Paul to go down to Jerusalem and Paul said that not only did the Church want him to go, but it was made known to him by revelation that he should go (Gal. 2). It was the will of God for him to go. Hence, Paul went. He took with him certain other brethren. You read about that in Acts 15.

When they came down to the city of Jerusalem, they called together the Apostles of Christ. The Apostles of Christ had not yet spread out. All of them were not yet gone from the city of Jerusalem. Peter, James, and John were still present. When the brethren from Antioch came into the city of Jerusalem, they called those Apostles together and laid before them this matter, this Judaistic teaching that a man had to be circumcised before he could become a Christian. When they laid that before the Apostles of Christ, the Apostles of Christ rendered a decision on it. That decision was written down in a letter that James himself penned. That letter was sent out from the city of Jerusalem to all of the Churches. It represented the decision of the Supreme Court of the Church of God.

The Apostles constituted the Supreme Court of the Church of God. Jesus said in Matthew 19:29, "In the regeneration, when the Son of man shall sit upon the throne of his glory, ye also shall sit upon twelve thrones judging the twelve tribes of Israel." The Apostles of Christ are seated tonight on those twelve thrones. *Through the work of divine revelation*—as ambassadors of the Lord Jesus Christ with all of his authority, as his representatives to the nations of the earth, with the power and authority of Christ behind them to sustain them, through the Word of God revealed by them in the New Testament—*they sit in judgment upon the Church and the affairs of the Church tonight exactly as they did then.*

Paul said in Galatians 3, referring to that Jerusalem Conference of the Apostles, "We laid it before them who were of repute, lest by any means we had run in vain." Now that, friends, is the way a question was settled in New Testament days pertaining to doctrine. They simply carried it to the Apostles for an inspired decision. When the Apostles made that decision, there was no appeal from it. Jesus said, "He that receiveth you receiveth me. He that rejecteth you rejecteth me." When Jesus sent his Apostles out and said, "Whatsoever you shall bind on earth shall be bound in heaven, whatsoever you shall loose upon the earth shall be loosed in heaven," those Apostles had no successors. The contention of the Roman Catholic priests to the contrary notwithstanding.

The claim of the Catholic priest to be a successor to any Apostle is perfectly ridiculous. There is not one single ounce of truth from any point of view that can sustain a claim of that kind. There is not any perpetuation of the office. Certainly not! The qualifications of an Apostle today could not be met by any living man. Peter said that from among those who have companied with us since the baptism of John until Jesus ascended into heaven must one be chosen to take the place of Judas (Acts 1:15-26). Do you think anybody on earth today could meet that qualification? Certainly not. No priest on earth, no preacher on earth, no individual on earth was an eyewitness of Jesus Christ, or is today an eyewitness of Jesus Christ.

The same Apostles who were in the New Testament Church in those days are in it now. This is the period of regeneration, when men are born again, made the children of God, born into God's family. This is the age of spiritual regeneration. Peter said that Jesus Christ having suffered has entered into his glory and is seated upon the throne of his glory at the right hand of God. In Ephesians 1:21, Paul described it, "Far above all principality, and power, and rule and dominion and every name that is named."

Christ is seated on the throne of his glory at the right hand of God in this period of regeneration, and his ambassadors are upon their thrones, twelve thrones, judging the twelve tribes of spiritual Israel—not fleshly Israel, for fleshly Israel and its relationship has been forgotten and gone. In Christ Jesus there is neither Jew nor Greek, bond nor free, male nor female. He is not a Jew who is one outwardly. Neither is circumcision of the flesh; he is a Jew who is one inwardly and circumcision is of the heart, Paul argued in Romans 2. James wrote to the twelve tribes of the dispersion. The twelve tribes of Israel represent the whole of fleshly Israel. The twelve tibes of spiritual Israel represent the whole of spiritual Israel. Paul tells us in Galatians 3, "If ye be Christ's, then are ye Abraham's seed, and heirs according to the promise." An Israelite today is an Israelite spiritually before God, walking in the steps of Abraham's faith.

All of spiritual Israel, the Church of God, is ruled over by the twelve Apostles of the Lord, with the authority of him who is the ruler of all of the kings of the earth, Jesus Christ himself, the King of Kings, and the Lord of Lords. Every decision that must be made, every decision that can be made with reference to doctrine must come from them by the inspiration of God. Religious questions cannot be decided by religious councils. They cannot be decided by a popular vote. They cannot be decided by a multitude of opinions upon the part of men.

Our Rule of Faith And Practice: Human Or Divine?
Paul said, "Let God be true and every man a liar" (Rom. 3:4). If every man and woman in the city of Lufkin, Texas, disagreed with what the Bible taught, with what the Apostles of Christ preached, what those Apostles preached would yet be the truth. What we need to do today is to get away from the idea that Christianity can be ruled by popular wisdom, that a spiritual question can be determined by what men think, or by the wisdom of man. We need to remember that God through divine revelation has made his truth known, and the doctrine that was preached by the Apostles, the ambassadors of Christ, is the truth and *the only truth* that can guide the souls of men and women in obedience to the will of God. Christ is our creed. His word is our rule of faith and practice and the only one that we have if we are Christians.

The Church of God today can no more accept human teaching than God permitted it to accept such in the New Testament days. We can no more follow the doctrines and the commandments that men may authorize now than Christians could then. When the time comes that men will get back to the Bible, be willing to put their faith in it, to believe what it teaches, and be willing to take it as their sole rule of faith and practice, every human creed on the face of the earth will be forgotten.

The human creeds are unreliable in the first place *because they are human*. The way of man is not in himself. It is not in man that walketh to direct his steps. There is a way that seemeth right unto man, but the end thereof are the ways of death. That is the way the Bible talks about it. Jesus said in Matthew 15:14 that if the blind lead the blind they shall both fall into the ditch. Human creeds are unreliable because they are human. *The Word of God is reliable because it is divine.*

Human creeds are unreliable and unacceptable for the reason that they are insufficient and *constantly have to be amended.* Always in every human creed there is provision for amendment, and they are constantly being amended. New situations arise and human creeds are unable to adapt themselves to the change—cannot foresee enough to provide for emergencies that come. God's wisdom was able to premeditate, to foresee, to foreknow everything that the Church would need throughout all the ages of its existence. The Word of God is the creed that will not countenance amendment to it. John said in Revelation, "If any man add unto the words of the prophecy of this book, to him shall be added the plagues that are written therein." You cannot add to the Word of God. You cannot take from the Word of God. You cannot modify or change or pervert the Word of God without destroying your acceptability in God's sight. You stand condemned when you do so. That is exactly what the Bible teaches.

Human creeds not only constantly have to be amended, but they must *be constantly revised.* If we had the time tonight, we could give you instance after instance of denominational creeds actually reversing themselves by the vote of the governing council of the denomination. Frequently, their doctrines are changed and stated in exactly the reverse to what they have been, and that is true of almost every human creed upon the face of the earth. The Word of God does not contradict itself. There is not any reversal of the teachings of the Bible. It is the same tomorrow as it is today, the same today as it was yesterday, and ever since the gospel has been revealed that has been true. It will be the same in the Judgment that it is now.

So human creeds are constantly revised and the man whose confidence is in them would have his faith constantly changing. You can put your faith in the Word of God and it cannot and should not know any change. Human creeds are unreliable again and ought not to be accepted because they cannot be enforced. Preachers can make you promises and preachers can give you assurances, church councils can make decisions and extend privileges, but they cannot enforce them in the Judgment. They are unenforceable and will be when you stand in the presence of God. For that reason, *you and I ought not to accept anything that any man teaches that does not come from God's Word.*

Further Study On Chapter Twelve

1. A pre-assigned student should read 3 review questions on chapter 11, give the class a few moments to write answers, then announce correct answers.

2. Memorize Acts 2:38,42 and be ready to quote it. (Give the class 1-2 minutes to write down their passage, then call on a few to recite.)

3. Outline chapter 12 at home (main points and scriptures). The teacher will call on class members to briefly explain what each heading means (such as "Acts 2: The Beginning of Christianity") and how some passage was used to support the heading.

4. List in separate columns the facts, the commands, and the promises of the gospel proclaimed in Acts 2.

5. Why is it impossible to find historical records of the true Church reaching all the way from the present time to the first century? Without such records, how can we know or recognize the true Church today?

6. Explain how the authority of God is expressed and exercised in order to guide and save men today.

7. Contrast some strengths of the divine creed with weaknesses of human creeds.

8. Discuss and illustrate the danger of exalting one Bible doctrine while excluding another in the rise of the Baptist denomination.

9. Explain from Acts 15 what false doctrine arose in the early church and how brethren found the proper solution to religious division.

10. What are some trends and danger signs which we need to watch and which could gradually change the Lord's people into a sect or denomination today? What can we do to avoid or to reverse such

dangers? (If possible, the teacher may break the class into smaller groups of 3-5 for about 5-7 minutes of discussion; then let each group leader tell the whole class one or two important points developed by the group.)

NOTE: If this book is used in a 13-week class, the last week should be used to review. The following assignment will help the class itself to conduct the review. Each student should prepare 1 review question on each chapter, and also write a paragraph which begins, "My study of *Faith and The Faith* has helped me in the following ways. First, my favorite memory verse was _____ because...." The teacher should call on various class members to ask some questions and to read some of their statements.

NOTE: Reflecting brother Cogdill's style of capitalization in the sermon manuscripts (which were not always uniform), Church is capitalized when referring to the spiritual relationship and the people of God in the universal sense, to the concept of the local church (as in discussing the work of the church), and to the local meeting place of saints, but not when referring to a specific local assembly. On this and some other words, editing may fail to consistently reflect brother Cogdill's desired style. Therefore, a word of caution is in order to those who are prone to make a special point of capitalization procedures on words such as church. Brother Cogdill never expressed to me any strong feelings on the matter. R.H.

Biographical Sketch of Roy E. Cogdill

Born 24 April 1907 in Hobart, Oklahoma, young Roy Edward Cogdill lost his father in 1915 but always drew great strength and courage from his mother. Roy was a mature and sincere twelve year old when O.E. Phillips baptized him in a pond near the grave of the boy's father. "Just as my father is buried yonder in a grave," the young man reflected, "I am buried in water. Just as he will be raised to live again, I am being raised to newness of life." Senior high school and freshman college courses were taken concurrently by Roy at Western Oklahoma Christian College (Cordell, Okla.), during the 1922-23 session. W.O.C.C. faculty members Robert M. Alexander (1894-1969), Byron Fullerton (1889-1978), and W. Claude Hall taught the Bible courses he took.

After Roy's first sermon on 26 November 1922 at Hobart, he preached the next summer at Mountain View and then went to Texas for the 1923-24 session at Abilene Christian College. Premillennialists and sympathizers were well represented in the faculty of Pres. Jesse P. Sewell (1876-1969) — men like Charles R. Brewer (1890-1971), Morgan Higdon Carter, David L. Cooper (b. 1886), and O.E. Phillips (b. 1886). None of them weakened Roy's convictions. He had learned early the great value of truth and the grave danger of error. Summer found him in gospel meetings and fall in San Antonio selling Bibles. The money earned helped to care for his sick mother. The new year found him in located work at Frederick, Oklahoma. On 21 July 1925 his A.C.C. sweetheart, Loraine Burke (1905-1960), became his bride. The next January they went to Oklahoma and both enrolled at W.O.C.C. He preached in meetings that summer and settled with the Sunset Church of Christ in Dallas, Texas in the Fall.

Preaching Christ in Gospel Meetings and in Located Work
Roy moved to work with the Johnston and Hemphill Church in

Greenville, Texas in May of 1927, but resigned the local pulpit to do full-time meeting work while living there during 1929-30. His next move was to Cleburne in October of 1930, where the building was filled at times to its capacity of 900. Roy's meetings often had been "held in the open air, with an 'acre of people' in attendance" (*Gospel Advocate,* 30 Apr. 1931, p. 516). He kept a punishing schedule much of the time. In May 1931 his throat played out, but the hope of preaching was renewed in July when a tumor was removed from his vocal cords. Disappointed by softness and corruption in the church at Cleburne, he went back to Dallas.

Supporting himself as a coffee distributor in Dallas, Roy earned a law degree by attending school at night (1933-37). His law practice with Jack Johannes during 1937-43 equipped him to help brethren with legal matters through the ensuing years, but preaching was always his first love! He preached at Terrell in 1933, at Sears and Summitt in Dallas during 1933-37, and in meeting work for the next several years. Around 1940, a small group left Sears and Summitt peacefully to plant a church in the University Park area and engaged Roy for about a year and a half.

Roy defended the gospel against millennial speculations about the return of Jesus to earth to complete his mission in a physical kingdom. "Nothing can be added to the present power and glory of Christ at the right hand of God," Roy argued in the October 1935 *Gospel Guardian* (p. 33). "The mission of Christ into the world was fully accomplished. He will not be reincarnated to dwell on earth. He will come a second time to award salvation to them that wait for him" (*G.G.,* Feb. 1936, p. 27). Such teaching was a scandal to men like E.L. Jorgenson (1886-1968), minister at the premillennial Highland Church of Christ in Louisville, Kentucky. His 16 April 1942 letter to radio station WGRC tried but failed to shut down the Bardstown Rd. Church's program with Morton T. Utley. The nefarious letter was exposed in the June *Bible Banner* by Foy E. Wallace, Jr. (1896-1979) and Cogdill preached both in person and by tape on WGRC during May and June, leaving Jorgenson enraged. He complained of "the Cogdill attack" in a 30 June letter to Cecil B. Douthitt (1896-1971), and received "confidential" sympathy from J.N. Armstrong (1870-1944) in a letter dated 24 June. Though Jorgenson professed a sweet spirit, his correspondence and his essay entitled "Analysis of an Air Attack" bitterly referred to the programs by Utley and Cogdill as repugnant, crass, vicious, ignorant, slavish, and legalistic. Roy was never ashamed to suffer such abuse for the truth, nor did it ever intimidate him.

After a good year with the South National Church in Springfield, Missouri (1943), the Cogdills enjoyed a successful work with the Norhill Church in Houston during 1944-46. Luther Blackmon (1907-77) was Roy's co-laborer there. In response to Seventh-Day Adventist propaganda, Norhill engaged Foy E. Wallace, Jr. to expose millennial theories in January of 1945 — and both Catholic and Protestant doctrines the next January — in the "Music Hall" meetings. Roy published the first series as *God's Prophetic Word* (1946), then prepared galley proofs of the second series which Wallace later published as *Bulwarks of the Faith* (1951). Both are classics! During his last few months in Houston, Roy started a journal named *Ancient Landmarks* and then moved it to Lufkin.

Triumphs and Tragedy at Lufkin
Roy and Luther were hired to labor with the Fourth and Groesbeck Church in Lufkin in 1946. With Roy D. Spears, they formed the Roy E. Cogdill Publishing Company to keep the monthly *Bible Banner* in print. Wallace was the official editor, but he left most of the work to Cogdill during this period. In April 1949 the *Banner* became a weekly under the name of the old *Gospel Guardian* (1935-36), with Yater Tant as editor. Roy held two debates and many gospel meetings during the Lufkin years and finally tendered his resignation to the elders on 19 June 1949 to be free to help in other places where he was needed. On Cogdill's recommendation, Foy's brother Cled Wallace (1892-1962) filled the pulpit in Lufkin.

The active elders at Lufkin proposed in May 1950 that Roy return to share pulpit duties with Cled and he came with that intention the next January. The elder who previously had been inactive became vocal against Roy. Seeing that one of the six elders and Cled were unhappy with the plan, Roy notified the eldership by letter on 24 February of his decision to move on rather than "to precipitate a disruption." Local county churches and meeting work beckoned.

Soon a large group of brethren who were distressed over the recalcitrant elder, long a reproach to the church, showed up at Roy's house asking advice. They prevailed upon him to frame a letter stating their last plea for a correction of the man's life and their plan to "establish a new congregation...peacefully and without any malice toward" Fourth and Groesbeck. The letter dated 12 March 1951 presents itself "not as a petition" nor a resort to "majority rule," and Roy cautioned against circulating it as such. Since over one hundred brethren signed the letter as expressing their sentiments, charges of majority rule, petition, and faction were made. The new group became the Timberland Dr. Church of Christ.

The *Gospel Advocate* publicized the Lufkin tragedy in a diversionary maneuver to counter the attacks of Cogdill and the *Gospel Guardian* on centralized cooperation in the work of many churches through one eldership. Hot articles were exchanged during the summer of 1951. Despite the *Advocate's* interference, the two churches issued a joint "Statement" of reconciliation in the 1 April 1954 *Guardian*. Since some brethren had misinterpreted the letter of 1951 as a petition or an ultimatum, an apology was offered for it. The troublesome elder was gone by 1954 and Fourth and Groesbeck apologized for having branded Timberland Dr. The two churches are at peace to this day.

The Cogdills preached Christ from June 1953 well into 1954 in Ontario, Canada, often in "towns and villages where the religion of Christ is utterly unknown" (*G.G.*, 19 Nov. 1953, p. 437). While back in the States for meetings, both Roy and Loraine were injured in a car wreck during March of 1954; a hip fracture left him with a limp at times. After two years with the West Ave. Church in San Antonio, Texas, Roy spent part of 1956 and into 1958 in meeting work again, with Lufkin as home base.

During 1958-60 the Cogdills located with the Mound and Star Church in Nacogdoches. It was a good work, but death took Loraine on 23 June 1960. The Cogdills had been married nearly thirty-five years and had raised one adopted daughter (Mrs. Martha Nell Davis). Loraine was an ideal preacher's wife. Roy sorely missed her and moved to Oklahoma City, Oklahoma to resume meeting work.

A New Lease on Life: Venita Williams Faulkner

The void was filled on 25 December 1960 when Roy wed Venita Williams Faulkner who lived in Oklahoma City. She was a strong Christian, a competent business woman, and a good companion. Her children by a deceased husband were Pam (Mrs. Doug Northcutt) and Jon; she and Roy later adopted Philip (1961). Years later

Roy reflected, "If a man is unfortunate enough to need two companions in a lifetime, he could not be more fortunate in the selection of a wife than I've been" (6 Jan. 1984 interview by R.H.). With Nita's moral support, he criss-crossed the country in twenty-eight gospel meetings and a six-night debate during their first year of marriage!

The Cogdills settled with the Winnetka Ave. Church of Christ in Canoga Park, California for the years 1963-early 1967. The church grew and its bulletin reached all over the country with articles on "a wide spectrum" of subjects and with emphasis on "human innovations in the church" (elders' commendation, 29 Jan. 1967 bulletin). At the Par Ave. Church in Orlando, Florida during 1967-71, Roy's pace would have kept three men busy. He edited a popular bulletin, taught Bible in Florida College at Temple Terrace (1969-71), wrote in *Truth Magazine,* conducted the magazine's bookstore for a time (mostly done by Nita), served as President of the Cogdill Foundation (publishing religious materials), worked on a uniform Bible class literature project, delivered three speeches at "the Arlington (Texas) meeting" on institutionalism, preached in the Philippine Islands during all of May 1970, and held gospel meetings for about three months each year.

Roy's close friend James Yates urged him to help rebuild the Spring Branch Church in Houston, Texas. After a year there, elders and deacons had been appointed and both attendance and contribution figures had grown. Then some generous friends helped to support Roy for a year (1972-73) to labor with the church in Henderson until it could provide for a preacher. During 30 July-5 August 1973 he held a gospel meeting with the Broadmoor Church in Nashville, Tennessee (where I had just moved). His series on "Faith" was excellent, but everyone noticed his discomfort in negotiating the two steps onto the pulpit platform. When he got home, cancer was discovered. He waged a courageous fight against it and various complications until his death. With financial help from Spring Branch, Roy left Henderson and went to Conroe in 1973 to establish a congregation. (Their basic building plan was patterned after Broadmoor's.)

During 1975 several brethren made contact with Alessandro Corazza of Rome, Italy, the first man converted by Americans after

World War II. He had translated Cogdill's *New Testament Church* in the mid-1950s. Dissatisfied with the control of Italian churches by American "sponsoring" churches, Corazza broke with the Americans about 1963. Cogdill helped Italian brethren in many ways after visiting them on three trips beginning in May 1976.

In August 1977 the Cogdills moved into their new home at 21606 Park Rock Lane, Katy—in the Houston area. Roy aided Harold Fite in teaching duties at the Fry Rd. Church in Katy, the new meeting place of the old Spring Branch group, and held occasional meetings. After spending most of November 1981 in Jordan, Ontario, he left home for Midfield, Alabama on 10 December to preach to a troubled church on the need for peace, unity, and scriptural church government. Trouble had erupted when the same elders who had asked a man to come preach at Midfield asked him to leave after a couple of years. The elders were faced with a petition-signing movement. In spite of health problems and personal abuse, the Cogdills stayed through March 1982. The faction at Midfield was withdrawn from and in time left. The remaining brethren were at peace, and I accepted the elders' invitation to move there by early June. The Cogdills returned to Katy with the special love and gratitude of the Midfield Church. He came back for a meeting 19-26 September, but was never able to fulfill a meeting engagement after that occasion

Preaching Christ Through Journals, Debates, and Books
Roy Cogdill has used every possible ability and avenue to preach Christ. His first journal article—"It Is Written"—appeared in the *Herald of Truth* dated 12-19 April 1923. Roy handled Texas subscriptions for the *Gospel Advocate* during the time of his throat trouble and edited the "Texas News and Notes" column (30 Apr.-26 Nov. 1931). The first column chided brethren who could afford daily papers and current magazines but "cannot afford our good religious papers" which aid in preaching the gospel (p. 517). Articles by Roy appeared in Foy E. Wallace, Jr.'s original *Gospel Guardian* (Oct. 1935-June 1936), helping to fight premillennialism. Shortly, Wallace started the *Bible Banner* (July 1938-Apr. 1949), broadening the battle lines against institutionalism and centralization in the churches' work. Not only did Roy write, but also beginning in March 1947 the Roy E. Cogdill Publishing Company printed the paper and he did editorial work for Wallace.

Ancient Landmarks was established and edited by Roy in March 1946 as a monthly subscription paper focused on first principles of the Gospel. After a couple of years, he had Yater Tant edit it. (Eventually it merged with the *Gospel Guardian*.)

Warning in the *Bible Banner* against church donations to colleges, Roy clashed with N.B. Hardeman (1872-1965), Robert Alexander of A.C.C., and G.C. Brewer (1884-1956). The *Banner* also protested one church collecting funds from other churches to "sponsor" an evangelist to go overseas. Each church was encouraged to have direct fellowship with the evangelist in the field. Church programs of social and recreational activity were opposed as a prostitution of the church's spiritual nature and mission. The *Banner* correctly detected trends pointing toward what professional historian David E. Harrell, Jr. later called the "Emergence of The 'Church of Christ' Denomination" (*G.G.*, 16 Feb.—2 Mar. 1967). Wallace's cry, "They shall not pass," was amened in the 30s—40s and then amplified in the 50s—60s by younger men like James W. Adams, Yater Tant, and Roy E. Cogdill.

In 1949 Wallace agreed for the monthly *Bible Banner* to become a weekly under the name *Gospel Guardian*. Cogdill Publishing owned the new paper and Tant was editor with Wallace as co-editor. Wallace soon faded out of view as a writer for the *Guardian,* but it grew and became synonymous with Cogdill and Tant in the fight against institutionalism and centralized cooperation.

The Bible pattern was Roy's plea as he met institutionalism's strongest apologists — Cecil N. Wright, James D. Bales, G.C. Brewer, B.C. Goodpasture (1895-1977), E.R. Harper, Roy H. Lanier, Guy N. Woods, J.D. Thomas, and William S. Banowsky. Thousands of brethren (including my own family) were awakened to preserve the Bible plan for church organization in the face of apostasy. But Roy wrote extensively on many other themes as well — Christ, his trial and death, gospel preaching, unity, Christian journalism, faith, baptism, the Holy Spirit, prayer, and others. The deaths of R.L. Whiteside (1869-1951) and John T. Lewis (1876-1967) were reported by Roy.

When Cogdill sold the Gospel Guardian Co. to Tant in 1962, Roy set up a Gospel Guardian Foundation to keep a few books in print. In 1969 it became the Cogdill Foundation and owner of *Truth*

Magazine (established 1956). Meanwhile, the *Guardian* passed through several owners and editors until it merged with *Truth* to appear as the *Guardian of Truth* beginning in 1981. In December 1980 the Board of the Cogdill Foundation accepted with regret his resignation and acquiesed to his advice that the name be changed to Guardian of Truth (rather than be tied to any one individual). His counsel and encouragement played a continuing role in the paper and other operations of the Foundation. Only eternity will reveal the good accomplished by brother Cogdill as he has preached Jesus Christ through gospel papers!

The Guardian of Truth Foundation is the result of an effort by brother Cogdill and others to publish *a sound, effective gospel paper* along with other Bible study aids. The bookstore helps to financially underwrite that work. This Foundation was envisioned as a nonprofit business to serve brethren's needs for good literature. It is in no sense a church, a cooperative or centralizing agent for churches, or a substitute for congregational activities. Churches may purchase the goods and services of the Foundation (just as they buy things from newspapers, lumber yards, and other businesses), but it accepts *no church donations*. Institutional-minded brethren have tried unsuccessfully to parallel their human organizations which are tied to church donations and Roy's publication efforts involving individuals only. He has proven through the years that brethren can and must operate their own business enterprises, whether primarily for profit or as a service, *without making them leeches on the churches.*

Debates have always been an effective method of preaching Christ and of defending the gospel. Just as the Prince of Peace drew the sword of the Spirit "and threw the scabbard away," the life of Roy E. Cogdill has been one continued scene of controversy for the gospel's sake (A. Campbell, *Millennial Harbinger,* 4 Jan. 1830, p. 41). Men like J. Early Arceneaux (1883-1970), Joe S. Warlick (1866-1941), C.R. Nichol (1876-1961), R.L. Whiteside, and Foy E. Wallace, Jr. inspired and armed Roy to contend earnestly for the faith. Wallace's 1934 debate in Ft. Worth, Texas with the Baptist "giant" J. Frank Norris (1877-1952) strengthened Roy's confidence in the power of truth over error.

The week of 24 June 1935 Roy answered the call of his brethren in Carnegie, Oklahoma to meet the Christian Church preacher Edwin L. Kirtley, Jr. (b. 1909) in a debate on instrumental music in worship. Unintimidated by Kirtley's appeal to Greek, the fledgling debator reacted "like a veteran" and met every quibble (M.C. Cuthbertson, *Gospel Advocate,* 18 July 1935, p. 691). The "Landmark" or "Association" Baptists brought D.N. Jackson to Lufkin to debate Roy on baptism and the impossibility of apostasy 10-13 December 1946. The *Cogdill-Jackson Debate* appeared in two editions in 1949 and a third in 1977, and is still in print. They met again in Houston's Music Hall later. The week of 9-13 February 1948 Roy and A.J. Kirkland, President of a Baptist college at Henderson, Texas, discussed baptism, apostasy, and instrumental music at Clute. The book Kirkland published in June on the debate gave a partial and inaccurate account.

On 5 October 1952 Cogdill contested the sensational claims of "faith healer" Charles Jessup before 12-15,000 people gathered at the revivalist's five-pole circus tent in Bowling Green, Kentucky. Roy's speech powerfully contrasted Bible miracles with the modern "system of racketeering. People are worked into a state of frenzied excitement and drained of their money." This sermon is still available in tract form.

Hundreds of brethren heard Roy E. Cogdill and Guy N. Woods in a six-night debate (18-23 Nov. 1957) at Phillips High School auditorium in Birmingham, Alabama, on church support of benevolent institutions and on sponsoring church programs such as the Herald of Truth Radio Program of the Highland Church in Abilene, Texas. This classic exchange was published in 1958 by both the Gospel Advocate Co. of Nashville, Tennessee and the Gospel Guardian Co. of Lufkin, Texas. The latter edition was reprinted by the Cogdill Foundation in 1976 and can be had today. The two men repeated their debate at the Main St. Church in Newbern, Tennessee during 18-23 December 1961. Many well informed brethren judged "that Cogdill did the most thorough job in exposing the unscripturalness of the Herald of Truth, to date" (Connie W. Adams, *G.G.,* 1 Feb. 1962, p. 605).

In a series of 15 *Gospel Guardian* articles from 20 August 1959 through 20 August 1960, Roy reviewed J.D. Thomas' book *We Be Brethren.* The book defended centralized church cooperation, church support of various institutions, and church-sponsored recreation.

Tant considered Roy's series "a reply to the whole philosophy of the modern movement" (*G.G.*, 24 Sept. 1959, p. 308). His wife's fatal illness cut the series short.

Nine men including James W. Adams and Reuel Lemmons met in April of 1967 at Buchanan Dam, Texas in an effort to re-open lines of communication through a round table discussion of the differences dividing brethren all across the country. During January 1968 at Arlington, Texas, 26 men met in a similar style — 13 from each side of the breach. Roy Cogdill and J.D. Thomas made opening speeches on "How to Establish Bible Authority" and exchanged rebuttals. Roy delivered a masterpiece on the principle difference between the two groups. He also spoke on "Co-operation of Churches." Communication between the estranged groups was congenial but brief because each was already far down two divergent roads. *The Arlington Meeting* book, still in print, is an excellent resource for study.

Christ and the church in the plan of salvation are proclaimed in Cogdill's book of fifty-two lessons on *The New Testament Church*. The outlines and questions on the church's nature, origin, mission, membership, government, unity, identity, worship, and early history are designed "to familiarize the student with the texts of the Bible itself" (p. v.). First published in 1938, this book had been translated into many languages and dialects and had sold about a quarter million copies by 1975. In 1957 a sequal volume entitled *Walking by Faith* offered an expanded study on "the nature, organization, and work of the church and...scriptural cooperation among the churches of Christ" (p. 4). By 1975 it too was widely translated and had sold some 50,000 copies. Both of these books are used by brethren today in private and in class studies, and for sermon outlines.

The first book published by the Old Paths Book Club was entitled *Preaching in the Twentieth Century* (1945, 2nd ed. 1955) and included a section of six chapters by Roy E. Cogdill on "The Bible in Preaching." Preachers must feed their own souls on the Word of God and make it the "center and circumference of all preaching" (p. 155). Roy's most recent book, *The New Testament: Book by Book* (1975), provides in 26 lessons "an overall view of the New Testament" (p. 2). This book reflects the heart of brother Cogdill's emphasis as a gospel preacher: *to exalt and teach the Bible as the final, perfect, all-sufficient revelation of God's Word.* His tracts and booklets on such themes as the Bible's authority, its perfection, man's obedience, and the Church of Christ all reflect that very same emphasis.

Brother Cogdill has preached Christ through the printed page for many years. A tremendous amount of publishing has been done at great personal sacrifice and with the help of devoted friends, through business arrangements known as the Roy E. Cogdill Publishing Co. (1946-54), Gospel Guardian Co. (1954-62), Gospel Guardian Foundation (1963-69), Cogdill Foundation (1969-80), and Guardian of Truth Foundation (1981-   ). As people continue reading the journals, debates, and other publications which bear brother Cogdill's imprint, he shall yet be doing the work of an evangelist — proclaiming salvation by faith in Jesus Christ.

Roy E. Cogdill's Style of Preaching

The style of Roy Cogdill's preaching was *forceful, plain,* and *straightforward.* In 1946 Roy reflected upon the style and content of Foy E. Wallace Jr.'s preaching during the 30s-40s, and enumerated the qualities which every gospel preacher ought to have. The preacher's ideals ought to include "devotion to the Lord,...loyalty to the church,...fidelity to the truth," thorough preparation, "unflinching courage," preaching the truth without concern for popularity or personal friendship, fighting for truth "on the plane of the issues" rather than attacking a man's personal character, boldness for truth but humility in personal matters, willingness to "announce his mistake" and apologize when shown to be wrong, and willingness to labor wherever needed "at the sacrifice of his own welfare, physically, financially, and otherwise" (*God's Prophetic Word,* orig. ed. of 1946, pp. vii.-viii.). Having watched Roy develop, Wallace mused, "As a pulpiteer he is without a peer in his generation of preachers" (p. iv.).

Price Billingsley (1877-1958) gave a description of Roy's preaching style in 1940 which agreed with Wallace's estimate. "Without lost motion or repetition, but with growing clarity and force," Roy preached at length with a remarkable "grasp of Biblical data" and an "unwavering fidelity to simple New Testament truth and practice" (*Gospel Advocate,* 12 Dec. 1940, p. 1181). Responding to a wave of desire for short and shallow sermons, Wallace often said,

"I have *never* seen a strong church created by serving 15 minute sugar sticks" (29 Dec. 1982 interview of Cogdill by R.H.). Cogdill's preaching helped to build many a *strong* church.

Roy never sought controversy for its own sake nor shirked it when truth was at stake. His preaching united *the theme of inner love, devotion, and zeal* with *the theme of strict obedience to God's Word.* Never enamored with the platitudes of a Dale Carnegie positive-mental-attitude approach to preaching, Roy drew the line between truth and error clearly enough for everyone to see. Yet, his attitude was not pessimistic, abusive, or morose. He was vibrant, confident, and victorious in proclaiming the gospel because he had faith in it as God's power to save. His style was *militant* for truth and against error, *dignified* before his fellowman and his Maker, and *sympathetic* to the plight of the lost.

Training in controversy came to Roy in his youth when the premillennial battle was taking shape. At the age of twenty-four, he saw the danger of trends toward institutionalized religion and stressed the importance of personal responsibility. "How long has it been since you had a private, face-to-face, heart-to-heart talk with some friend about the salvation of his soul?" (*Gospel Advocate,* 27 Aug. 1931, p. 1061) Roy always fought centralization and institutionalism because they lessen the sense of individual service to God. Many other controversies over "the faith" and contentions over opinions have been faced in his 62 years of preaching. His article on "Handling Aright the Word of Truth" discussed "basic rules of Bible study" which brethren must learn in order to "contend earnestly for the faith" without being "contentious about our own opinions or human customs and traditions" (*Searching the Scriptures,* 16 Oct. 1968, pp. 153-55).

A trail of split churches has been left by occasional efforts to settle internal congregational problems by appealing to petitions, votes, and majorities. The Cogdill Publishing Co. reprinted B.M. Strother's booklet on *The Church and A Faction,* a defense by Nichol, Wallace, and Whiteside of oversight by elders against the encroachments of majority rule at McAlester, Oklahoma in the late 1930s. During the problems at Lufkin, Roy consistently urged brethren to avoid the desire to seek majority rule through petitions. Majority rule tactics such as votes and petitions were used at times to promote institutionalism during the 1950s-60s. As at McAlester, irate brethren resorted to such devices at Midfield, Alabama in late 1981 and the elders called upon brother Cogdill to preach on God's plan for church government and peace.

Honesty in controversy requires apologies, clarifications, and corrections at one time or another. Early editions of *The New Testament Church* said the benevolence sent from Antioch to brethren in Judea was placed "in hands of Elders of Jerusalem Church to be administered by them" (Acts 11:29-30). During the disturbance over centralized cooperation, it was pointed out that the statement means that all Judean saints were in Jerusalem or that the Jerusalem church was a centralized agent for Judean churches. Subsequent editions replaced "Jerusalem Church" with "Judean elders" in keeping with the biblical text (p. 39 of early eds., p. 47 in later eds.).

No more significant or difficult change was ever faced by Roy than one involving the Music Hall meetings in Houston. Norhill had planned and guaranteed the work as its own, but had received aid from twenty area churches and had handled their funds through its treasury. When Roy became deeply involved in the fight for congregational autonomy and against centralized cooperation in the support of foreign evangelism, the major response of his opponents was that he had approved their plan in principle during the Norhill days. He had never thought of Norhill planning or acting as the agent of other churches, but later conceded the difficulty in establishing a clear difference in principle between the Music Hall and the Herald of Truth programs. "...I have long ago surrendered the ground and henceforth will hold no more such meetings lest I lead my brethren to sin" (*G.G.*, 29 July 1954, pp. 10-11).

E.R. Harper repeatedly brought up the Music Hall meetings again in a 1956 debate with Tant. When Guy Woods harped on it again the next year in Birmingham, Roy laid it to rest. Re-study of Bible principles Roy had always believed had clarified that it was wrong for other churches to send their money to Norhill, and he had long ago given up the practice.

> And if you think it embarrasses me, to the least degree, to acknowledge that I made a mistake in the manner in which that thing was handled, you are wrong about it. I'm sorry the mistake was made. I'm trying to avoid it now (*Cogdill-Woods Debate*, pp. 214-15).

When convinced he was wrong, Roy tried to make the correction.

Brethren who knew brother Cogdill well have often observed that he had the heart of a child. A strong stand for truth does not preclude a tender heart. Roy was not ashamed to shed tears where the cause of the Lord was concerned. After rebuking equally G.C. Brewer's plea for church support of schools and W. Carl Ketcherside's denial of a school's right to teach the Bible, Roy said he had no personal issue with either of them.

> I am sure God is just as interested in the salvation of one as he is the other and therefore I should be. I love both of them and wish that I could persuade them to accept and stand only for the truth so that there would not be any factionalism and we could all stand together. Brethren, why not? (*G.G.*, 5 Nov. 1953, p. 409).

The combination of factors in Roy's preaching style — forceful, plain, straightforward, controversial when needed, open to correction, and tenderhearted—made him equally powerful as proponent for truth and opponent of error. Bill Cavender noted that "few men have been possessed of native ability so lavishly poured out by God on individuals as has Roy E. Cogdill." "He has been one of the ablest students of the Bible and preachers among us" (bulletin of South Cullman, Ala. Church of Christ, *Bible Facts,* Feb. 1982, p. 1).

Outlook in Sunset Years
In the sunset years of life, Roy Cogdill's desire was to press on with unabated confidence in the power of God's Word. He stedfastly refused to apologize for the lines drawn by preaching the truth.

He remembered too well the sad lessons of the James DeForest Murch (1892-1973) and Claude F. Witty (1877-1952) unity meetings of 1938-42 when some brethren thought themselves wise enough to improve on debate and controversy as the God-given means to destroy error and to save souls. Rapproachment was sought by the soft-soap, positive-mental-attitude, eternal-optimist, slip-up-on-their-blind-side, Dale Carnegie approach to those in apostasy. Brother Cogdill and some who are wavering *now* did not believe thirty or forty years ago that the plain and straightforward methods of Christ and of his Apostles could be improved upon. Roy maintained that confidence to the end (and expressed himself to me on this point numerous times in recent years).

After "Fifty Years As A Gospel Preacher," brother Cogdill made some observations which reflect devotion to the Lord and His Word as the guiding principle of Roy's life:

> There have been several occasions in my life when the temptation came to turn aside from preaching and get into some profession or business that offered tempting financial reward, but it has never been a problem to make the decision that I would continue to give my full time to preaching the word of the Lord [though he explains that a time or two he temporarily "made tents" to provide for his family, RH].
>
> I have earnestly tried to preach and contend for what I have believed to be the truth through these years without compromise. As I face the future I pray that it may continue to be so. Nothing has been sadder to me than to witness some stalwart servant of the Lord live to reach such years in which he destroys all for which he ever stood. I pray that I may not do so.
>
> That does not mean that I have not erred in what I have believed and taught. On more than one occasion I have found myself out of harmony with what I have learned to be the truth and been brought to alter my position to bring it in harmony with the truth I learned. I intend to continue to learn and whenever I learn anything that is contrary to what I have believed, I will make whatever change may be demanded by truth. I pray that God may continue to give me the strength to do so. It does mean, though, that my convictions and conscience have not been for sale. Personal authority, the influence of even the closest of friends, personal ambition to be a "big preacher," financial advantage, nor any other personal consideration has been a determining factor in any stand taken or position occupied, or in any course of action.
>
> On the other hand, there is the persuasion that in many cases a vastly different course would have been taken had such things entered into the decision. I have never rejoiced in making enemies but I have never weighed the preaching of the gospel by the measuring of its impression or result. Preaching it has been my obligation and the results of truth belong to God (*Truth Magazine,* 11 Jan. 1973, pp. 151-53).

We all will do well to remember that it is our duty to preach, to defend, and to propagate the gospel of Christ by every scriptural means. Since God and not man is the author of the gospel, *it is not our place to trim back the truth or to apologize for its effects.* "The results of truth belong to God." As brother Cogdill sought to do through a lifetime of preaching salvation by faith in Christ, let all who follow determine to preach the unsearchable riches of Christ without shame, without fear, without apology.

Roy E. Cogdill passed away on Monday, 13 May 1985 at 12:57 a.m. in the Katy Memorial Hospital at Katy, Texas. After a good Lord's Day, during which he worshipped with the saints both morning and evening, he suffered a sudden heart attack at 11:30 p.m. in his home. It seems providential that on 23 April, the day before his seventy-eighth birthday, many members of both his physical and his spiritual families gathered to express their respect and love for him. Brethren from near and far, some of whom he had not seen for many years, met with him at the Fry Road Church building to sing, to pray, to meditate upon the Bible, and to remember.

Sitting in a wheelchair, pale and wearing a neck brace, all because of injuries received in a fall, brother Cogdill gave and received the refreshments of spiritual fellowship. James W. Adams, the prime mover of the occasion, gave an overview of Roy's life. I reflected upon his influence on younger preachers, Leon Odom recalled humorous incidents in Roy's life, and James Yates spoke from the viewpoint of an elder.

Little could any of us realize that Adams and Yates with Clinton Hamilton would be speaking at Roy Cogdill's funeral twenty-two days later, on 15 May, in the same building. He is buried near his beloved mother and other loved ones in the Municipal Cemetery at Hobart, Oklahoma to await the Resurrection Day.

Ron Halbrook

West Columbia, Texas
June 1986

www.ingramcontent.com/pod-product-compliance
Lightning Source LLC
Chambersburg PA
CBHW070328090426
42733CB00012B/2405